GLEIM®

2023 EDITION

CIA REVIEW

PART 1: ESSENTIALS OF INTERNAL AUDITING

by

Irvin N. Gleim, Ph.D., CPA, CIA, CMA, CFM

Aligned with the 2019 CIA exam reorganization

Gleim Publications, Inc.
PO Box 12848
Gainesville, Florida 32604
(800) 874-5346
(352) 375-0772
www.gleim.com/cia
CIA@gleim.com

For updates to the first printing of the 2023 edition of *CIA Review: Part 1*

Go To: www.gleim.com/updates

Or: Email update@gleim.com with **CIA 1 2023-1** in the subject line. You will receive our current update as a reply.

Updates are available until the next edition is published.

ISSN: 2638-8154

ISBN: 978-1-61854-529-9 *CIA Review: Part 1*
ISBN: 978-1-61854-531-2 *CIA Review: Part 2*
ISBN: 978-1-61854-532-9 *CIA Review: Part 3*
ISBN: 978-1-61854-463-6 *CIA Exam Guide: A System for Success*

ACKNOWLEDGMENTS FOR PART 1

The author is grateful for permission to reproduce the following materials copyrighted by The Institute of Internal Auditors: Certified Internal Auditor Examination Questions and Suggested Solutions (copyright © 1980-2021), excerpts from *Sawyer's Internal Auditing* (5th, 6th, and 7th editions), parts of the 2022 *Certification Candidate Handbook*, and the International Professional Practices Framework.

CIA® is a Registered Trademark of The Institute of Internal Auditors, Inc. All rights reserved.

ABOUT THE AUTHOR

Irvin N. Gleim, Ph.D., CIA, CPA, CMA, CFM, who authored the first edition of the Gleim CIA Review over 40 years ago, was Professor Emeritus in the Fisher School of Accounting at the University of Florida and a member of the American Accounting Association, Academy of Legal Studies in Business, American Institute of Certified Public Accountants, Association of Government Accountants, Florida Institute of Certified Public Accountants, The Institute of Internal Auditors, and the Institute of Management Accountants. The late Dr. Gleim published articles in the *Journal of Accountancy*, *The Accounting Review*, and the *American Business Law Journal* and authored numerous accounting books, aviation books, and CPE courses.

A PERSONAL THANKS

This edition would not have been possible without the extraordinary effort and dedication of Jedidiah Arnold, Jacob Bennett, Julie Cutlip, Ethan Good, Fernanda Martinez, Bree Rodriguez, Veronica Rodriguez, Bobbie Stanley, Joanne Strong, Elmer Tucker, and Ryan Van Tress, who typed the entire manuscript and all revisions and drafted and laid out the diagrams, illustrations, and cover for this book.

We also appreciate the production and editorial assistance of Andre Alford, Brianna Barnett, Michaela Giampaolo, Doug Green, Jessica Hatker, Sonora Hospital-Medina, Bryce Owen, David Sox, and Alyssa Thomas.

We are also thankful for the critical reading assistance of Amanda Allen, Ryan Guard, Mark Jones, Melissa Leonard, Andrew Schreiber, and Maris Silvestri.

We are also grateful for the video production expertise of Gary Brook, Philip Brubaker, Matthew Church, and Chris Vigilante, who helped produce and edit our Gleim Instruct Video Series.

Finally, we appreciate the encouragement, support, and tolerance of our families throughout this project.

REVIEWERS AND CONTRIBUTORS

Garrett W. Gleim, CIA, CPA, CGMA, leads production of the Gleim CPA, CMA, CIA, and EA exam review systems. He is a member of the American Institute of Certified Public Accountants and the Florida Institute of Certified Public Accountants and holds a Bachelor of Science in Economics with a Concentration in Accounting from The Wharton School, University of Pennsylvania. Mr. Gleim is coauthor of numerous accounting and aviation books and the inventor of multiple patents with educational applications. He is also an avid pilot who holds a commercial pilot rating and is a flight instructor. In addition, as an active supporter of the local business community, Mr. Gleim serves as an advisor to several start-ups with ties to the University of Florida.

Charles M. Day, CPA, CA(SA), MCompt, holds a Bachelor of Commerce in Accounting from KwaZulu-Natal University and a Master of Accounting Sciences from the University of South Africa. Prior to joining Gleim, he taught accounting and finance at the University of Exeter and Oxford Brookes University. He has also worked as an external auditor, internal auditor, management accountant, finance systems consultant, and accounting policy and internal controls coordinator. He was awarded the William S. Smith Certificate of Honor by The Institute of Internal Auditors for outstanding performance on the May 2005 Certified Internal Auditor exam. He used Gleim materials to prepare for the exam. Mr. Day provided substantial editorial assistance throughout the project.

Grady M. Irwin, J.D., is a graduate of the University of Florida College of Law, and he has taught in the University of Florida College of Business. Mr. Irwin provided substantial editorial assistance throughout the project.

Joseph Mauriello, Ph.D., CIA, CISA, CPA, CFE, CMA, CFSA, CRMA, is a Senior Lecturer as well as the Director of the Center for Internal Auditing Excellence at the University of Texas at Dallas. He is also active in his local chapter of The IIA and currently holds the title of Past President. Dr. Mauriello is the lead CIA Gleim Instruct lecturer and provided substantial editorial assistance throughout the project.

Mark S. Modas, M.S.T., CPA, holds a Bachelor of Arts in Accounting from Florida Atlantic University and a Master of Science in Taxation from Nova Southeastern University. He is currently an Assistant Professor of Accounting at Santa Fe College and was formerly the head of the Internal Audit department of Perry Ellis International and the Director of Accounting and Financial Reporting for the School Board of Broward County, Florida. Additionally, Mark worked as the corporate tax compliance supervisor for Ryder Systems, Inc., and has worked as a tax practitioner for more than 25 years. Mr. Modas provided substantial editorial assistance throughout the project.

Floran Syler-Woods, Ph.D., CIA, CPA, is an Associate Professor of Accounting and Data Analytics and Director of the Business Department Assessment and Accreditation at Stillman College. She has over 30 years of experience in management and accounting, having worked as a partner of a public accounting practice, director of finance, director of audit, and regional operations director. Dr. Syler-Woods provided substantial editorial assistance throughout the project.

TABLE OF CONTENTS

DETAILED TABLE OF CONTENTS

GLEIM

ACCOUNTING TITLES FROM GLEIM PUBLICATIONS

CIA Review:

- Part 1: Essentials of Internal Auditing
- Part 2: Practice of Internal Auditing
- Part 3: Business Knowledge for Internal Auditing
- CIA Challenge Exam

CMA Review:

- Part 1: Financial Planning, Performance, and Analytics
- Part 2: Strategic Financial Management

CPA Review:

- Auditing & Attestation (AUD)
- Business Environment & Concepts (BEC)
- Financial Accounting & Reporting (FAR)
- Regulation (REG)

EA Review:

- Part 1: Individuals
- Part 2: Businesses
- Part 3: Representation, Practices and Procedures

Exam Questions and Explanations (EQE) Series:

- Auditing & Systems
- Business Law & Legal Studies
- Cost/Managerial Accounting
- Federal Tax
- Financial Accounting

Gleim also publishes aviation training materials. Go to www.GleimAviation.com for a complete listing of our aviation titles.

A MESSAGE FROM OUR AUTHORS

In 1980, we set out with one goal: to help **you** prepare to pass the CIA exam. We were **the first** CIA review course, and our mission was and continues to be to provide an affordable, effective, and easy-to-use study program. Gleim CIA Review materials comprehensively cover The IIA's CIA Exam Syllabus. While the delivery and technology have changed over the years and are always evolving, our mission and the core learning techniques that we have perfected over the last 40+ years remain the same.

The outline presentation, the spacing, and the question-and-answer formats in this book are designed to facilitate readability, learning, understanding, and your success on the CIA exam. Our most successful candidates use the Gleim Premium CIA Review System*, which includes this book, our innovative SmartAdapt technology, first-of-their-kind Gleim Instruct video lectures, the Gleim Access Until You Pass guarantee, and comprehensive exam-emulating test questions. Our course

- ✓ Teaches how to optimize your score through learning strategies and exam-taking techniques.
- ✓ Defines the subject matter tested on Part 1 of the CIA exam.
- ✓ Outlines all of the Part 1 subject matter in 8 easy-to-use study units, including all relevant authoritative pronouncements.
- ✓ Presents multiple-choice questions taken or modeled from past CIA examinations to prepare you for the types of questions you will see on your CIA exams.
    - In our book, our answer explanations are presented to the immediate right of each multiple-choice question for your convenience. Use a piece of paper to cover our detailed explanations as you answer the question and then review all answer choices to learn why the correct answer is correct and why the other choices are incorrect.
    - You also should practice answering questions through our online platform so you are comfortable answering questions online like you will do on test day. Our adaptive course will focus and target your weak areas.
- ✓ Contains The IIA Glossary and a cross-reference between The IIA CIA Exam Syllabus and the Gleim CIA materials.

Thank you for trusting us as your CIA review provider. Gleim continues to celebrate 40+ years of being the leading CIA review course. We look forward to helping you pass the CIA exam and achieve career success.

We appreciate any and all feedback from candidates like you. Please go to www.gleim.com/feedbackCIA1 to share suggestions on how we can improve this edition.

Please reach out to us immediately after the exam upon receipt of your exam scores. While the CIA exam is nondisclosed, and you must maintain confidentiality of any CIA questions or answers and agree not to divulge the nature of its content, we ask for you to provide information about our materials, such as the topics that need to be added or expanded, so that we are providing the best review materials possible.

Good Luck on the Exam,

Irvin N. Gleim

---

*Visit www.gleimcia.com or call (800) 874-5346 to order.

PREPARING FOR AND TAKING THE CIA EXAM

READ THE *CIA EXAM GUIDE:* *A SYSTEM FOR SUCCESS*

In addition to this book, access the free Gleim *CIA Exam Guide* at www.gleim.com/passCIA and reference it as needed throughout your studying process to obtain a deeper understanding of the attributes that make up the CIA exam. This booklet is your system for success.

OVERVIEW OF THE CIA EXAMINATION

The total exam is 6.5 hours of testing (including 5 minutes per part for a survey). It is divided into three parts, as follows:

CIA Exam (3-Part)			
Part	Title	Exam Length	Number of Questions
1	Essentials of Internal Auditing	2.5 hrs	125 multiple-choice
2	Practice of Internal Auditing	2 hrs	100 multiple-choice
3	Business Knowledge for Internal Auditing	2 hrs	100 multiple-choice

All CIA questions are multiple-choice. The exam is offered continually throughout the year. The CIA exam is computerized to facilitate easier and more convenient testing. Pearson VUE, the testing company that The IIA contracts to proctor the exams, has hundreds of testing centers worldwide. Online testing is also available in select countries/territories, making testing more convenient. The online components of Gleim CIA Review provide exact exam emulations, or mirrors, of the Pearson VUE computer screens and procedures so you feel comfortable at the testing center on exam day.

SUBJECT MATTER FOR PART 1

Below, we have provided The IIA's abbreviated CIA Exam Syllabus for Part 1. This syllabus is for the revised CIA exam offered since January 1, 2019. The percentage coverage and approximate questions for each topic are indicated to its right. We adjust the content of our materials to any interim changes in The IIA's CIA Exam Syllabus announced by The IIA.

Part 1: Essentials of Internal Auditing

		Approximate Questions
I. Foundations of Internal Auditing	15%	19
II. Independence and Objectivity	15%	19
III. Proficiency and Due Professional Care	18%	23
IV. Quality Assurance and Improvement Program	7%	9
V. Governance, Risk Management, and Control	35%	43
VI. Fraud Risks	10%	12
		125

At the time of print, exams for the revised syllabus are currently available in Arabic, Simplified Chinese, Traditional Chinese, English, French, German, Japanese, Korean, Polish, Portuguese, Spanish, Thai, and Turkish. Candidates taking the exam in these languages should use this 2023 edition of Gleim CIA Review.

Appendix B contains the CIA Exam Syllabus in its entirety as well as cross-references to the subunits in our text where topics are covered. Remember that we have studied the syllabus in developing our CIA Review materials. Accordingly, you do not need to spend time with Appendix B. Rather, it should give you confidence that Gleim CIA Review is the best and most comprehensive review course available to help you PASS the CIA exam.

SUCCESS TIP

The IIA has reported concerns from Part 1 candidates that Part 1 has tested topics that should be tested in Part 2 or Part 3. The IIA has clarified that while a Part 1 question may mention a Part 3 topic, such as IT terminology, the question is not testing the IT concept. Rather, it is testing a candidate's understanding and interpretation of a Part 1 concept, such as objectivity, using an industry-related scenario, such as IT.

The takeaway is that candidates should read each question carefully and focus on the concepts in Part 1 and how the material relates to ethics, proficiency, governance, risk management and control, and fraud.

WHICH PRONOUNCEMENTS ARE TESTED?

New pronouncements are eligible to be tested on the CIA exam beginning 6 months after a pronouncement's effective date. Rest assured that Gleim updates these materials as appropriate when any new standard is testable and will only cover what candidates need for the current CIA exam.

NONDISCLOSED EXAM

As part of The IIA's nondisclosure policy and to prove each candidate's willingness to adhere to this policy, a Nondisclosure Agreement and General Terms of Use must be accepted by each candidate before each part is taken. This statement is reproduced here to remind all CIA candidates about The IIA's strict policy of nondisclosure, which Gleim consistently supports and upholds.

I agree to comply with and be bound by The IIA's rules, including this nondisclosure agreement and general terms of use.

I understand that The IIA's exam is confidential and secure, protected by civil and criminal laws of the United States and elsewhere. This exam is confidential and is protected by copyright law.

I have not accessed live questions that might appear on my exam. I agree not to discuss the content of the exam with anyone.

I will not record, copy, disclose, publish, or reproduce any exam questions or answers, in whole or in part, in any form or by any means before, during, or after I take an exam, including orally; in writing; in any internet chat room, message board, or forum; by SMS or text; or otherwise.

I have read, understand, and agree to the terms and conditions set forth in The IIA's Certification Candidate Handbook, including fees, policies, and score invalidations for misconduct, irregularities, or breaches of The IIA's Code of Ethics.

I agree that The IIA has the right to withhold or invalidate any exam score when, in The IIA's judgment, there is a good faith basis to question the validity of a score for any reason, and I will forfeit my exam fee.

I understand that if I do not agree to this nondisclosure agreement and these conditions, I will not be permitted to take the exam, and I will forfeit my exam fee.

THE IIA'S REQUIREMENTS FOR CIA DESIGNATIONS

The CIA designation is granted only by The IIA. Candidates must complete the following steps to become a CIA®:

- ✓ Complete the appropriate certification application form and register for the part(s) you are going to take. Check the CIA blog at www.gleim.com/CIAApply for more information on the application and registration process. The CIA Review course provides a useful checklist to help you keep track of your progress and organize what you need for exam day.

- ✓ Pass all three parts of the CIA exam within 3 years of application approval (4 years if approved before September 1, 2019).

- ✓ Fulfill or expect to fulfill the education and experience requirements (see the free Gleim *CIA Exam Guide* for details).

- ✓ Provide a character reference proving you are of good moral character.

- ✓ Comply with The IIA's Code of Ethics.

ELIGIBILITY PERIOD

Credits for parts passed can be retained as long as the requirements are fulfilled. Candidates accepted into the certification program **on or after September 1, 2019,** must complete the program certification process within **3 years** of application approval. Candidates should note that this time period begins with application approval and not when they pass the first part. If a candidate has not completed the certification process within 3 years, all fees and previously passed exam parts will be forfeited. Candidates who received application approval **before September 1, 2019,** have **4 years** to complete the certification process.

Eligibility Extension: Candidates who have not successfully completed their exam(s), or who have been accepted into the program but have not taken their exam(s), have the opportunity to extend their program eligibility by 12 months. To take advantage of The IIA's one-time Certification Candidate Program Extension, candidates must pay a set fee per applicant and apply through the Candidate Management System.

Transition Information: Candidates who passed one or two parts of the exam prior to 2019 and still need to pass one or two parts will not lose credit for the part(s) already passed. Credit for any part(s) passed in the pre-2019 version of the exam remains valid for the 4-year eligibility window that begins with the application date.

MAINTAINING YOUR CIA DESIGNATION

After passing all three parts, you will receive an email confirming your certification. This email will let you know if any CPE has been awarded and what year you will need to submit information regarding CPE.

CIAs are required to take CPE to maintain and update their knowledge and skills. Practicing CIAs must complete and report 40 hours of Continuing Professional Education (CPE)–including 2 hours of ethics training–every year.

The reporting deadline is December 31. Complete your CPE Reporting Form through the online Certification Candidate Management System. Processing fees vary based on location, membership status, and the method you use to report. Contact Gleim for all of your CPE needs at www.gleim.com/cpe.

GLEIM CIA REVIEW WITH SMARTADAPT

Gleim Premium CIA Review features the most comprehensive coverage of exam content and employs learning techniques that help you prepare for the CIA exam with confidence. The Gleim CIA Review System is powered by our SmartAdapt technology, an innovative learning platform that continually identifies areas you should focus on and guides you through the learning process. Follow these steps for an optimized CIA review:

Step 1: Complete a Diagnostic Quiz.

As you work through this quiz, you will get immediate feedback on your answer choices. This allows you to learn by studying the detailed answer explanations while the quiz sets a baseline that our SmartAdapt technology will use to create a custom learning track.

Step 2: Read, watch, or listen based on your weak areas.

Study identified areas. Learn concepts from our streamlined outlines with detailed examples, topic summaries, tips, and color-coded standards. Watch selections identified from our highly acclaimed Gleim Instruct videos, featuring Dr. Joseph Mauriello, CIA, CPA, CMA. This will ensure you master the required skills.

Step 3: Practice answering multiple-choice questions.

Practice and perfect your question-answering techniques by taking the adaptive quizzes SmartAdapt has created for you to optimize your learning.

Final Review: Complete Mock Exams to complete your final review leading up to your exam.

After completing all study units, take the first Mock Exam, a full-length practice exam. Then, SmartAdapt will guide you through a Final Review based on your results. Finally, a few days before your exam date, take the second Mock Exam. SmartAdapt will tell you when you are ready so you can pass with confidence.

To facilitate your studies, the Gleim Premium CIA Review System uses the most comprehensive test bank of exam-quality CIA questions on the market. Our system's content and presentation are the most realistic representation of the whole exam environment allowing you to feel completely at ease on test day.

GLEIM KNOWLEDGE TRANSFER OUTLINES

This edition of the Gleim CIA Review books has the following features to make studying easier:

Examples

We use illustrative examples, set off in shaded boxes, to make the concepts more relatable.

EXAMPLE 2-1   Scope Limitation

An internal audit activity was recently engaged to audit the final balance of inventory for the financial statements. During the audit, senior management contacted the lead auditor and stated that the internal audit activity would not be given access to the physical inventory.

The denial of access to the inventory is a scope limitation. The internal audit activity needs to communicate the nature of the scope limitation and its potential effects to the board. This communication should preferably be in writing.

Gleim Success Tips

These tips supplement the core exam material by suggesting how certain topics might be presented on the exam or how you should prepare for an issue.

SUCCESS TIP

Knowledge of the IPPF is important for understanding and distinguishing among the elements of the authoritative guidance on internal auditing. But it is more important that you **understand** and can accurately **apply** the **content** contained in the IPPF. Parts 1 and 2 of the CIA exam primarily test understanding and application of IPPF content.

Flowcharts and Visuals

These images help to conceptualize ideas and make procedures clear.

- Governance does not exist independently of risk management and control. Rather, governance, risk management, and control (collectively referred to as GRC) are interrelated.

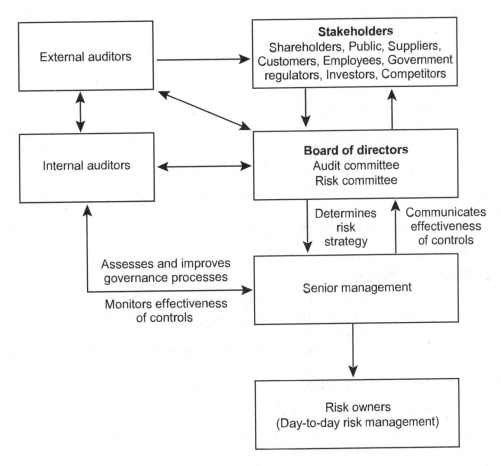

Figure 4-1

Memory Aids

We offer mnemonic devices to help you remember important concepts.

- A useful memory aid for the COSO components of internal control is "Controls stop **CRIME**."

C	**C**ontrol activities
R	**R**isk assessment
I	**I**nformation and communication
M	**M**onitoring
E	Control **e**nvironment

Guidance Designations

In an effort to help CIA candidates better grasp The IIA's authoritative literature, we have come up with visual indicators to help candidates easily identify each type of guidance.

Attribute Standard 1000
Purpose, Authority, and Responsibility

The purpose, authority, and responsibility of the internal audit activity must be formally defined in an internal audit charter, consistent with the Mission of Internal Audit and the mandatory elements of the International Professional Practices Framework (the Core Principles for the Professional Practice of Internal Auditing, the Code of Ethics, the *Standards*, and the Definition of Internal Auditing). The chief audit executive must periodically review the internal audit charter and present it to senior management and the board for approval.

Performance Standard 2120
Risk Management

The internal audit activity must evaluate the effectiveness and contribute to the improvement of risk management processes.

Interpretation of Standard 1000

The internal audit charter is a formal document that defines the internal audit activity's purpose, authority, and responsibility. The internal audit charter establishes the internal audit activity's position within the organization, including the nature of the chief audit executive's functional reporting relationship with the board; authorizes access to records, personnel, and physical properties relevant to the performance of engagements; and defines the scope of internal audit activities. Final approval of the internal audit charter resides with the board.

Implementation Standard 1110.A1

The internal audit activity must be free from interference in determining the scope of internal auditing, performing work, and communicating results. The chief audit executive must disclose such interference to the board and discuss the implications.

TIME-BUDGETING AND QUESTION-ANSWERING TECHNIQUES FOR THE EXAM

Having a solid multiple-choice answering technique will help you maximize your score on each part of the CIA exam. Remember, knowing how to take the exam and how to answer individual questions is as important as studying/reviewing the subject matter tested on the exam. Competency in both will reduce your stress and the number of surprises you experience on exam day.

- **Budget your time so you can finish before time expires.**

  - Spend about 1 minute per question. This would result in completing 125 questions in 125 minutes to give you 25 minutes to review your answers and questions that you have marked.

- **Ignore the answer choices so that they will not affect your precise reading of the question.**

  - Only one answer option is best. In the MCQs, four answer choices are presented, and you know one of them is correct. The remaining choices are distractors and are meant to appear correct at first glance. *They are called distractors for a reason.* Eliminate them as quickly as you can.

  - In computational items, the distractors are carefully calculated to be the result of common mistakes. Be careful and double-check your computations if time permits.

- **Read the question carefully to discover exactly what is being asked.**

  - Focusing on what is required allows you to
    - ✓ Reject extraneous information
    - ✓ Concentrate on relevant facts
    - ✓ Proceed directly to determining the best answer

  - Be careful! The requirement may be an **exception** that features a negative word.

- **Decide the correct answer before looking at the answer choices.**

- **Read the answer choices, paying attention to small details.**

  - Even if an answer choice appears to be correct, do not skip the remaining answer choices. Each choice requires consideration because you are looking for the best answer provided.

  - Tip: Treat each answer choice like a true/false question as you analyze it.

  - Be careful choosing answer choices that include absolutes such as "always" or "never."

  - Often an answer choice is a correct statement but is outside the scope of the question. For example, a question may ask for procedures, and the incorrect answer choices are procedures, albeit not the correct procedures for the topic.

- **Click on the best answer.**

  - You have a 25% chance of answering the question correctly by guessing blindly, but you can improve your odds with an educated guess.

  - For many MCQs, you can eliminate two answer choices with minimal effort and increase your educated guess to a 50/50 proposition.
    - ▸ Rule out answers that you think are incorrect.
    - ▸ Speculate what The IIA is looking for and/or why the question is being asked.
    - ▸ Select the best answer or guess between equally appealing answers. Your first guess is usually the most intuitive.

- **Answer the questions in consecutive order.**

  - Do **not** agonize over any one item or question. Stay within your time budget.

  - Never leave a multiple-choice question (MCQ) unanswered. Your score is based on the number of correct responses. You will not be penalized for answering incorrectly. If you are unsure about a question, do the following:
    - ✓ Make an educated guess,
    - ✓ Mark it for review at the bottom of the screen, and
    - ✓ Return to it before you submit your exam as time allows.

LEARNING FROM YOUR MISTAKES

During your studies, do not get frustrated if you score low on a practice quiz. It is an opportunity to learn, and learning from questions you answer incorrectly is very important. Each question you answer incorrectly is an **opportunity** to avoid missing actual test questions on your CIA exam. Thus, you should carefully study the answer explanations provided until you understand why the original answer you chose is wrong, as well as why the correct answer indicated is correct. This study technique is clearly the difference between passing and failing for many CIA candidates.

Also, you **must** determine why you answered questions incorrectly and learn how to avoid the same error in the future. Reasons for missing questions include

- ⊘ Misreading the requirement (stem)
- ⊘ Not understanding what is required
- ⊘ Making a math error
- ⊘ Applying the wrong rule or concept
- ⊘ Being distracted by one or more of the answers
- ⊘ Incorrectly eliminating answers from consideration
- ⊘ Not having any knowledge of the topic tested
- ⊘ Employing bad intuition when guessing

It is also important to verify that you answered correctly for the right reasons. Otherwise, if the material is tested on the CIA exam in a different manner, you may not answer it correctly.

HOW TO BE IN CONTROL
WHILE TAKING THE EXAM

You have to be in control to be successful during exam preparation and execution. Control can also contribute greatly to your personal and other professional goals. Control is a process whereby you

- Develop expectations, standards, budgets, and plans
- Undertake activity, production, study, and learning
- Measure the activity, production, output, and knowledge
- Compare actual activity with expected and budgeted activity
- Modify the activity, behavior, or study to better achieve the desired outcome
- Revise expectations and standards in light of actual experience
- Continue the process or restart the process in the future

Exercising control will ultimately develop the confidence you need to outperform most other CIA candidates and PASS the CIA exam! Obtain our *CIA Exam Guide* for a more detailed discussion of control and other exam tactics.

IF YOU HAVE QUESTIONS ABOUT GLEIM MATERIALS

Gleim has an efficient and effective way for candidates who have purchased the Premium CIA Review System to submit an inquiry and receive a response regarding Gleim materials directly through their course. This system also allows you to view your Q&A session in your Gleim Personal Classroom.

Questions regarding the **information in this introduction and/or the *CIA Exam Guide* (study suggestions, studying plans, exam specifics)** should be emailed to personalcounselor@gleim.com.

Questions concerning **orders, prices, shipments, or payments** should be sent via email to customerservice@gleim.com and will be promptly handled by our competent and courteous customer service staff.

For **technical support**, you may use our automated technical support service at www.gleim.com/support, email us at support@gleim.com, or call us at (800) 874-5346.

FEEDBACK

Please fill out our online feedback form (www.gleim.com/feedbackCIA1) immediately after you take the CIA exam so we can adapt to changes in the exam. Our approach has been approved by The IIA.

GLEIM CIA REVIEW

We make it easier to keep your CIA materials current.

gleim.com/CIAupdate

Updates are available until the next edition is released.

STUDY UNIT ONE

FOUNDATIONS OF INTERNAL AUDITING

(26 pages of outline)

This study unit covers **Domain I: Foundations of Internal Auditing** from The IIA's CIA Exam Syllabus. This domain makes up 15% of Part 1 of the CIA exam and is tested at the **basic** and **proficient** cognitive levels.

The **learning objectives** of Study Unit 1 are

- Interpret The IIA's Mission of Internal Audit, Definition of Internal Auditing, and Core Principles for the Professional Practice of Internal Auditing, as well as the purpose, authority, and responsibility of the internal audit activity

- Explain the requirements of an internal audit charter (required components, board approval, communication of the charter, etc.)

- Interpret the difference between assurance and consulting services provided by the internal audit activity

- Demonstrate conformance with The IIA Code of Ethics

Internal auditors perform assurance and consulting activities designed to evaluate and improve the effectiveness of the entity's governance, risk management, and internal control processes using a systematic, disciplined, and risk-based approach. This may include evaluation of internal control, examination of financial and operating information, review of compliance with laws and regulations, and the assessment of fraud risk.

1.1 APPLICABLE GUIDANCE

International Professional Practices Framework (IPPF)

The Institute of Internal Auditors (The IIA) defines the **mission** of internal audit as follows:

- "To enhance and protect organizational value by providing risk-based and objective assurance, advice, and insight."

- Facilitating the achievement of this mission is the IPPF.

The IPPF contains **mandatory** guidance and **recommended** guidance.

Figure 1-1

Mandatory Guidance

Adherence to the mandatory guidance is essential for the professional practice of internal auditing.

- The mandatory guidance consists of four elements:

    1. The **Core Principles** for the Professional Practice of Internal Auditing
    2. The **Definition of Internal Auditing**
    3. The **Code of Ethics**
    4. The *Standards*

- The Core Principles and the Definition of Internal Auditing are reflected in the Code of Ethics and the *Standards*. Thus, conformance with the Code and the *Standards* demonstrates conformance with all mandatory elements of the IPPF.

- If the *Standards* are used with requirements of other authoritative bodies, internal audit communications also may cite the other requirements. But, if the *Standards* and other requirements are inconsistent, internal auditors must conform with the *Standards* and may conform with the other requirements if they are more restrictive.

Figure 1-2

Element 1 of 4

The **Core Principles** are the basis for internal audit effectiveness. The internal audit function is effective if all principles are present and operating effectively. The following are the 10 Core Principles:

1. "Demonstrates integrity.
2. Demonstrates competence and due professional care.
3. Is objective and free from undue influence (independent).
4. Aligns with the strategies, objectives, and risks of the organization.
5. Is appropriately positioned and adequately resourced.
6. Demonstrates quality and continuous improvement.
7. Communicates effectively.
8. Provides risk-based assurance.
9. Is insightful, proactive, and future-focused.
10. Promotes organizational improvement."

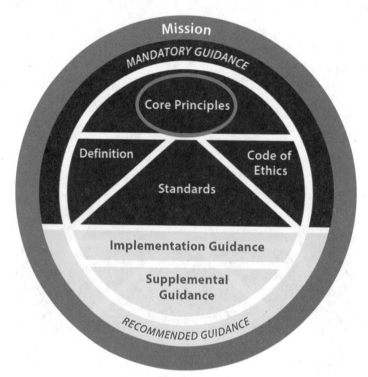

Figure 1-3

Element 2 of 4

The **Definition of Internal Auditing** is a concise statement of the role of the internal audit activity in the organization.

> "Internal auditing is an independent, objective assurance and consulting activity designed to add value and improve an organization's operations. It helps an organization accomplish its objectives by bringing a systematic, disciplined approach to evaluate and improve the effectiveness of **risk management, control, and governance processes**."

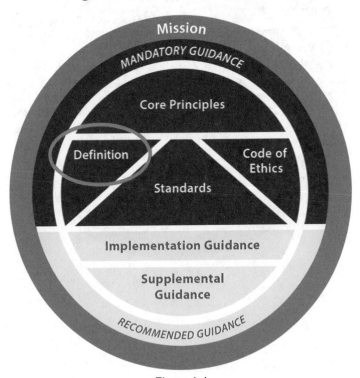

Figure 1-4

Element 3 of 4

The **Code of Ethics** is covered in detail in later subunits.

Figure 1-5

Element 4 of 4

The **Standards** (known formally as the *International Standards for the Professional Practice of Internal Auditing*) serve the following four purposes described by The IIA:

1. "Guide adherence with the mandatory elements of the International Professional Practices Framework.

2. Provide a framework for performing and promoting a broad range of value-added internal auditing services.

3. Establish the basis for the evaluation of internal audit performance.

4. Foster improved organizational processes and operations."

The *Standards* are vital to the practice of internal auditing, but CIA candidates need not memorize them. However, the principles they establish should be thoroughly understood and appropriately applied.

Figure 1-6

Types of Standards

Attribute Standards describe the characteristics of organizations and parties providing internal auditing services. They govern the responsibilities, attitudes, and actions of the organization's internal audit activity and the people who serve as internal auditors. Attribute Standards are displayed in green boxes throughout this text to emphasize their importance.

Performance Standards describe the nature of internal auditing and provide quality criteria for evaluation of internal audit performance. They govern the nature of internal auditing and provide quality criteria for evaluating the internal audit function's performance.

Interpretations of Attribute or Performance Standards are provided by The IIA to clarify terms and concepts. They are displayed in blue boxes.

Implementation Standards apply to specific types of engagements. They expand upon the individual Attribute or Performance Standards by providing the requirements applicable to assurance (A) or consulting (C) services. They are displayed in gray boxes throughout this text.

Recommended Guidance

Implementation Guidance and Supplemental Guidance constitute recommended guidance. They describe practices for effective implementation of the mandatory elements of the IPPF: (1) the Core Principles, (2) the Definition of Internal Auditing, (3) the Code of Ethics, and (4) the *Standards*.

Figure 1-7

Purpose, Authority, and Responsibility of the Internal Audit Activity

Each organization's internal audit charter lays out the purpose, authority, and responsibility of the internal audit activity for that organization.

Purpose

The purpose of the internal audit activity is to provide "independent, objective assurance and consulting services designed to add value and improve an organization's operations.

- The internal audit activity helps an organization accomplish its objectives by bringing a systematic, disciplined approach to evaluate and improve the effectiveness of governance, risk management and control processes" (The IIA Glossary).

There are two general types of internal audit activities: assurance services and consulting services.

1. **Assurance services** involve the internal auditor's objective assessment of evidence to provide opinions or conclusions regarding an entity, operation, function, process, system, or other subject matters. It is an objective examination of evidence for the purpose of providing an independent assessment of governance, risk management, and control processes for the organization.

    - The **nature and scope** of an assurance engagement are determined by the internal auditor.
    - Generally, the process owner, the internal auditor, and the user are the three participants in assurance services.

        1. The **process owner** is the person or group directly involved with the entity, operation, function, process, system, or other subject matter.
        2. The **internal auditor** is the person or group making the assessment).
        3. The **user** is the person or group using the assessment.

    - Examples of assurance services include

        - Financial
        - Performance
        - Compliance
        - System security
        - Due diligence

2. **Consulting services** are advisory in nature and generally are performed at the specific request of an engagement client. Consulting services are activities intended to add value and improve an organization's governance, risk management, and control processes without the internal auditor's assumption of management responsibility.

    ■   The **nature and scope** of the consulting engagement are subject to agreement with the engagement client.

    ■   Generally, the internal auditor and the engagement client are the two participants in consulting services.

        1. The **internal auditor** is the person or group offering the advice.

            ●   When performing consulting services, the internal auditor should maintain objectivity and not assume management responsibility.

        2. The **engagement client** is the person or group seeking and receiving the advice.

    ■   Consulting services include providing counsel, advice, facilitation, and training.

Authority

The board of directors adopts a formal charter that grants sufficient authority to a chief audit executive and the internal audit activity.

The support of management and the board is crucial when inevitable conflicts arise between the internal audit activity and the department or function under review. Thus, the internal audit activity should be empowered to require auditees to grant access to all records, personnel, and physical properties relevant to the performance of every engagement. ·

●   A formal **charter** that defines the internal audit activity's authority must be adopted. The authority granted should be sufficient. Final approval of the charter resides with the board.

Responsibility

The internal audit activity's responsibility also is defined in the charter. It should provide the organization with assurance and consulting services that will add value and improve the organization's operations.

●   Specifically, the internal audit activity must evaluate and improve the effectiveness of the organization's governance, risk management, and control processes.

You have completed the outline for this subunit.
Study multiple-choice questions 1 through 3 on page 39.

STOP & REVIEW

1.2 ETHICS -- INTRODUCTION AND PRINCIPLES

Author's Note: The gray boxes throughout the rest of this study unit are quotes from The IIA's Code of Ethics.

Introduction

The IIA incorporates the Definition of Internal Auditing into the Introduction to the Code of Ethics and specifies the reasons for establishing the Code.

Introduction to The IIA's Code of Ethics

The purpose of The Institute's Code of Ethics is to promote an ethical culture in the profession of internal auditing.

Internal auditing is an independent, objective assurance and consulting activity designed to add value and improve an organization's operations. It helps an organization accomplish its objectives by bringing a systematic, disciplined approach to evaluate and improve the effectiveness of risk management, control, and governance processes.

A code of ethics is necessary and appropriate for the profession of internal auditing, founded as it is on the trust placed in its objective assurance about governance, risk management, and control.

The Institute's Code of Ethics extends beyond the Definition of Internal Auditing to include two essential components:

1. Principles that are relevant to the profession and practice of internal auditing.

2. Rules of Conduct that describe behavior norms expected of internal auditors. These rules are an aid to interpreting the Principles into practical applications and are intended to guide the ethical conduct of internal auditors.

"Internal auditors" refers to Institute members, recipients of or candidates for IIA professional certifications, and those who perform internal audit services within the Definition of Internal Auditing.

Applicability

The provisions of the Code are applied broadly to all organizations and persons who perform internal audit services, not just CIAs and members of The IIA.

Applicability and Enforcement of the Code of Ethics

This Code of Ethics applies to both entities and individuals that perform internal audit services.

For IIA members and recipients of or candidates for IIA professional certifications, breaches of the Code of Ethics will be evaluated and administered according to The Institute's Bylaws and Administrative Directives. The fact that a particular conduct is not mentioned in the Rules of Conduct does not prevent it from being unacceptable or discreditable, and therefore, the member, certification holder, or candidate can be liable for disciplinary action.

- Violations of rules of ethics should be reported to The IIA's board of directors.

Principles

The Rules of Conduct in the Code are organized based on the principles of integrity, objectivity, confidentiality, and competency.

Principles

Internal auditors are expected to apply and uphold the following principles:

1. **Integrity**
   The integrity of internal auditors establishes trust and thus provides the basis for reliance on their judgment.

2. **Objectivity**
   Internal auditors exhibit the highest level of professional objectivity in gathering, evaluating, and communicating information about the activity or process being examined. Internal auditors make a balanced assessment of all the relevant circumstances and are not unduly influenced by their own interests or by others in forming judgments.

3. **Confidentiality**
   Internal auditors respect the value and ownership of information they receive and do not disclose information without appropriate authority unless there is a legal or professional obligation to do so.

4. **Competency**
   Internal auditors apply the knowledge, skills, and experience needed in the performance of internal audit services.

Rules of Conduct

1. **Integrity**

Internal auditors:

1.1. Shall perform their work with honesty, diligence, and responsibility.

1.2. Shall observe the law and make disclosures expected by the law and the profession.

1.3. Shall not knowingly be a party to any illegal activity, or engage in acts that are discreditable to the profession of internal auditing or to the organization.

1.4. Shall respect and contribute to the legitimate and ethical objectives of the organization.

2. **Objectivity**

Internal auditors:

2.1. Shall not participate in any activity or relationship that may impair or be presumed to impair their unbiased assessment. This participation includes those activities or relationships that may be in conflict with the interests of the organization.

2.2. Shall not accept anything that may impair or be presumed to impair their professional judgment.

2.3. Shall disclose all material facts known to them that, if not disclosed, may distort the reporting of activities under review.

3. **Confidentiality**

Internal auditors:

3.1. Shall be prudent in the use and protection of information acquired in the course of their duties.

3.2. Shall not use information for any personal gain or in any manner that would be contrary to the law or detrimental to the legitimate and ethical objectives of the organization.

4. **Competency**

Internal auditors:

4.1. Shall engage only in those services for which they have the necessary knowledge, skills, and experience.

4.2. Shall perform internal audit services in accordance with the *International Standards for the Professional Practice of Internal Auditing*.

4.3. Shall continually improve their proficiency and the effectiveness and quality of their services.

To remember the above principles on the CIA exam, use the memory aid **I O**nly **C**arry **C**ash.

STOP & REVIEW

You have completed the outline for this subunit.
Study multiple-choice questions 4 and 5 on page 40.

1.3 ETHICS -- INTEGRITY

Rules of Conduct – Integrity

Integrity
Internal auditors:

1.1. Shall perform their work with honesty, diligence, and responsibility.

1.2. Shall observe the law and make disclosures expected by the law and the profession.

1.3. Shall not knowingly be a party to any illegal activity, or engage in acts that are discreditable to the profession of internal auditing or to the organization.

1.4. Shall respect and contribute to the legitimate and ethical objectives of the organization.

Further guidance on integrity is provided in Implementation Guide, *Code of Ethics: Integrity*.

- "Integrity is the **foundation** of the other three principles in The IIA's Code of Ethics. Objectivity, confidentiality, and competency all depend on integrity. Integrity also underpins the *Standards*."

- The chief audit executive's (CAE's) responsibility for implementing integrity includes the following:

  - "[T]he CAE should cultivate a culture of integrity by acting with integrity and adhering to the Code of Ethics."

  - "The CAE also establishes policies and procedures to guide the internal audit activity . . . to show diligence and responsibility."

  - "[T]he CAE also may emphasize the importance of integrity by providing training that demonstrates integrity and other ethical principles in action."

- For internal auditors, "the best attempts to identify and measure integrity likely involve astute awareness and understanding of the Code of Ethics' rules of conduct for integrity, the IPPF's Mandatory Guidance, and supporting practices."

- "For internal auditors, behaviors that may not be illegal but may be **discreditable** include:

  - Behavior that may be considered bullying, harassing, or discriminatory.

  - Failing to accept responsibility for making mistakes.

  - Issuing false reports or permitting others to do so.

  - Lying.

  - Making claims about one's competency in a manner that is deceptive, false, or misleading.

  - Making disparaging comments about the organization, fellow employees, or its stakeholders, either in person or via media (e.g., in publications or social media posts).

- Minimizing, concealing, or omitting observations or unsatisfactory conclusions and ratings from engagement reports or overall assessments.
- Noncompliance with the *Standards* and other IPPF Mandatory Guidance.
  - Performing internal audit services with undeclared impairments to independence and objectivity.
  - Performing internal audit services for which one is not competent.
  - Soliciting or disclosing confidential information without proper authorization.
  - Stating that the internal audit activity is operating in conformance with the *Standards* when the assertion is not supported by the results of the quality assurance and improvement program.
- Overlooking illegal activities that the organization may tolerate or condone.
- Using the CIA designation or other credentials after they have expired or been revoked."

How to Comply with the Integrity Rule

Maintenance, and reporting on, a quality assurance and improvement program (QAIP) by the CAE and participation of internal auditors in continuing professional education (CPE)

Internal auditor accountability demonstrated by the following:

- The organization's ethics policies or code of conduct
- Relevant laws and regulations
- The IIA's Code of Ethics
- IPPF Mandatory Guidance

Diligent supervision of engagements and performance of the self-assessments required by the *Standards* demonstrate the integrity of the internal audit activity as a whole.

EXAMPLE 1-1	Conformance with the Integrity Rule

An internal auditor is working for a cosmetics manufacturer that may be inappropriately testing cosmetics on animals. If, out of loyalty to the employer, no information about the testing is gathered, the auditor violated the Rules of Conduct by

- Knowingly becoming a party to an illegal act,
- Engaging in an act discreditable to the profession,
- Failing to make disclosures expected by the law, and
- Not performing the work diligently.

You have completed the outline for this subunit.
Study multiple-choice questions 6 and 7 on page 41.

STOP & REVIEW

1.4   ETHICS -- OBJECTIVITY

Rules of Conduct – Objectivity

Objectivity
Internal auditors:

    2.1. Shall not participate in any activity or relationship that may impair or be presumed to impair their unbiased assessment. This participation includes those activities or relationships that may be in conflict with the interests of the organization.

    2.2. Shall not accept anything that may impair or be presumed to impair their professional judgment.

    2.3. Shall disclose all material facts known to them that, if not disclosed, may distort the reporting of activities under review.

SUCCESS TIP

The objectivity principle is a frequently tested ethics topic. Being able to apply the rules of conduct related to objectivity to scenarios will increase your success on the exam. To do this, a higher level of understanding beyond memorization is required.

A material ownership interest in a competitor is allowable. An internal auditor seldom can during the course of employment take action to enhance the value of the ownership interest.

For example, if management override of an important control creates exposure to a material risk, the internal auditor is ethically obligated to report the matter to senior officials charged with performing the governance function. Disclosure is not limited by time constraints.

An internal auditor cannot assure anonymity. Information communicated to an internal auditor is not deemed to be privileged. However, promising merely to attempt to keep the source of the information confidential is allowed.

Disclosure is not required when the internal auditor gathers sufficient information to dispel the suspicion of fraud.

The CAE should share information and coordinate activities with other internal and external providers of relevant assurance and consulting services.

Conflict of Interest Policy

A conflict of interest policy should prohibit the transfer of benefits between an employee and those with whom the organization deals.

Examples of violations of Rules 2.1., 2.2., and 2.3. include the following:

- **Rule of Conduct 2.1.**

  1. Excessive individual fraternizing outside of work with the organization's employees, management, third-party suppliers, and vendors.

  2. Certain dealings in commercial properties (excluding rental activity).

  3. Sales of services or products by the internal auditor to the organization.

  4. Participation in non-public service organizations may not be allowed, for example, serving as a consultant to third parties (vendors, suppliers, etc.) with which the organization conducts business.

  5. Performing an audit in a department managed by a family member.

  6. Accepting a bonus based on work accomplished during an audit.

  7. Assuming management responsibilities and auditing an area in which the auditor had such responsibilities within 1 year.

- **Rule of Conduct 2.2.**

  1. Accepting gifts, meals, trips, and special treatment that exceed policy limits or are not disclosed and approved

  2. Working in a non-audit position and accepting gifts not permitted by IIA code of conduct

- **Rule of Conduct 2.3.**

  1. Intentional omission of disclosures of illegal activity from final engagement communications

  2. Withholding pertinent information

  3. Not communicating pertinent information to the chief audit executive

  4. Distorting facts reported in final engagement communications

Conformance with objectivity is demonstrated by the following:

- The CAE provides relevant policies and procedures for the internal audit activity.

- The CAE requires internal auditors attend meetings or training sessions about objectivity (for example, CPE).

- The CAE documents the rationale for allocation of resources to the internal audit plan, including potential impairments.

- Other evidence may include documentation of research into potential conflicts of interest involving outsourced and cosourced activities.

- Approval of the CAE or a designated engagement supervisor of engagement workpapers may evidence that internal auditors have conducted a balanced assessment.

- Feedback from post-engagement surveys and supervisory reviews of engagements may provide additional evidence that the internal auditors' work appeared to be performed objectively.

- Assessments as part of the internal audit activity's quality assurance and improvement program also lend support that appropriate objectivity was used in arriving at internal audit conclusions and opinions.

EXAMPLE 1-2 Conformance with the Objectivity Rule

At the end of the year, an internal auditing team made observations and recommendations that an organization can use to improve operating efficiency. To express gratitude, the division manager presented the internal audit team with a gift of moderate value. The internal audit team meets to discuss whether to accept the gift. The following reasons for accepting or not accepting the gift were discussed:

One auditor said, "we *should* accept the gift because its value is insignificant."

Another auditor said, "we *should not* accept the gift until after we submit our final engagement communication."

A third auditor said, "we *should not* accept the gift."

The lead auditor considered the opinions of the other auditors and the intent of the Rules of Conduct. The lead auditor then decided that acceptance of the gift would be inappropriate because of the presumed impairment of the internal auditor's professional judgment.

STOP & REVIEW

You have completed the outline for this subunit.
Study multiple-choice questions 8 through 12 beginning on page 42.

1.5 ETHICS -- CONFIDENTIALITY

Rules of Conduct – Confidentiality

Confidentiality

Internal auditors:

    3.1. Shall be prudent in the use and protection of information acquired in the course of their duties.

    3.2. Shall not use information for any personal gain or in any manner that would be contrary to the law or detrimental to the legitimate and ethical objectives of the organization.

Further guidance on confidentiality is provided in Implementation Guide, *Code of Ethics: Confidentiality*:

- "Organizations usually issue **information security policies** to protect the data they acquire, use, and produce and to ensure compliance with the laws and regulations that pertain to the industry and jurisdiction within which they operate."

    - "To protect proprietary information, policies and procedures may require internal auditors to take the following precautions, even when handling information internally:

        ‣ Collect only the data required to perform the assigned engagement and use this information only for the engagement's intended purposes.

        ‣ Protect information from intentional or unintentional disclosure through the use of controls such as data encryption, email distribution restrictions, and restriction of physical access to the information.

        ‣ Eliminate copies of or access to such data when it is no longer needed."

- "To better understand the effects of legal and regulatory requirements and protections (e.g., legal privilege or attorney-client privilege), the chief audit executive (CAE) should **consult with legal counsel**. The organization's policies and procedures may require that specific authorities review and approve business information before external release."

- "Rule of Conduct 3.2 emphasizes that internal auditors must not use any information for personal gain.

- For example, internal auditors should not use insider financial, strategic, or operational knowledge of an organization to bring about personal financial gain by purchasing or selling shares in the organization.

- Another example is releasing insider knowledge to journalists or via other media without proper authorization. Using **insider information** to develop a competitive product or selling proprietary information to a competitor also violates this confidentiality rule.

- Furthermore, internal auditors should not abuse their privilege to access information, such as using access to customer records to look up a neighbor's recent purchases or to view the health records of a celebrity."

- Conformance with confidentiality is demonstrated as follows:
    - "The CAE may demonstrate support of internal audit confidentiality through evidence of policies, processes, procedures, and training materials implemented to cover confidentiality as it applies to the internal audit activity and the organization."
    - "Regarding the release of engagement results, reports, or related information, the CAE demonstrates conformance with the confidentiality principle and rules of conduct by documenting and retaining records of disclosures approved by legal counsel, if applicable, and by senior management and the board."
    - "Internal auditors demonstrate conformance with engagement record confidentiality by documenting distribution restrictions in engagement workpapers and reports and by retaining authorizations of all disclosures and approved distribution lists."
    - Given no reports or investigations of individual auditors' violations of policies, procedures, and rules related to confidentiality, the internal audit activity as a whole most likely is in conformance with the principle.

EXAMPLE 1-3	Conformance with the Confidentiality Rule

Which of the following violate(s) The IIA's Code of Ethics?

- Investigating a lead sales person's expense reports based on rumors of overstatement.
    - Investigating potential instances of fraud is within the internal auditor's normal responsibilities. It is not a violation.
- Purchasing stock in a target organization after reading company reports that it may be acquired.
    - Rule of Conduct 3.2 states, "Internal auditors shall not use information for any personal gain." The stock purchase is a violation.
- Disclosing confidential information in response to a court order.
    - The principle of confidentiality permits the disclosure of confidential information given a legal or professional obligation to do so. This disclosure is not a violation.

STOP & REVIEW

You have completed the outline for this subunit.
Study multiple-choice questions 13 and 14 on page 44.

1.6 ETHICS -- COMPETENCY

Rules of Conduct – Competency

Competency
Internal auditors:

4.1. Shall engage only in those services for which they have the necessary knowledge, skills, and experience.

4.2. Shall perform internal audit services in accordance with the *International Standards for the Professional Practice of Internal Auditing*.

4.3. Shall continually improve their proficiency and the effectiveness and quality of their services.

Further guidance on competency is provided in Implementation Guide, *Code of Ethics: Competency*:

- Conformance with competency is demonstrated by the following:

  - "The CAE may demonstrate a culture supportive of competency and the continual improvement of proficiency, effectiveness, and quality through evidence that:

    ‣ Engagements have been properly resourced and supervised.

    ‣ Feedback has been solicited from internal audit stakeholders and sufficiently considered.

    ‣ Performance reviews of internal auditors have been conducted regularly.

    ‣ Opportunities for training, mentoring, and professional education have been provided.

    ‣ A quality assurance and improvement program is active.

    ‣ Internal audit services are performed in conformance with the IPPF's Mandatory Guidance."

- "The knowledge, skills, and experience of individual internal auditors may be evidenced, in part, through

  1. Credentialed qualifications, such as university degrees and certifications, and

  2. Relevant work history as detailed on the internal auditor's resume, which the CAE or the organization's human resources department should have on file."

- "[I]nternal auditors may maintain documentation of a skills self-assessment, a plan for professional development, and the completion of continuing professional education/ development courses or trainings."

- To expand their competencies, internal auditors may provide evidence of experiences undertaken, for example, specific work assignments (that is, on-the-job training) or volunteering in professional organizations.

- Also, pursuing and completing professional education, whether for new certifications or continuing professional education, further evidences internal auditors' commitment to continual improvement of their proficiency and the effectiveness and quality of their services.

EXAMPLE 1-4   Conformance with the Competency Rule

Which of the following violate(s) The IIA's Code of Ethics?

- After obtaining evidence that an employee is embezzling funds, the internal auditor interrogates the suspect. The organization has a security department.

  - Internal auditors generally lack the knowledge, skills, or experience regarding interrogation of suspects possessed by security specialists. The lack of proficiency most likely is a violation.

- An internal auditor has been assigned to perform an engagement in the warehousing department next year. The auditor currently has no expertise in this area but accepted the assignment and plans to take continuing professional education courses in warehousing.

  - The internal auditor plans to acquire the required knowledge and skills prior to the start of this engagement. The internal auditor most likely did not violate the Code of Ethics.

STOP & REVIEW

You have completed the outline for this subunit.
Study multiple-choice questions 15 through 17 beginning on page 45.

1.7 INTERNAL AUDIT CHARTER

Internal Audit Charter

Attribute Standard 1000
Purpose, Authority, and Responsibility

The purpose, authority, and responsibility of the internal audit activity must be formally defined in an internal audit charter, consistent with the Mission of Internal Audit and the mandatory elements of the International Professional Practices Framework (the Core Principles for the Professional Practice of Internal Auditing, the Code of Ethics, the *Standards*, and the Definition of Internal Auditing). The chief audit executive must periodically review the internal audit charter and present it to senior management and the board for approval.

The following Interpretation was issued by The IIA:

Interpretation of Standard 1000

The internal audit charter is a formal document that defines the internal audit activity's purpose, authority, and responsibility. The internal audit charter establishes the internal audit activity's position within the organization, including the nature of the chief audit executive's functional reporting relationship with the board; authorizes access to records, personnel, and physical properties relevant to the performance of engagements; and defines the scope of internal audit activities. Final approval of the internal audit charter resides with the board.

Engagement clients must be informed of the internal audit activity's purpose, authority, and responsibility to prevent misunderstandings about access to records and personnel.

An auditee must not be able to place a **scope limitation** on the internal audit activity by refusing to make relevant records, personnel, and physical properties available to the internal auditors.

Implementation Guide 1000, *Purpose, Authority, and Responsibility*, further addresses the charter.

- "To create [the internal audit charter], the chief audit executive (CAE) must understand the Mission of Internal Audit and the mandatory elements of The IIA's International Professional Practices Framework (IPPF), including

    - The Core Principles for the Professional Practice of Internal Auditing,
    - The Code of Ethics,
    - The *International Standards for the Professional Practice of Internal Auditing*, and
    - The Definition of Internal Auditing.

- The charter is the understanding that provides the foundation for a discussion among the CAE, senior management, and the board to **mutually agree upon**

    - Internal audit objectives and responsibilities
    - The expectations for the internal audit activity
    - The CAE's functional and administrative reporting lines
    - The level of authority (including access to physical property, personnel, and records) required for the internal audit activity to perform engagements and fulfill its agreed-upon objectives and responsibilities"

- "The CAE may need to confer with the organization's legal counsel or the board secretary regarding the preferred format for charters and how to effectively and efficiently submit the proposed internal audit charter for board approval.

- Once **drafted**, the proposed internal audit charter should be discussed with senior management and the board to confirm that it accurately describes the agreed-upon role and expectations or to identify desired changes. Once the draft has been **accepted**, the CAE **formally presents** it during a board meeting to be discussed and approve.

- The **minutes** of the board meetings during which the CAE initially discusses and then formally presents the internal audit charter provide documentation of conformance. In addition, the **CAE retains the approved charter**."

The charter must define the nature of assurance and consulting services provided by the internal audit activity. Two Implementation Standards state this.

Implementation Standard 1000.A1

The nature of assurance services provided to the organization must be defined in the internal audit charter. If assurances are to be provided to parties outside the organization, the nature of these assurances must also be defined in the internal audit charter.

Implementation Standard 1000.C1

The nature of consulting services must be defined in the internal audit charter.

The charter also must refer to the four elements of the mandatory guidance portion of the IPPF: (1) the Core Principles, (2) the Code of Ethics, (3) the *Standards*, and (4) the Definition of Internal Auditing.

Attribute Standard 1010
Recognizing Mandatory Guidance in the Internal Audit Charter

The mandatory nature of the Core Principles for the Professional Practice of Internal Auditing, the Code of Ethics, the *Standards*, and the Definition of Internal Auditing must be recognized in the internal audit charter. The chief audit executive should discuss the Mission of Internal Audit and the mandatory elements of the International Professional Practices Framework with senior management and the board.

The IIA's model internal audit charter is available from The IIA; however, it is restricted to IIA members only.

Key Definitions from the Glossary

The complete IIA Glossary is in Appendix A. The definitions do not need to be memorized, but they should be understood so candidates can apply them to multiple-choice questions.

Chief audit executive (CAE) describes the role of a person in a senior position responsible for effectively managing the internal audit activity in accordance with the internal audit charter and the mandatory elements of the International Professional Practices Framework.

- The chief audit executive or others reporting to the chief audit executive will have appropriate professional certifications and qualifications.

- The specific job title or responsibilities of the chief audit executive may vary across organizations.

The **board** is the highest-level governing body (e.g., a board of directors, a supervisory board, or a board of governors or trustees) charged with the responsibility to direct or oversee the organization's activities and hold senior management accountable.

- Although governance arrangements vary among jurisdictions and sectors, typically the board includes members who are not part of management.

- If a board does not exist, the word "board" in the *Standards* refers to a group or person charged with governance of the organization.

- Furthermore, "board" in the *Standards* may refer to a committee or another body to which the governing body has delegated certain functions (e.g., an audit committee).

STOP & REVIEW

You have completed the outline for this subunit.
Study multiple-choice questions 18 through 21 beginning on page 46.

QUESTIONS

1.1 Applicable Guidance

1. Which Standards expand upon the other categories of Standards?

    A. Performance Standards.

    B. Attribute Standards.

    C. Implementation Standards.

    D. All of the choices are correct.

Answer (C) is correct.
    REQUIRED: The Standards that expand upon other Standards.
    DISCUSSION: Implementation Standards expand upon the Attribute and Performance Standards. They provide requirements applicable to assurance or consulting engagements.
    Answer (A) is incorrect. Performance Standards apply to all internal audit services. **Answer (B) is incorrect.** Attribute Standards apply to all internal audit services. **Answer (D) is incorrect.** Only Implementation Standards expand upon the standards in other categories.

2. The purpose of the internal audit activity can be best described as

    A. Adding value to the organization.

    B. Providing additional assurance regarding fair presentation of financial statements.

    C. Expressing an opinion on the adequate design and functioning of the system of internal control.

    D. Assuring the absence of any fraud that would materially affect the financial statements.

Answer (A) is correct.
    REQUIRED: The best description of the internal audit activity.
    DISCUSSION: Internal auditing is an independent, objective assurance and consulting activity designed to add value and improve an organization's operations (Definition of Internal Auditing).

3. The *Standards* consist of three types of Standards. Which Standards apply to the characteristics of providers of internal auditing services?

    A. Implementation Standards.

    B. Performance Standards.

    C. Attribute Standards.

    D. Independence Standards.

Answer (C) is correct.
    REQUIRED: The Standards describing the traits of entities and individuals providing internal auditing services.
    DISCUSSION: Attribute Standards describe the characteristics of organizations and parties providing internal auditing services.
    Answer (A) is incorrect. Implementation Standards apply to specific types of engagements. **Answer (B) is incorrect.** Performance Standards describe the nature of internal auditing and provide quality criteria for evaluation of internal audit performance. **Answer (D) is incorrect.** The IPPF does not contain Independence Standards.

1.2 Ethics -- Introduction and Principles

4. In complying with The IIA's Code of Ethics, an internal auditor should

    A. Use individual judgment in the application of the principles set forth in the Code.

    B. Respect and contribute to the objectives of the organization even if it is engaged in illegal activities.

    C. Go beyond the limitation of personal technical skills to advance the interest of the organization.

    D. Primarily apply the competency principle in establishing trust.

Answer (A) is correct.
    REQUIRED: The action complying with The IIA's Code of Ethics.
    DISCUSSION: The IIA's Code of Ethics includes principles that internal auditors are expected to apply and uphold. They are interpreted by the Rules of Conduct, behavior norms expected of internal auditors. That a particular conduct is not mentioned in the Rules of Conduct does not prevent it from being unacceptable or discreditable. Consequently, a reasonable inference is that individual judgment is necessary in the application of the principles and the Rules of Conduct.
    Answer (B) is incorrect. An internal auditor "shall not knowingly be a party to any illegal activity." Furthermore, an internal auditor is bound to respect and contribute only to the legitimate and ethical objectives of the organization. **Answer (C) is incorrect.** Internal auditors "shall engage only in those services for which they have the necessary knowledge, skills, and experience." **Answer (D) is incorrect.** Applying and upholding the integrity principle is the means by which an internal auditor establishes trust as a basis for reliance on his or her judgment.

5. An internal auditor who encounters an ethical dilemma **not** explicitly addressed by The IIA's Code of Ethics should always

    A. Seek counsel from an independent attorney to determine the personal consequences of potential actions.

    B. Take action consistent with the principles embodied in The IIA's Code of Ethics.

    C. Seek the counsel of the audit committee before deciding on an action.

    D. Act consistently with the employing organization's code of ethics even if such action would not be consistent with The IIA's Code of Ethics.

Answer (B) is correct.
    REQUIRED: The action that must be taken by an internal auditor regarding an ethical dilemma not explicitly addressed by The IIA's Code of Ethics.
    DISCUSSION: The IIA's Code of Ethics is based on principles relevant to the profession and practice of internal auditing that internal auditors are expected to apply and uphold: integrity, objectivity, confidentiality, and competency. Furthermore, the Code states that particular conduct may be unacceptable or discreditable even if it is not mentioned in the Rules of Conduct.
    Answer (A) is incorrect. The auditor must act consistently with the spirit of The IIA's Code of Ethics. It is not practical to seek the advice of legal counsel for all ethical decisions. Moreover, unethical behavior may not be illegal. **Answer (C) is incorrect.** It is not feasible to seek the audit committee's advice for all potential dilemmas. Furthermore, the advice might not be consistent with the profession's standards. **Answer (D) is incorrect.** If the organization's standards are not consistent with, or as high as, the profession's standards, the internal auditor should abide by the latter.

1.3 Ethics -- Integrity

6. Which situation is most likely a violation of The IIA's Code of Ethics?

A. Reporting apparent violations of antitrust statutes by officers to government regulators.

B. Cooperating with the government's criminal investigation of the organization.

C. Reporting apparent violations of antitrust statutes by officers to the board of directors.

D. Immediately reporting a violent crime observed at work to local law enforcement agencies.

Answer (A) is correct.
   REQUIRED: The violation of The IIA's Code of Ethics.
   DISCUSSION: An internal auditor must (1) not knowingly be a party to any illegal activity (Rule of Conduct 1.3); (2) disclose all material facts known to him or her that, if not disclosed, might distort the reporting of activities under review (Rule of Conduct 2.3); and (3) respect and contribute to the legitimate and ethical objectives of the organization (Rule of Conduct 1.4). Thus, when apparent violations of antitrust statutes by officers come to the internal auditor's attention, (s)he should report to the board of directors rather than directly to the government regulators. An internal auditor also must observe the law and make any disclosures required by the law or by the profession (Rule of Conduct 1.2).
   Answer (B) is incorrect. Everyone has a legal obligation to cooperate with a criminal investigation. An internal auditor must observe the law and make any disclosures required by the law or by the profession (Rule of Conduct 1.2). **Answer (C) is incorrect.** An internal auditor should report apparent improprieties to the board. **Answer (D) is incorrect.** Everyone has a legal and moral obligation to report violent crimes immediately.

7. The IIA's Code of Ethics requires internal auditors to perform their work with

A. Honesty, diligence, and responsibility.

B. Timeliness, sobriety, and clarity.

C. Knowledge, skills, and competencies.

D. Punctuality, objectivity, and responsibility.

Answer (A) is correct.
   REQUIRED: The qualities internal auditors should exhibit in the performance of their work.
   DISCUSSION: Rule of Conduct 1.1 under the integrity principle states, "Internal auditors shall perform their work with honesty, diligence, and responsibility."
   Answer (B) is incorrect. Timeliness, sobriety, and clarity are not mentioned in the Code. **Answer (C) is incorrect.** Knowledge, skills, and competencies are mentioned in the *Standards*. **Answer (D) is incorrect.** Punctuality is not mentioned in the Code.

1.4 Ethics -- Objectivity

8. Which of the following situations is a violation of The IIA's Code of Ethics?

- A. An internal auditor, with the knowledge and consent of management, accepted a token gift from a customer of the organization that was not presumed to impair and did not impair judgment.
- B. Knowing that management was aware of the situation, an internal auditor purposely left a description of an unlawful practice out of the final engagement communication.
- C. An internal auditor shared techniques with internal auditors from another organization.
- D. Based upon knowledge of the probable success of the employer's business, an internal auditor invested in a mutual fund that specialized in the same industry.

Answer (B) is correct.
REQUIRED: The violation of The IIA's Code of Ethics.
DISCUSSION: Rule of Conduct 2.3 under the objectivity principle states, "Internal auditors shall disclose all material facts known to them that, if not disclosed, may distort the reporting of activities under review." Moreover, Rule of Conduct 1.3 under the integrity principle states, "Internal auditors shall not knowingly be a party to any illegal activity, or engage in acts that are discreditable to the profession of internal auditing or to the organization."
Answer (A) is incorrect. Acceptance of anything from a customer is prohibited but only if it would impair or be presumed to impair professional judgment.
Answer (C) is incorrect. Rule of Conduct 4.3 under the competency principle states, "Internal auditors shall continually improve their proficiency and the effectiveness and quality of their services." **Answer (D) is incorrect.** Although an internal auditor is prohibited from using confidential information for personal gain, and an investment in the organization's stock would be questionable, an investment in a mutual fund is acceptable.

9. Which of the following concurrent occupations could appear to subvert the ethical behavior of an internal auditor?

- A. Internal auditor and a well-known charitable organization's local in-house chairperson.
- B. Internal auditor and part-time business insurance broker.
- C. Internal auditor and adjunct faculty member of a local business college that educates potential employees.
- D. Internal auditor and landlord of multiple housing that publicly advertises for tenants in a local community newspaper listing monthly rental fees.

Answer (B) is correct.
REQUIRED: The concurrent occupations that could create an ethical issue.
DISCUSSION: Rule of Conduct 2.1 under the objectivity principle states, "Internal auditors shall not participate in any activity or relationship that may impair or be presumed to impair their unbiased assessment. This participation includes those activities or relationships that may be in conflict with the interests of the organization." As a business insurance broker, the internal auditor may lose his or her objectivity because (s)he might benefit from a change in the employer's insurance coverage.
Answer (A) is incorrect. The activities of a charity are unlikely to be contrary to the interests of the organization. **Answer (C) is incorrect.** Teaching is compatible with internal auditing. **Answer (D) is incorrect.** Whereas dealing in commercial properties might involve a conflict, renting residential units most likely does not.

10. Which of the following activities of an internal auditor is most likely to be acceptable under The IIA's Code of Ethics?

    A. Late arrivals and early departures from work because this practice is common in the organization.

    B. Frequent luncheons and other socializing with major suppliers of the organization without the consent of senior management.

    C. Conducting an unrelated business outside of office hours.

    D. Acceptance of a material gift from a supplier.

Answer (C) is correct.

    REQUIRED: The acceptable activity under The IIA's Code of Ethics.

    DISCUSSION: Nothing in The IIA's Code of Ethics prohibits operating an unrelated business outside of regular office hours. The activity is not, in itself, (1) a conflict of interest, (2) a use of information for personal gain, or (3) an impairment of the internal auditor's unbiased assessment.

    Answer (A) is incorrect. Internal auditors should exercise diligence in performing their duties. **Answer (B) is incorrect.** Rule of Conduct 2.1 under the objectivity principle states, "Internal auditors shall not participate in any activity or relationship that may impair or be presumed to impair their unbiased assessment. This participation includes those activities or relationships that may be in conflict with the interests of the organization." **Answer (D) is incorrect.** Rule of Conduct 2.2 under the objectivity principle states, "Internal auditors shall not accept anything that may impair or be presumed to impair their professional judgment."

11. In their reporting, internal auditors are required by The IIA's Code of Ethics to

    A. Present sufficient factual information without revealing confidential matters that could be detrimental to the organization.

    B. Disclose all material information obtained by the auditor as of the date of the final engagement communication.

    C. Obtain factual information within the established time and budget parameters.

    D. Disclose material facts known to the internal auditor that could distort the final engagement communication if not revealed.

Answer (D) is correct.

    REQUIRED: The reporting responsibility under The IIA's Code of Ethics.

    DISCUSSION: Rule of Conduct 2.3 under the objectivity principle states, "Internal auditors shall disclose all material facts known to them that, if not disclosed, may distort the reporting of activities under review."

    Answer (A) is incorrect. The Code requires only that internal auditors be prudent in the use and protection of information. **Answer (B) is incorrect.** The Code does not address disclosure this specifically. **Answer (C) is incorrect.** Time and budget parameters are not addressed in the Code.

12. Objectivity is an ethical requirement for all persons engaged in the professional practice of internal auditing. One aspect of objectivity requires

    A. Performance of professional duties in accordance with relevant laws.

    B. Avoidance of conflict of interest.

    C. Refraining from using confidential information for unethical or illegal advantage.

    D. Maintenance of an appropriate level of professional expertise.

Answer (B) is correct.

    REQUIRED: The aspect of the objectivity requirement.

    DISCUSSION: Commitment to independence from conflicts of economic or professional interest is an aspect of objectivity.

    Answer (A) is incorrect. Observing the law is a component of integrity. **Answer (C) is incorrect.** Not using confidential information for unethical or illegal advantage is an aspect of confidentiality. **Answer (D) is incorrect.** Maintenance of an appropriate level of professional expertise is an aspect of competency.

1.5 Ethics -- Confidentiality

13. Which of the following actions taken by a chief audit executive (CAE) could be considered professionally ethical under The IIA's Code of Ethics?

- A. The CAE decides to delay an engagement at a branch so that his nephew, the branch manager, will have time to "clean things up."
- B. To save organizational resources, the CAE cancels all staff training for the next 2 years on the basis that all staff are too new to benefit from training.
- C. To save organizational resources, the CAE limits procedures at foreign branches to confirmations from branch managers that no major personnel changes have occurred.
- D. The CAE refuses to provide information about organizational operations to his father, who is a part owner.

Answer (D) is correct.

REQUIRED: The action considered ethical under The IIA's Code of Ethics.

DISCUSSION: Rule of Conduct 3.1 under the confidentiality principle states, "Internal auditors shall be prudent in the use and protection of information acquired in the course of their duties." Additionally, Rule of Conduct 3.2 states, "Internal auditors shall not use information for any personal gain or in any manner that would be contrary to the law or detrimental to the legitimate and ethical objectives of the organization." Thus, such use of information by the CAE might be illegal under insider trading rules.

Answer (A) is incorrect. According to Rule of Conduct 1.1, "Internal auditors shall perform their work with honesty, diligence, and responsibility." **Answer (B) is incorrect.** According to Rule of Conduct 4.3, "Internal auditors shall continually improve their proficiency and the effectiveness and quality of their services." **Answer (C) is incorrect.** According to Rule of Conduct 4.2, "Internal auditors shall perform internal audit services in accordance with the *International Standards for the Professional Practice of Internal Auditing (Standards).*" The *Standards* require supporting information to be sufficient, reliable, relevant, and useful.

14. An internal auditor is performing services in a division in which the chief financial officer is a close personal friend, and the internal auditor learns that the friend is to be replaced after a series of critical labor negotiations. The internal auditor relays this information to the friend. Has a violation of The IIA's Code of Ethics occurred?

- A. No. The use of the confidential information resulted in no personal gain to the internal auditor.
- B. No. The internal auditor was just being honest with his or her friend.
- C. Yes. The internal auditor had a conflict of interest with the organization.
- D. Yes. The internal auditor was not prudent in the use of information acquired in the course of his or her duties.

Answer (D) is correct.

REQUIRED: The basis for the violation, if any, of The IIA's Code of Ethics.

DISCUSSION: Rule of Conduct 3.1 under the confidentiality principle states, "Internal auditors shall be prudent in the use and protection of information acquired in the course of their duties." Rule of Conduct 3.2 states, "Internal auditors shall not use information for any personal gain or in any manner that would be contrary to the law or detrimental to the legitimate and ethical objectives of the organization." In this case, the decision whether to notify the financial officer of his or her replacement was properly the organization's. Accordingly, the internal auditor was bound not to tell his or her friend.

Answer (A) is incorrect. The Rules of Conduct specifically prohibit using information in a manner that would be detrimental to the legitimate and ethical objectives of the organization. **Answer (B) is incorrect.** The Rules of Conduct specifically prohibit using information in a manner that would be detrimental to the legitimate and ethical objectives of the organization. **Answer (C) is incorrect.** The facts do not suggest that a conflict of interest with the organization existed. However, such a conflict would be present, for example, if the internal auditor used confidential information to seize a business opportunity that rightfully belonged to the organization. Furthermore, the internal auditor's objectivity was impaired by auditing a division in which a relative or close personal friend was employed. The impairment, whether in fact or appearance, requires disclosure of the details to appropriate parties.

1.6 Ethics -- Competency

15. Under The IIA's Code of Ethics, an entity that provides internal auditing services is specifically required to

A. Maintain certain predetermined staffing requirements for engagements.

B. Comply with the *International Standards for the Professional Practice of Internal Auditing.*

C. Comply with organizational policy.

D. Participate in a formal continuing education program.

Answer (B) is correct.
    REQUIRED: The requirement of The IIA's Code of Ethics.
    DISCUSSION: The IIA's Code of Ethics applies not only to individuals but also to entities that provide internal auditing services. Rule of Conduct 4.2 under the competency principle states, "Internal auditors shall perform internal audit services in accordance with the *International Standards for the Professional Practice of Internal Auditing*."
    Answer (A) is incorrect. Staffing requirements must be determined based on the circumstances of each engagement. **Answer (C) is incorrect.** The Code requires internal auditors to respect and contribute to the legitimate and ethical objectives of the organization and not engage in acts discreditable to the organization. However, the Code does not specifically mention compliance with organizational policy. **Answer (D) is incorrect.** The Code requires compliance with the *Standards*, and the *Standards* require internal auditors to enhance their knowledge, skills, and other competencies through continuing professional development, but neither the Code nor the *Standards* require formal continuing education.

16. A new staff internal auditor was told to perform an engagement in an area with which the internal auditor was not familiar. Because of time constraints, no supervision was provided. The assignment represented a good learning experience, but the area was clearly beyond the internal auditor's competence. Nonetheless, the internal auditor prepared comprehensive working papers and communicated the results to management. In this situation,

A. The internal audit activity violated the *Standards* by hiring an internal auditor without proficiency in the area.

B. The internal audit activity violated the *Standards* by not providing adequate supervision.

C. The chief audit executive has not violated The IIA's Code of Ethics because it does not address supervision.

D. The *Standards* and The IIA's Code of Ethics were followed by the internal audit activity.

Answer (B) is correct.
    REQUIRED: The effect of failing to supervise an internal auditor who lacks proficiency in the area of the engagement.
    DISCUSSION: Rule of Conduct 4.2 under the competency principle requires internal auditing services to be performed in accordance with the *Standards*. Attr. Std. 1200 requires engagements to be performed with proficiency and due professional care. They also should be properly supervised to ensure that objectives are achieved, quality is assured, and staff is developed (Perf. Std. 2340).
    Answer (A) is incorrect. All internal auditors need not be proficient in all areas. The internal audit activity as a whole should have an appropriate mix of skills. **Answer (C) is incorrect.** The Code requires compliance with the *Standards*, and the *Standards* require proper supervision. **Answer (D) is incorrect.** The *Standards* and the Code were not followed.

17. Which of the following most likely constitutes a violation of The IIA's Code of Ethics?

 A. Auditor A has accepted an assignment to perform an engagement at the electronics manufacturing division. Auditor A has recently joined the internal audit activity. But Auditor A was senior auditor for the external audit of that division and has audited many electronics organizations during the past 2 years.

 B. Auditor B has been assigned to perform an engagement at the warehousing function 6 months from now. Auditor B has no expertise in that area but accepted the assignment anyway. Auditor B has signed up for continuing professional education courses in warehousing that will be completed before the assignment begins.

 C. Auditor C is content as an internal auditor and has come to look at it as a regular 9-to-5 job. Auditor C has not engaged in continuing professional education or other activities to improve effectiveness during the last 3 years. However, Auditor C feels performance of quality work is the same as before.

 D. Auditor D discovered an internal financial fraud during the year. The books were adjusted to properly reflect the loss associated with the fraud. Auditor D discussed the fraud with the external auditor when the external auditor reviewed working papers detailing the incident.

Answer (C) is correct.
 REQUIRED: The violation of The IIA's Code of Ethics.
 DISCUSSION: Rule of Conduct 4.3 under the competency principle states, "Internal auditors shall continually improve their proficiency and the effectiveness and quality of their services."
 Answer (A) is incorrect. No professional conflict of interest exists per se, especially given that the internal auditor was previously in public accounting. However, the internal auditor should be aware of potential conflicts. **Answer (B) is incorrect.** An internal auditor must possess the necessary knowledge, skills, and competencies at the time an engagement is conducted, not the time it is accepted. **Answer (D) is incorrect.** The information was disclosed as part of the normal process of cooperation between the internal and external auditor. Because the books were adjusted, the external auditor was expected to inquire as to the nature of the adjustment.

1.7 Internal Audit Charter

18. The authority of the internal audit activity is limited to that granted by

 A. The board and the controller.

 B. Senior management and the *Standards*.

 C. Management and the board.

 D. The board and the chief financial officer.

Answer (C) is correct.
 REQUIRED: The source of authority of the internal audit activity.
 DISCUSSION: The purpose, authority, and responsibility of the internal audit activity must be formally defined in a charter. The CAE must periodically review and present the charter to senior management and the board for approval (Attr. Std. 1000).
 Answer (A) is incorrect. The controller is not the only member of management. **Answer (B) is incorrect.** The *Standards* cannot provide actual authority to an internal audit activity. **Answer (D) is incorrect.** Management and the board, not a particular manager, give the internal audit activity its authority.

19. The chief audit executive (CAE) is best defined as the

    A. Inspector general.

    B. Person responsible for the internal audit function.

    C. Outside provider of internal audit services.

    D. Person responsible for overseeing the contract with the outside provider of internal audit services.

Answer (B) is correct.
    REQUIRED: The best definition of the CAE.
    DISCUSSION: The CAE is a person in a senior position responsible for effectively managing the internal audit activity in accordance with the internal audit charter and the mandatory elements of the IPPF (The IIA Glossary).
    Answer (A) is incorrect. The specific job title of the chief audit executive may vary across organizations (The IIA Glossary). **Answer (C) is incorrect.** The internal audit activity may be insourced. **Answer (D) is incorrect.** The term "chief audit executive" is defined broadly because (1) the internal audit activity may be insourced or outsourced and (2) many different titles are used in practice.

20. Which one of the following must be included in the internal audit charter?

    A. Internal audit objectivity.

    B. Internal audit responsibility.

    C. Chief audit executive's compensation plan.

    D. Number of full-time internal audit employees deemed to be the necessary minimum.

Answer (B) is correct.
    REQUIRED: The item required to be included in the internal audit charter.
    DISCUSSION: The purpose, authority, and responsibility of the internal audit activity must be formally defined in an internal audit charter.
    Answer (A) is incorrect. Objectivity is an attribute of individual auditors and is not included in the internal audit charter. **Answer (C) is incorrect.** The CAE's compensation plan is not an appropriate matter to include in the internal audit charter. **Answer (D) is incorrect.** The staffing of the internal audit activity is determined by the CAE and the board; it is not an appropriate matter to include in the internal audit charter.

21. The chief audit executive meets with the members of the internal audit activity at scheduled staff meetings. Which of the following is the most appropriate function of such a staff meeting?

    A. Developing the engagement work schedule.

    B. Revising travel, promotion, and compensation policies.

    C. Explaining administrative policies and obtaining suggestions from the staff.

    D. Developing long-range training programs that will meet the staff's needs.

Answer (C) is correct.
    REQUIRED: The most appropriate activity at an audit staff meeting.
    DISCUSSION: One reason for staff meetings is to explain routine administrative matters, to teach new techniques, and even to let off steam. For example, staff members should be able to raise questions about ineffective procedures, promotions, salaries, or other problems.
    Answer (A) is incorrect. Management of the internal audit activity should develop engagement work schedules. **Answer (B) is incorrect.** Management of the internal audit activity should revise travel, promotion, and compensation policies. **Answer (D) is incorrect.** Developing long-range training programs that will meet the staff's needs should be done by management of the internal audit activity.

GO TO ONLINE COURSE

Access the **Gleim CIA Premium Review System** featuring our SmartAdapt technology from your Gleim Personal Classroom to continue your studies. You will experience a personalized study environment with exam-emulating multiple-choice questions.

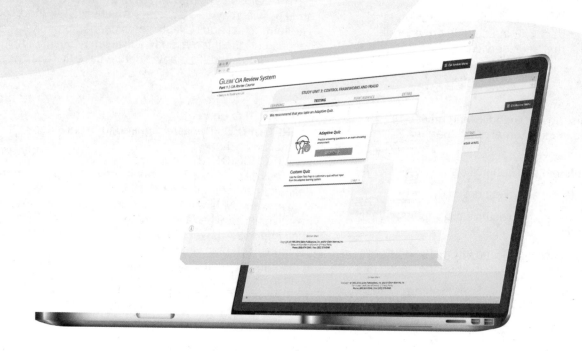

STUDY UNIT TWO

INDEPENDENCE, OBJECTIVITY, AND PROFICIENCY

(24 pages of outline)

This study unit covers all of **Domain II: Independence and Objectivity** (Subunits 2.1-2.3) and the "Proficiency" section of **Domain III: Proficiency and Due Professional Care** (Subunits 2.4-2.5) from The IIA's CIA Exam Syllabus. Domains II and III make up 15% and 18%, respectively, of Part 1 of the CIA exam and are tested at the **basic** and **proficient** cognitive levels. The study units covering Domains II and III are

- **Study Unit 2: Independence, Objectivity, and Proficiency**
- Study Unit 3: Due Professional Care and Quality Assurance and Improvement Program

The **learning objectives** of Study Unit 2 are

- Interpret organizational independence of the internal audit activity (importance of independence, functional reporting, etc.)

- Identify whether the internal audit activity has any impairments to its independence

- Assess and maintain an individual internal auditor's objectivity, including determining whether an individual internal auditor has any impairments to his/her objectivity

- Analyze policies that promote objectivity

- Recognize the knowledge, skills, and competencies required to fulfill the responsibilities of the internal audit activity

- Demonstrate the knowledge and competencies that an internal auditor needs to possess to perform his/her individual responsibilities, including technical skills and soft skills (communication, critical thinking, persuasion/negotiation, collaboration, etc.)

To inspire confidence, an internal auditor must be not only independent (intellectually honest) but also recognized as independent (free of any obligation to, or interest in, the client, management, or owners). An internal auditor must have independence of mind (fact) and independence in appearance. Objectivity, the ability to perform tasks without bias, is judged by the function's organizational status and relevant policies and procedures that support objectivity. Internal auditors and the internal audit activity must possess the knowledge, skills, and other competencies needed to perform assigned responsibilities.

2.1 INDEPENDENCE OF THE INTERNAL AUDIT ACTIVITY

While Attribute Standard 1100 defines independence and objectivity, this subunit focuses on independence of the internal audit activity. (Objectivity is the subject of Subunit 2.2.)

Attribute Standard 1100

Independence and Objectivity

The internal audit activity must be independent, and internal auditors must be objective in performing their work.

Independence

Independence is an organizational attribute of the internal audit activity as a whole. The IIA clarifies this distinction in the Interpretation below.

Interpretation of Standard 1100 (para. 1)

Independence is the freedom from conditions that threaten the ability of the internal audit activity to carry out internal audit responsibilities in an unbiased manner. To achieve the degree of independence necessary to effectively carry out the responsibilities of the internal audit activity, the chief audit executive has direct and unrestricted access to senior management and the board. This can be achieved through a **dual-reporting** relationship. Threats to independence must be managed at the individual auditor, engagement, functional, and organizational levels.

Dual reporting separates reporting into two parts:

1. **Functional** reporting and
2. **Administrative** reporting.

Achieving Independence through Functional Reporting to the Board

In this Standard, the reporting level that assures independence is identified in general terms:

Attribute Standard 1110

Organizational Independence

The chief audit executive must report to a level within the organization that allows the internal audit activity to fulfill its responsibilities. The chief audit executive must confirm to the board, at least annually, the organizational independence of the internal audit activity.

The related Interpretation specifies a reporting relationship that effectively achieves independence:

Interpretation of Standard 1110

Organizational independence is effectively achieved when the chief audit executive reports functionally to the board. Examples of functional reporting to the board involve the board:

- Approving the internal audit charter.

- Approving the risk based internal audit plan.

- Approving the internal audit budget and resource plan.

- Receiving communications from the chief audit executive on the internal audit activity's performance relative to its plan and other matters.

- Approving decisions regarding the appointment and removal of the chief audit executive.

- Approving the remuneration of the chief audit executive.

- Making appropriate inquiries of management and the chief audit executive to determine whether there are inappropriate scope or resource limitations.

Board Interaction

The CAE's access to the board must not be limited.

Attribute Standard 1111
Direct Interaction with the Board
The chief audit executive must communicate and interact directly with the board.

Further guidance on the CAE's direct communication with the board is provided in Implementation Guide 1111, *Direct Interaction with the Board*:

- "If the CAE has a direct functional reporting relationship with the board, then the board assumes responsibility for approving the internal audit charter, internal audit plan, internal audit budget and resource plan, evaluation and compensation of the CAE, and appointment and removal of the CAE. Further, the board monitors the ability of internal audit to operate independently and fulfill its charter."

- "Under a functional reporting relationship, the CAE will have many opportunities to communicate and interact directly with the board, as required by Attribute Standard 1111 *(Direct Interaction with the Board)*."

  - "For example, the CAE will participate in audit committee and/or full board meetings, generally quarterly, to communicate such things as the proposed internal audit plan, budget, progress, and any challenges."

  - "Further, the CAE will have the ability to contact the chair or any member of the board to communicate sensitive matters or issues facing internal audit or the organization."

  - "Typically, and **at least annually**, a private meeting with the board or audit committee and the CAE (without senior management present) is formally conducted to discuss such matters or issues."

  - "It is also helpful for the CAE to participate in one-on-one meetings or phone calls periodically with the board or audit committee chair, either prior to scheduled meetings or routinely during the year, to ensure direct and open communication."

- "Board meeting agendas and minutes are often sufficient to demonstrate whether the CAE has communicated and interacted directly with the board."

Facilitating Independence through Dual Reporting

SUCCESS TIP

The dual-reporting relationship is the most frequently tested aspect of the independence attribute. The organizational independence of the internal audit activity is achieved when it reports functionally to the board and administratively to senior management.

Further guidance on the dual-reporting relationship is provided in Implementation Guide 1110, *Organizational Independence*:

- "[T]he CAE works with the board and senior management to determine organizational placement of internal audit, including the CAE's reporting relationships. To ensure effective organizational independence, the CAE has a direct functional reporting line to the board."

    - But the CAE cannot solely determine organizational independence and placement.

- "A **functional reporting** line to the **board** provides the CAE with direct board access for sensitive matters and enables sufficient organizational status. It ensures that the CAE has unrestricted access to the board, typically the highest level of governance in the organization."

- "Generally, the CAE also has an **administrative reporting** line to senior management, which further enables the requisite stature and authority of internal audit to fulfill responsibilities."

    - "For example, the CAE typically **would not** report to a controller, accounting manager, or mid-level functional manager."

    - "To enhance stature and credibility, The IIA recommends that the CAE report administratively to the **chief executive officer (CEO)** so that the CAE is clearly in a senior position, with the authority to perform duties unimpeded."

- Conformance with *Organizational Independence* may be demonstrated, among other means, through

    - "[T]he internal audit charter and the audit committee charter, which would describe the audit committee's oversight duties."

    - "The CAE's job description and performance evaluation[, which] would note reporting relationships and supervisory oversight."

    - "[A]n internal audit policy manual that addresses policies like independence and board communication requirements or an organization chart with reporting responsibilities . . . "

The following Implementation Standard clarifies how internal audit's independence is applied as a practical matter:

Implementation Standard 1110.A1

The internal audit activity must be free from interference in determining the scope of internal auditing, performing work, and communicating results. The chief audit executive must disclose such interference to the board and discuss the implications.

STOP & REVIEW

You have completed the outline for this subunit.
Study multiple-choice questions 1 through 4 beginning on page 73.

2.2 OBJECTIVITY OF INTERNAL AUDITORS

This subunit focuses on the objectivity of the internal auditor as defined in Attribute Standard 1100.

Objectivity

SUCCESS TIP

Independence is an attribute of the internal audit activity. In contrast, objectivity is an attribute of individual internal auditors. Knowledge of this distinction will increase your success on the exam.

Internal auditors must be objective in performing their work.

Objectivity is an attribute of individual internal auditors. The IIA clarifies this distinction in the following Interpretation:

Interpretation of Standard 1100 (para. 2)

Objectivity is an unbiased mental attitude that allows internal auditors to perform engagements in such a manner that they believe in their work product and that no quality compromises are made. Objectivity requires that internal auditors do not subordinate their judgment on audit matters to others. Threats to objectivity must be managed at the individual auditor, engagement, functional, and organizational levels.

The importance of objectivity as an attribute of individual internal auditors is embodied in the following Standard:

Attribute Standard 1120
Individual Objectivity

Internal auditors must have an impartial, unbiased attitude and avoid any conflict of interest.

Conflict of Interest

The IIA Glossary defines conflict of interest as any relationship that is, or appears to be, not in the best interest of the organization. A conflict of interest would prejudice an individual's ability to perform his or her duties and responsibilities objectively.

The importance of identifying potential conflicts of interest of individual internal auditors is clarified in the following Interpretation:

Interpretation of Standard 1120

Conflict of interest is a situation in which an internal auditor, who is in a position of trust, has a competing professional or personal interest. Such competing interests can make it difficult to fulfill his or her duties impartially. A conflict of interest exists even if no unethical or improper act results. A conflict of interest can create an appearance of impropriety that can undermine confidence in the internal auditor, the internal audit activity, and the profession. A conflict of interest could impair an individual's ability to perform his or her duties and responsibilities objectively.

Aspects of Objectivity

Further guidance on the objectivity of internal auditors is provided in Implementation Guide 1120, *Individual Objectivity*:

- "Objectivity refers to an internal auditor's **impartial and unbiased mindset**, which is facilitated by avoiding conflicts of interest."

- "To manage internal audit objectivity effectively, many CAEs have an internal audit **policy manual or handbook** that describes the expectation and requirements for an unbiased mindset for every internal auditor. Such a policy manual may describe

    - The critical importance of objectivity to the internal audit profession.
    - Typical situations that could undermine objectivity, such as
        ▸ Auditing in an area in which an internal auditor recently worked;
        ▸ Auditing a family member or a close friend; or
        ▸ Assuming, without evidence, that an area under audit is acceptable based solely on prior positive experiences.
    - Actions the internal auditor should take if he or she becomes aware of a current or potential objectivity concern, such as discussing the concern with an internal audit manager or the CAE.
    - Reporting requirements, where each internal auditor periodically considers and discloses conflicts of interest."
        ▸ Policies often require internal auditors to indicate that they understand the conflict of interest policy, disclose potential conflicts, and sign annual statements indicating that no potential threats exist or acknowledging any known potential threats.

- "To reinforce the importance of these policies and help ensure all internal auditors internalize their importance, many CAEs will hold **routine workshops or training** on these fundamental concepts. . . . For example, more senior auditors and managers may share personal experiences where objectivity was called into question or where they self-disclosed a relationship or experience that was a conflict. Another common related training topic is professional skepticism. Such training reinforces the nature of skepticism and the criticality of avoiding bias and maintaining an open and curious mindset."

- "[W]hen **assigning internal auditors** to specific engagements, the CAE (or delegate) will consider potential objectivity impairments and avoid assigning team members who may have a conflict . . . "

- Because "**performance and compensation** practices can significantly and negatively affect an individual's objectivity[,] . . . the CAE needs to be thoughtful in designing the internal audit performance evaluation and compensation system and consider whether the measurements used could impair an internal auditor's objectivity."

Review of internal audit work results before the related engagement communications are released assists in providing reasonable assurance that the work was performed objectively.

Assess Individual Objectivity

The CAE must establish policies and procedures to assess the objectivity of individual internal auditors.

- These can take the form of periodic reviews of conflicts of interest or as-needed assessments during the staffing requirements phase of each engagement.

Maintain Individual Objectivity

The responsibility to maintain objectivity rests with the CAE **and with internal auditors themselves**.

- Internal auditors should be aware of the possibility of new conflicts of interest that may result from changes in personal circumstances or the particular auditees to which an auditor may be assigned.

STOP & REVIEW | You have completed the outline for this subunit.
Study multiple-choice questions 5 through 8 beginning on page 74.

Quick Study Guide
Subunits 2.1 and 2.2
Independence and Objectivity
Attribute Standard 1100

The internal audit activity must be independent, and internal auditors must be objective in performing their work.

Attribute of internal audit activity

Organizational Independence

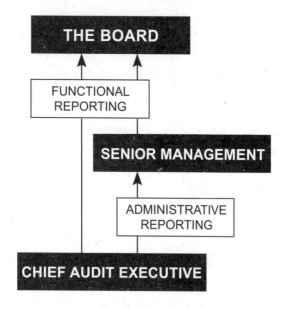

1. The internal audit activity must be free from interference in determining the scope of internal auditing, performing work, and communicating results. The chief audit executive must disclose such interference to the board and discuss the implications.

2. The chief audit executive must have opportunities to interact with the board to communicate sensitive matters.

3. The chief audit executive must interact directly with the board at least annually.

4. Board meeting minutes prove whether the chief audit executive communicated directly with the board.

Attribute of internal auditor

Individual Objectivity

1. Internal auditors must have an impartial, unbiased attitude and avoid any conflict of interest.

2. Objectivity is an unbiased mental attitude that allows internal auditors to perform engagements in such a manner that they believe in their work product and that no quality compromises are made.

3. Objectivity requires that internal auditors do not subordinate their judgment on audit matters to others.

4. Threats to objectivity must be managed at the individual auditor, engagement, functional, and organizational levels.

Conflict of Interest

1. A conflict of interest is any "relationship that is, **or appears to be**, not in the best interest of the organization. A conflict of interest would impair an individual's ability to perform his or her duties and responsibilities objectively."

2. A conflict of interest is a situation in which an internal auditor has a competing professional or personal interest that makes it difficult to fulfill his or her duties impartially.

3. A conflict of interest exists even if no unethical or improper act results.

4. A conflict of interest can create **an appearance of impropriety** that can undermine confidence in the internal auditor, the internal audit activity, and the profession.

2.3 IMPAIRMENT TO INDEPENDENCE AND OBJECTIVITY

SUCCESS TIP

The impairments frequently tested on the exam are those caused by the internal auditor or internal audit activity assessing activities for which they were previously responsible or will have responsibility over.

The disclosure requirements related to impairments are also frequently tested. Note that all impairments must be disclosed to the "appropriate" party.

Mastery of both of these frequently tested aspects of impairments will increase your success on the exam.

Attribute Standard 1130
Impairment to Independence or Objectivity

If independence or objectivity is impaired in fact or appearance, the details of the impairment must be disclosed to appropriate parties. The nature of the disclosure will depend upon the impairment.

Interpretation of Standard 1130

Impairment to organizational independence and individual objectivity may include, but is not limited to, personal conflict of interest; scope limitations; restrictions on access to records, personnel, and properties; and resource limitations, such as funding.

The determination of appropriate parties to which the details of an impairment to independence or objectivity must be disclosed is dependent upon the expectations of the internal audit activity's and the chief audit executive's responsibilities to senior management and the board as described in the internal audit charter, as well as the nature of the impairment.

Specific Circumstances that Cause Impairment

The IIA provides examples of and responses to impairments to both independence and objectivity in Implementation Guide 1130, *Impairment to Independence or Objectivity*:

- "Impairment situations generally include self-interest, self-review, familiarity, bias, or undue influence."

- "Internal audit examples of organizational **independence impairments** include the following, which, if in effect, can also undermine internal auditor objectivity:
  - The CAE has broader functional responsibility than internal audit and executes an audit of a functional area that is also under the CAE's oversight.
  - The CAE's supervisor has broader responsibility than internal audit, and the CAE executes an audit within his or her supervisor's functional responsibility.
  - The CAE does not have direct communication or interaction with the board.
  - The budget for the internal audit activity is reduced to the point that internal audit cannot fulfill its responsibilities as outlined in the charter."

- "Examples of **objectivity impairments** include:
  - An internal auditor audits an area in which he or she recently worked, such as when an employee transfers into internal audit from a different functional area of the organization and then is assigned to an audit of that function . . .
  - An internal auditor audits an area where a relative or close friend is employed.
  - An internal auditor assumes, without evidence, that an area being audited has effectively mitigated risks based solely on prior positive audit or personal experiences (e.g., a lack of professional skepticism).
  - An internal auditor modifies the planned approach or results based on the undue influence of another person, often someone senior to the internal auditor, without appropriate justification."

- "Both the nature of the impairment and board/senior management expectations will determine the **appropriate parties to be notified** of the impairment and the ideal **communication approach**. For example:

    - When the CAE believes the impairment is **not real**, but recognizes there could be a *perception* of impairment, the CAE may choose to discuss the concern in engagement planning meetings with the operating management, document the discussion (such as in an audit planning memo), and explain why the concern is without merit. Such a disclosure may also be appropriate for a final engagement report.

    - When the CAE believes the impairment is **real** and is affecting the ability of internal audit to perform its duties independently and objectively, the CAE is likely to discuss the impairment with the board and senior management and seek their support to resolve the situation.

    - When an impairment comes to light **after an audit has been executed**, and it impacts the reliability (or perceived reliability) of the engagement results, the CAE will discuss it with operating and senior management, as well as the board."

A **scope limitation** is a restriction placed on the internal audit activity that precludes the activity from accomplishing its objectives and plans. Among other things, a scope limitation may restrict

- The scope defined in the internal audit **c**harter.

- The internal audit activity's **a**ccess to records, personnel, and physical properties relevant to the performance of engagements.

- The approved engagement work **s**chedule.

- The performance of necessary engagement **p**rocedures.

- The approved **s**taffing plan and financial budget.

Use the following memory aid "CASPS" to recall examples of scope limitations:

Charter
Access
Schedule
Procedures
Staffing

EXAMPLE 2-1	Scope Limitation

An internal audit activity was recently engaged to audit the final balance of inventory for the financial statements. During the audit, senior management contacted the lead auditor and stated that the internal audit activity would not be given access to the physical inventory.

The denial of access to the inventory is a scope limitation. The internal audit activity needs to communicate the nature of the scope limitation and its potential effects to the board. This communication should preferably be in writing.

Internal auditors are not to **accept fees, gifts, or entertainment** from an employee, client, customer, supplier, or business associate that may create the **appearance** that the auditor's objectivity has been impaired.

- The **appearance** that objectivity has been impaired may apply to current and future engagements conducted by the auditor.

- The status of engagements is not to be considered as justification for receiving fees, gifts, or entertainment.

- The receipt of promotional items (such as pens, calendars, or samples) that are available to employees and the general public and have minimal value does not hinder internal auditors' professional judgments.

- Internal auditors are to report immediately the offer of all material fees or gifts to their supervisors.

However, the internal auditor's objectivity is not impaired when the auditor **recommends** standards of control for systems or reviews procedures before they are implemented.

Certain responsibilities lead to the presumption that objectivity is impaired.

- These responsibilities include **designing, installing, implementing, or drafting** procedures for information systems.
    - The appearance of objectivity cannot be maintained when an internal auditor both (1) designs, installs, implements, or drafts procedures for an information system and (2) audits or reviews that system.

- The following chart contains examples of what may or may not be presumed to impair the objectivity of an internal auditor:

Responsibility	Presumption of Impairment
Recommending standards of control for a new information system application	**Not** presumed to impair objectivity
Performing reviews of the procedures for retiring capital equipment	**Not** presumed to impair objectivity
Drafting procedures for a new hiring system	Presumed to impair objectivity

Objectivity Impaired by Previous Assignment of Internal Audit Personnel

Employees often hold several different positions within the organization in sequence, on both temporary and permanent bases.

- Organizations build competence and gain the advantages of new perspectives by such cross-training.

On occasion, departments or functions in which current internal audit personnel were employed may be scheduled for an engagement in the internal audit work plan. These situations are addressed in the following Implementation Standard:

Implementation Standard 1130.A1

Internal auditors must refrain from assessing specific operations for which they were previously responsible. Objectivity is presumed to be impaired if an auditor provides assurance services for an activity for which the auditor had responsibility within the previous year.

Objectivity Impaired by Assignment of Nonaudit Functions to Internal Audit Personnel

The CAE may be assigned responsibility for one or more functions outside the scope of internal auditing. For example, if the payables department is understaffed and internal audit has been asked to cover 40 hours per week, the internal auditor who has been temporarily assigned to accounts payable will have his or her objectivity impaired.

Objectivity is presumed to be impaired if an internal auditor provides assurance services for an activity for which the internal auditor has responsibility within the previous year.

- This includes assumption of operational duties on a temporary basis.

- The internal audit activity should not be assigned to audit those activities they previously performed until at least 1 year has elapsed.

Attribute Standard 1112
Chief Audit Executive Roles Beyond Internal Auditing

Where the chief audit executive has or is expected to have roles and/or responsibilities that fall outside of internal auditing, safeguards must be in place to limit impairments to independence or objectivity.

Interpretation of Standard 1112

The chief audit executive may be asked to take on additional roles and responsibilities outside of internal auditing, such as responsibility for compliance or risk management activities. These roles and responsibilities may impair, or appear to impair, the organizational independence of the internal audit activity or the individual objectivity of the internal auditor. Safeguards are those oversight activities, often undertaken by the board, to address these potential impairments, and may include such activities as periodically evaluating reporting lines and responsibilities and developing alternative processes to obtain assurance related to the areas of additional responsibility.

The following Implementation Standard provides guidance for these situations:

Implementation Standard 1130.A2

Assurance engagements for functions over which the chief audit executive has responsibility must be overseen by a party outside the internal audit activity.

Objectivity Impaired by Performance of Consulting Services

Implementation Standard 1130.A3

The internal audit activity may provide assurance services where it had previously performed consulting services, provided the nature of the consulting did not impair objectivity and provided individual objectivity is managed when assigning resources to the engagement.

Implementation Standard 1130.C1

Internal auditors may provide consulting services relating to operations for which they had previous responsibilities.

Implementation Standard 1130.C2

If internal auditors have potential impairments to independence or objectivity relating to proposed consulting services, disclosure must be made to the engagement client prior to accepting the engagement.

STOP & REVIEW

You have completed the outline for this subunit.
Study multiple-choice questions 9 through 13 beginning on page 75.

Quick Study Guide
Subunit 2.3

Impairment to Independence and Objectivity

1. If independence or objectivity is impaired in fact or appearance, the details of the impairment must be disclosed to appropriate parties. The nature of the disclosure will depend upon the impairment.

2. Impairment to organizational independence and individual objectivity may include, but is not limited to, personal conflict of interest; scope limitations; restrictions on access to records, personnel, and properties; and resource limitations, such as funding.

3. The determination of appropriate parties to which the details of an impairment to independence or objectivity must be disclosed is dependent upon the expectations of the internal audit activity and the board as described in the internal audit charter, as well as the nature of the impairment.

Independence Impairments

1. The CAE has broader functional responsibility than internal audit and executes an audit of a functional area that is also under the CAE's oversight.

2. The CAE's supervisor has broader responsibility than internal audit, and the CAE executes an audit within his or her supervisor's functional responsibility.

3. The CAE does not have direct communication or interaction with the board.

4. The budget for the internal audit activity is reduced to the point that internal audit cannot fulfill its responsibilities as outlined in the charter.

Both the nature of the impairment and board/senior management expectations will determine the appropriate parties to be notified of the impairment and the ideal communication approach.

Objectivity Impairments

1. An internal auditor audits an area in which (s)he recently worked, such as when an employee transfers into internal audit from a different functional area of the organization and then is assigned to an audit of that function.

2. An internal auditor audits an area where a relative or close friend is employed.

3. An internal auditor assumes, without evidence, that an area being audited has effectively mitigated risks based solely on prior positive audit or personal experiences (e.g., a lack of professional skepticism).

4. An internal auditor modifies the planned approach or results based on the undue influence of another person, often someone senior to the internal auditor, without appropriate justification.

5. Accepting fees, gifts, or entertainment from an employee, client, customer, supplier, or business associate may create the appearance that the auditor's objectivity has been impaired.

6. Designing, installing, implementing, or drafting procedures for information systems impairs objectivity. However, recommending standards or performing a review of procedures does NOT impair objectivity.

7. Objectivity can be impaired by a previous assignment.

---

1. When the CAE believes the impairment is **not real** but recognizes there could be a perception of impairment, the CAE may choose to discuss the concern in engagement planning meetings with the operating management, document the discussion (such as in an audit planning memo), and explain why the concern is without merit. Such a disclosure may also be appropriate for a final engagement report.

2. When the CAE believes the impairment is **real** and is affecting the ability of internal audit to perform its duties independently and objectively, the CAE is likely to discuss the impairment with the board and senior management and seek their support to resolve the situation.

3. When an impairment comes to light **after an audit has been executed** and it impacts the reliability (or perceived reliability) of the engagement results, the CAE will discuss it with operating and senior management as well as the board.

4. **Scope Limitation.** Nature and effects written in report to board.

2.4 AUDITOR PROFICIENCY

Internal auditors and the internal audit activity must each be proficient. Both the individual and the team must meet proficiency requirements.

Attribute Standard 1200
Proficiency and Due Professional Care

Engagements must be performed with proficiency and due professional care.

Responsibility

According to Implementation Guide 1200, *Proficiency and Due Professional Care,*

- "The **CAE is responsible** for ensuring conformance with Attribute Standard 1200 by the internal audit activity as a whole."

- However, "[p]erforming engagements with proficiency and due professional care is the responsibility of **every internal auditor**."

Proficiency

SUCCESS TIP

In addition to individual auditor proficiency, the proficiency of the internal audit activity is frequently tested on the exam. To increase your success on the exam, remember the internal audit activity is considered proficient if the team **collectively** possesses or obtains the competencies needed to perform its responsibilities.

The internal audit activity as a whole, not each auditor individually, must be proficient in all necessary competencies.

Attribute Standard 1210
Proficiency

Internal auditors must possess the knowledge, skills, and other competencies needed to perform their individual responsibilities. The internal audit activity collectively must possess or obtain the knowledge, skills, and other competencies needed to perform its responsibilities.

The Interpretation of Attribute Standard 1210 states, "Proficiency is a collective term that refers to the knowledge, skills, and other competencies required of internal auditors to effectively carry out their professional responsibilities. It encompasses consideration of current activities, trends, and emerging issues, to enable relevant advice and recommendations."

Proficiency includes knowledge sufficient to evaluate fraud risks and IT risks and controls.

Implementation Standard 1210.A2

Internal auditors must have sufficient knowledge to evaluate the risk of fraud and the manner in which it is managed by the organization, but are not expected to have the expertise of a person whose primary responsibility is detecting and investigating fraud.

Implementation Standard 1210.A3

Internal auditors must have sufficient knowledge of key information technology risks and controls and available technology-based audit techniques to perform their assigned work. However, not all internal auditors are expected to have the expertise of an internal auditor whose primary responsibility is information technology auditing.

Implementation Standard 1210.C1

The chief audit executive must decline the consulting engagement or obtain competent advice and assistance if the internal auditors lack the knowledge, skills, or other competencies needed to perform all or part of the engagement.

Internal auditors become proficient through professional education (including continuing professional development), professional experience, and certifications.

The IIA's Competency Framework[©]

The internal audit activity can obtain and maintain the proficiency required by the *Standards* if it effectively applies The IIA's Competency Framework[©] (subsequently referred to as the framework).

- A **competency** is the ability to perform a task or job properly. It is a set of defined knowledge, skills, and behavior.

Implementation Guide 1210, *Proficiency*, provides guidance on the relationship between internal audit proficiency and the framework.

The framework defines the three competency levels needed for each of the four knowledge areas to fulfill International Professional Practices Framework (IPPF) requirements for all occupational levels of the internal audit profession.

The three competency levels are

1. General awareness (staff, entry-level personnel)
2. Applied knowledge (management, mid-level personnel)
3. Expert (executive, senior-level personnel)

The IPPF is the primary set of standards for internal auditors.

To build and maintain the proficiency of the internal audit activity, the CAE may develop a competency assessment tool or skills assessment based on the framework or another benchmark, such as a mature internal audit activity.

It is inferred an auditor at the mid-level, applied knowledge position also has the general awareness of the same knowledge area. Additionally, an auditor at the senior-level, expert position also has the general awareness and applied knowledge of the same knowledge area.

The four knowledge areas are as follows:

1. **Professionalism** addresses authority, credibility, and ethical conduct.

2. **Performance** is associated with planning, conducting, and delivering internal audit engagements in accordance with The IIA's *Standards*.

3. **Environment** involves the risk management of identifying and understanding specific risks within the industry and location the entity operates.

4. **Leadership and communication** comprises developing and managing the internal audit function, persuading and motivating others, and communicating with impact.

The organization of the framework can be accessed and reviewed in its entirety at https://theiia.org/en/standards/internal-audit-competency-framework/.

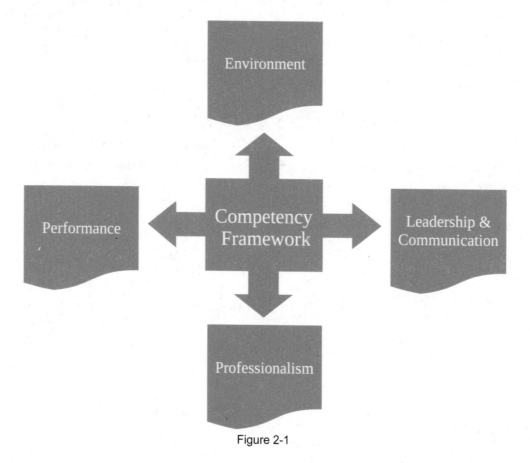

Figure 2-1

STOP & REVIEW

You have completed the outline for this subunit.
Study multiple-choice questions 14 through 16 on page 78.

2.5 INTERNAL AUDIT RESOURCES

Internal auditing resources include both internal resources and external resources.

Internal Resources

The CAE must ensure that the internal audit activity is able to fulfill its responsibilities.

- Identifying the available knowledge, skills, and competencies within the internal audit activity will help the CAE determine whether the current staff is sufficient to satisfy those responsibilities.

- Senior management is responsible for the hiring of internal audit staff.

The following practices help the CAE identify the available resources:

- Hiring practices are an essential part of understanding the background of the internal audit staff. During this process, the CAE identifies the internal auditor's education, previous experience, and specialized areas of knowledge.

- The CAE should conduct periodic skills assessments to determine the specific resources available. Assessments should be performed at least annually.

- Staff performance appraisals are completed at the end of any major internal audit engagement. These appraisals help the CAE assess future training needs and current staff abilities.

- Continuing professional development encourages continued growth. Acquired training also should be considered when identifying internal audit resources.

Databases can be used to store internal audit background information. The information stored can include lists of relevant skills, completed projects, acquired training, and development needs.

If the internal audit staff is not able to fulfill internal audit responsibilities, the use of external service providers must be considered.

External Resources

Outsourcing and Cosourcing

An organization may outsource none, all, or some of the functions of the internal audit activity. However, oversight of and responsibility for the internal audit activity must **not** be outsourced.

- Regardless of the degree of outsourcing, services still must be performed in accordance with the *Standards*, and the guidance for obtaining external service providers should be followed.

Outsourcing alternatives include the following:

- Partial or total external sourcing on an ongoing basis
- Cosourcing for a specific engagement or on an ongoing basis

  - Cosourcing is performance by internal audit staff of joint engagements with external service providers.

CAE's Responsibility

The following Implementation Standard requires the use of expertise from outside the internal audit activity during assurance engagements when the internal auditors lack the necessary expertise.

Implementation Standard 1210.A1

The chief audit executive must obtain competent advice and assistance if the internal auditors lack the knowledge, skills, or other competencies needed to perform all or part of the engagement.

- Each member of the internal audit activity need not be qualified in all disciplines. When necessary, the CAE can obtain necessary knowledge, skills, and competencies from external service providers.

External Service Providers

Qualified external service providers may be recruited from many sources, such as a public accounting firm, an external consulting firm, or a university.

However, an external service provider associated with the engagement client is unacceptable because the person would not be independent or objective.

External service providers may more easily accommodate engagement requirements in distant locations.

STOP & REVIEW

You have completed the outline for this subunit.
Study multiple-choice questions 17 through 20 beginning on page 79.

QUESTIONS

2.1 Independence of the Internal Audit Activity

1. To determine the organizational placement of internal audit, the CAE

1. Works with the board

2. Works with senior management

3. Has discretion to independently determine placement

    A. 1 only.

    B. 2 only.

    C. 1 and 2 only.

    D. 3 only.

Answer (C) is correct.
    REQUIRED: The process in which the internal audit function's organizational placement is determined.
    DISCUSSION: The CAE cannot solely determine the organizational independence and placement of internal audit. The CAE works with the board and senior management to determine the organizational placement of internal audit.
    Answer (A) is incorrect. The CAE also must work with senior management. **Answer (B) is incorrect.** The CAE also must work with the board. **Answer (D) is incorrect.** The CAE does not have discretion to independently determine the organizational placement of the internal audit function.

2. The CAE should report functionally to the board. The board is responsible for which of the following activities?

1. Internal communication and information flows

2. Approval of the internal audit risk assessment and related audit plan

3. Approval of annual compensation and salary adjustments for the CAE

    A. 1 and 2 only.

    B. 2 and 3 only.

    C. 1 and 3 only.

    D. 1, 2, and 3.

Answer (B) is correct.
    REQUIRED: The activities for which the board is responsible.
    DISCUSSION: Organizational independence is effectively achieved when the CAE reports functionally to the board. Examples of functional reporting to the board involve the board

- Approving the internal audit charter

- Approving the risk-based internal audit plan

- Receiving communications from the CAE on the internal audit activity's performance

- Approving decisions regarding the appointment and removal of the CAE

- Making appropriate inquiries of management and the CAE to determine whether there are inappropriate scope or resource limitations (Inter. Attr. Std. 1110)

    Answer (A) is incorrect. Internal communication and information flows are administrative reporting items. Administrative reporting is the reporting relationship within the management structure. Furthermore, functional reporting also involves the board's approval of annual compensation and salary adjustments for the CAE. **Answer (C) is incorrect.** Internal communication and information flows are administrative reporting items. Moreover, functional reporting also involves the board's approval of the internal audit risk assessment and related audit plan. **Answer (D) is incorrect.** Internal communication and information flows are administrative reporting items.

3. The optimal administrative reporting line of the CAE is to

    A. The audit committee.

    B. Line management.

    C. Board of directors.

    D. CEO or equivalent.

Answer (D) is correct.
    REQUIRED: The individual or group to whom the CAE should report administratively.
    DISCUSSION: The CAE should report administratively to the CEO or an equivalent so that the CAE (1) is clearly in a senior position and (2) has authority to perform duties unimpeded.
    Answer (A) is incorrect. Functional reporting is to the board. **Answer (B) is incorrect.** Administrative reporting preferably is to the CEO. **Answer (C) is incorrect.** The CAE must communicate and interact directly with the board. Functional reporting is to the board.

4. Independence permits internal auditors to render impartial and unbiased judgments. The best way to achieve independence is through

    A. Individual knowledge and skills.

    B. A dual-reporting relationship.

    C. Supervision within the organization.

    D. Organizational knowledge and skills.

Answer (B) is correct.
    REQUIRED: The best way to achieve independence.
    DISCUSSION: Independence is the freedom from conditions that threaten the ability of the internal audit activity to carry out internal audit responsibilities in an unbiased manner. To achieve the degree of independence necessary to effectively carry out the responsibilities of the internal audit activity, the CAE has direct and unrestricted access to senior management and the board. This can be achieved through a dual-reporting relationship (Inter. Std. 1100).
    Answer (A) is incorrect. Individual knowledge and skills allow individual auditors to achieve professional proficiency. **Answer (C) is incorrect.** Supervision ensures that engagement objectives are achieved, quality is assured, and staff is developed. **Answer (D) is incorrect.** Organizational knowledge and skills allow the internal audit activity collectively to achieve professional proficiency.

2.2 Objectivity of Internal Auditors

5. Assessing individual objectivity of internal auditors is the responsibility of

    A. The chief executive officer.

    B. The board.

    C. The audit committee.

    D. The chief audit executive.

Answer (D) is correct.
    REQUIRED: The party responsible for assessing the individual objectivity of internal auditors.
    DISCUSSION: The CAE must establish policies and procedures to assess the objectivity of individual internal auditors.

6. Which of the following actions is required of the CAE in regard to the objectivity of internal auditors?

    A. Maximize.

    B. Prioritize.

    C. Minimize.

    D. Assess.

Answer (D) is correct.
    REQUIRED: The CAE's responsibility with regard to internal auditor objectivity.
    DISCUSSION: The CAE must establish policies and procedures to assess the objectivity of individual internal auditors.

7. Internal auditors should be objective. Objectivity

   A. Requires internal auditors not to subordinate their judgment on audit matters to that of others.

   B. Is required only in assurance engagements.

   C. Is freedom from threats to the ability to perform audit work without bias.

   D. Prohibits internal auditors from providing consulting services relating to operations for which they had previous responsibility.

Answer (A) is correct.
   REQUIRED: The true statement regarding objectivity.
   DISCUSSION: Objectivity is "an unbiased mental attitude that allows internal auditors to perform engagements in such a manner that they believe in their work product and that no quality compromises are made. Objectivity requires that internal auditors do not subordinate their judgment on audit matters to others" (Inter. Attr. Std. 1100).
   Answer (B) is incorrect. Objectivity also is required in a consulting engagement. **Answer (C) is incorrect.** Independence is freedom from threats to the ability to perform audit work without bias. **Answer (D) is incorrect.** Internal auditors may provide consulting services relating to operations for which they had previous responsibility.

8. Maintaining individual objectivity is most dependent on

   A. Clearly informing auditee departments and functions of The IIA definition of conflict of interest.

   B. An annual evaluation by the board.

   C. An annual evaluation by an external assessment team.

   D. Internal auditors avoiding conflicts of interest.

Answer (D) is correct.
   REQUIRED: The factor most important to the maintenance of individual objectivity.
   DISCUSSION: Internal auditors should be aware of the possibility of new conflicts of interest that may arise owing to changes in personal circumstances or the particular auditees to which an auditor may be assigned.

2.3 Impairment to Independence and Objectivity

9. An internal auditor assigned to audit a vendor's compliance with product quality standards is the brother of the vendor's controller. The auditor should

   A. Accept the assignment but avoid contact with the controller during fieldwork.

   B. Accept the assignment but disclose the relationship in the engagement final communication.

   C. Notify the vendor of the potential conflict of interest.

   D. Notify the chief audit executive of the potential conflict of interest.

Answer (D) is correct.
   REQUIRED: The action the auditor should take, given a family connection with the auditee.
   DISCUSSION: Internal auditors are to report to the chief audit executive (CAE) any situations in which an actual or potential impairment to independence or objectivity may reasonably be inferred, or if they have questions about whether a situation constitutes an impairment to objectivity or independence.
   Answer (A) is incorrect. Given a family connection with the auditee, even if the auditor avoids contact with the controller, the appearance of a conflict of interest exists. **Answer (B) is incorrect.** Situations of potential conflict of interest or bias should be avoided, not merely disclosed. **Answer (C) is incorrect.** Conflicts of interest are to be reported to the chief audit executive, not the vendor or engagement client.

10. An internal auditor has recently received an offer from the manager of the marketing department of a weekend's free use of his beachfront condominium. No engagement is currently being conducted in the marketing department, and none is scheduled. The internal auditor

    A. Should reject the offer and report it to the appropriate supervisor.

    B. May accept the offer because its value is immaterial.

    C. May accept the offer because no engagement is being conducted or planned.

    D. May accept the offer if approved by the appropriate supervisor.

Answer (A) is correct.
    REQUIRED: The true statement about the offer of a gift by a nonclient member of the organization.
    DISCUSSION: An internal auditor is not to accept fees, gifts, or entertainment from an employee, client, customer, supplier, or business associate. Accepting a fee or gift may imply that the auditor's objectivity has been impaired. Even though an engagement is not being conducted in the applicable area at that time, a future engagement may result in the appearance of impairment of objectivity. Thus, no consideration should be given to the engagement status as justification for receiving fees or gifts. The receipt of promotional items (such as pens, calendars, or samples) that are available to the general public and have minimal value do not hinder internal auditors' professional judgments. Impairment of independence or objectivity, in fact or appearance, must be disclosed to appropriate parties (Attr. Std. 1130).
    Answer (B) is incorrect. The value of a weekend vacation is not immaterial. **Answer (C) is incorrect.** The status of engagements is not a justification for receiving fees or gifts. **Answer (D) is incorrect.** A supervisor may not approve unethical behavior.

11. The internal audit activity should be free to audit and report on any activity that also reports to its administrative head if it considers such coverage to be appropriate for its audit plan. Any limitation in scope or reporting of results of these activities should be brought to the attention of the

    A. Chief executive officer.

    B. Chief financial officer.

    C. External auditor.

    D. Board and senior management.

Answer (D) is correct.
    REQUIRED: The person or group to be notified when a scope or reporting limitation exists.
    DISCUSSION: Impairments of the internal audit activity's independence and objectivity should be communicated to the board and senior management.
    Answer (A) is incorrect. Although the CEO is a part of senior management and is the senior person in the administrative reporting line, impairments of independence and objectivity also should be communicated to the board. **Answer (B) is incorrect.** The CFO is also responsible for the organization's accounting functions. Thus, when a scope or reporting limitation exists, the CFO may be responsible for it. **Answer (C) is incorrect.** The external auditor should not be notified unless the board believes it is necessary.

12. As part of a company-sponsored award program, an internal auditor was offered an award of significant monetary value by a division in recognition of the cost savings that resulted from the auditor's recommendations. According to the International Professional Practices Framework, what is the most appropriate action for the auditor to take?

    A. Accept the gift because the engagement is already concluded and the report issued.

    B. Accept the award under the condition that any proceeds go to charity.

    C. Inform audit management and ask for direction on whether to accept the gift.

    D. Decline the gift and advise the division manager's superior.

Answer (C) is correct.
    REQUIRED: The most appropriate action for the auditor to take when offered an award of significant monetary value.
    DISCUSSION: Internal auditors are not to accept fees, gifts, or entertainment from an employee, client, customer, supplier, or business associate that may create the appearance that the auditor's objectivity has been impaired. The status of engagements is not to be considered as justification for receiving fees, gifts, or entertainment. Internal auditors are to report immediately the offer of all material fees or gifts to their supervisors.
    Answer (A) is incorrect. The auditor should not accept the gift, despite the previous completion of the engagement and issuance of the report. **Answer (B) is incorrect.** The auditor should not accept the award without first informing and consulting audit management. **Answer (D) is incorrect.** Declining the gift and advising the division manager's superior could erode the audit function's relationship with the division in question. The auditor should inform and consult audit management for guidance.

13. George is the new internal auditor for XYZ Corporation. George was in charge of payroll for XYZ just 10 months ago. Performing what services in regard to payroll is considered an impairment of independence or objectivity if performed by George?

    A. Consulting services.

    B. Assurance services.

    C. Assurance or consulting services.

    D. Neither assurance nor consulting services.

Answer (B) is correct.
    REQUIRED: The services that will impair independence or objectivity.
    DISCUSSION: Objectivity is presumed to be impaired if an internal auditor provides assurance services for an activity for which the internal auditor had responsibility within the previous year. Thus, if George provides assurance services for payroll, his objectivity is presumed to be impaired. However, internal auditors may provide consulting services relating to operations for which they had previous responsibilities (Impl. Std. 1130.C1).
    Answer (A) is incorrect. Internal auditors may provide consulting services relating to operations for which they had previous responsibilities (Impl. Std. 1130.C1). **Answer (C) is incorrect.** Providing assurance services regarding payroll will impair George's independence or objectivity. **Answer (D) is incorrect.** Providing consulting services regarding payroll will not impair George's objectivity.

2.4 Auditor Proficiency

14. Your organization has selected you to develop an internal audit activity. Your approach will most likely be to hire

A. Internal auditors, each of whom possesses all the skills required to handle all engagements.

B. Inexperienced personnel and train them the way the organization wants them trained.

C. Degreed accountants because most internal audit work is accounting related.

D. Internal auditors who collectively have the knowledge and skills needed to perform the responsibilities of the internal audit activity.

Answer (D) is correct.
  REQUIRED: The personnel required by an internal audit activity.
  DISCUSSION: The internal audit activity collectively must possess or obtain the knowledge, skills, and other competencies needed to perform its responsibilities (Attr. Std. 1210).
  Answer (A) is incorrect. The scope of internal auditing is so broad that one individual cannot have the requisite expertise in all areas. **Answer (B) is incorrect.** The internal audit activity should have personnel with various skill levels to permit appropriate matching of internal auditors with varying engagement complexities. Furthermore, experienced internal auditors should be available to train and supervise less experienced staff members. **Answer (C) is incorrect.** Many skills are needed in internal auditing. For example, computer skills are needed in engagements involving information technology.

15. The internal audit activity collectively must possess or obtain certain competencies. Internal audit staff should be competent in

A. The exercise of business acumen.

B. Applying tax laws to returns.

C. Determining whether personnel decisions reflect general management principles.

D. Evaluating marketing campaigns.

Answer (A) is correct.
  REQUIRED: The discipline which the internal audit activity must possess or obtain competence.
  DISCUSSION: The internal audit activity collectively must possess or obtain the knowledge, skills, and other competencies needed to perform its responsibilities (Attr. Std. 1210). The emphasis of internal auditors' technical expertise is on (1) the IPPF; (2) governance, risk, and control; and (3) business acumen. Internal auditors are competent regarding business acumen when they maintain expertise related to (1) the business environment, (2) industry practices, and (3) specific organizational factors.
  Answer (B) is incorrect. The Competency Framework does not specifically address the exercise of applying tax laws to returns. **Answer (C) is incorrect.** Internal audit staff should have certain competencies regarding internal audit management (e.g., maintaining up-to-date competencies), not general management principles. **Answer (D) is incorrect.** Internal auditors ordinarily need not be competent in marketing.

16. Internal auditors must possess the knowledge, skills, and other competencies essential to the performance of their individual responsibilities. Consequently, all internal auditors should be competent with regard to

A. Operating within the organization's framework for governance, risk management, and control.

B. Evaluating investments in securities.

C. Applying management principles at the operational level.

D. Performing structured systems analysis.

Answer (A) is correct.
  REQUIRED: The competency that all internal auditors should possess.
  DISCUSSION: The internal audit activity collectively must possess or obtain the knowledge, skills, and other competencies needed to perform its responsibilities (Attr. Std. 1210). Operating within the organization's framework for governance, risk management, and control is a detailed competency supporting the core competency of governance, risk, and control. This detailed competency is recommended for each broad job level (staff, manager, or CAE) of the internal audit activity.

2.5 Internal Audit Resources

17. Which one of the following is responsible for determining the appropriate levels of education and experience needed for the internal audit staff?

- A. Human resource manager.
- B. Chief audit executive.
- C. Chief executive officer.
- D. Chief financial officer.

Answer (B) is correct.
    REQUIRED: The person responsible for determining the internal audit knowledge, skills, and other competencies.
    DISCUSSION: The CAE must ensure that the internal audit activity is able to fulfill its responsibilities. The CAE must determine the appropriate levels of education and experience needed for the internal audit staff to fulfill that responsibility.
    Answer (A) is incorrect. Hiring practices are an essential part of understanding the internal audit staff's background, but the human resource manager is not responsible for determining the appropriate levels of education and experience needed for the internal audit staff. **Answer (C) is incorrect.** The chief executive officer is not directly responsible for determining the appropriate levels of education and experience needed for the internal audit staff. **Answer (D) is incorrect.** The chief financial officer is not responsible for determining the appropriate levels of education and experience needed for the internal audit staff.

18. How often should the skills of the internal audit staff be assessed?

- A. Periodically.
- B. Every 5 years.
- C. Annually.
- D. Semi-annually.

Answer (A) is correct.
    REQUIRED: The frequency with which assessments should be performed.
    DISCUSSION: According to IG 1210, *Proficiency*, the CAE may develop a competency assessment tool or skills assessment based on a benchmark such as The IIA's competency framework to build and maintain the proficiency of the internal audit activity. The CAE includes the criteria in job descriptions and recruitment material. The CAE also may use the assessment tool to make a periodic skills assessment to identify gaps.
    Answer (B) is incorrect. External assessments, not skills assessments, must be performed at least once every 5 years (Attr. Std. 1312). **Answer (C) is incorrect.** According to Attr. Std. 1110, the CAE must confirm to the board, at least annually, the internal audit activity's organizational independence, not the performance of a skills assessment. Also, the results of ongoing monitoring must be communicated at least annually (Interp. Std. 320). **Answer (D) is incorrect.** The *Standards* do not specify a definite frequency for skills assessments.

19. All of the following will help the CAE identify the available knowledge, skills, and competencies of the internal audit staff **except**

    A. Hiring practices.

    B. Periodic skills assessment.

    C. External service provider.

    D. Staff performance appraisals.

Answer (C) is correct.
    REQUIRED: The item that does not help the CAE identify internal audit resources.
    DISCUSSION: External service providers are used when the internal audit staff does not have the necessary knowledge, skills, and competencies to fulfill the responsibilities of the internal audit activity.
    Answer (A) is incorrect. Hiring practices are an essential part of understanding the background of the internal audit staff. **Answer (B) is incorrect.** The CAE should conduct periodic skills assessments to determine the specific resources available. **Answer (D) is incorrect.** Staff performance appraisals are completed at the end of any major internal audit engagement. These appraisals help the CAE assess future training needs and current staff abilities.

20. In some organizations, internal audit functions are outsourced. Management in a large organization should recognize that the external auditor may have an advantage, compared with the internal auditor, because of the external auditor's

    A. Familiarity with the organization. Its annual audits provide an in-depth knowledge of the organization.

    B. Size. It can hire experienced, knowledgeable, and certified staff.

    C. Size. It is able to offer continuous availability of staff unaffected by other priorities.

    D. Structure. It may more easily accommodate engagement requirements in distant locations.

Answer (D) is correct.
    REQUIRED: The advantage of outsourcing internal audit functions.
    DISCUSSION: Large organizations that are geographically dispersed may find outsourcing internal audit functions to external auditors to be effective. A major public accounting firm ordinarily has operations that are national or worldwide in scope.
    Answer (A) is incorrect. The internal auditors are likely to be more familiar with the organization than the external auditors, given the continuous nature of their responsibilities. **Answer (B) is incorrect.** The internal auditor also can hire experienced, knowledgeable, and certified staff. **Answer (C) is incorrect.** The internal auditor is more likely to be continuously available. The external auditor has responsibilities to many other clients.

STUDY UNIT THREE

DUE PROFESSIONAL CARE AND QUALITY ASSURANCE AND IMPROVEMENT PROGRAM

(16 pages of outline)

This study unit covers the "Due Professional Care" section of **Domain III: Proficiency and Due Professional Care** and all of **Domain IV: Quality Assurance and Improvement Program** from The IIA's CIA Exam Syllabus. Study Unit 2 covers the "Proficiency" section of Domain III. Domains III and IV make up 18% and 7%, respectively, of Part 1 of the CIA exam and are tested at the **basic** and **proficient** cognitive levels.

The **learning objectives** of Study Unit 3 are

- Demonstrate due professional care

- Demonstrate an individual internal auditor's competency through continuing professional development

- Describe the required elements of the quality assurance and improvement program (internal assessments, external assessments, etc.)

- Describe the requirement of reporting the results of the quality assurance and improvement program to the board or other governing body

- Identify appropriate disclosure of conformance vs. nonconformance with The IIA's *International Standards for the Professional Practice of Internal Auditing*

Internal auditors and the internal audit activity demonstrate due professional care by (1) following the profession's technical and ethical standards, (2) striving for improved competence and quality services, and (3) discharging professional responsibility to the best of their ability. A quality assurance and improvement program is designed to enable an evaluation of the internal audit activity's conformance with the *Standards* and an evaluation of whether internal auditors apply the Code of Ethics. The program also assesses the efficiency and effectiveness of the internal audit activity and identifies opportunities for improvement.

3.1 DUE PROFESSIONAL CARE AND CONTINUING PROFESSIONAL DEVELOPMENT

Attribute Standard 1220
Due Professional Care

Internal auditors must apply the care and skill expected of a **reasonably** prudent and competent internal auditor. Due professional care does not imply infallibility.

SUCCESS TIP

Due professional care questions on the exam frequently test the standard of care required of internal auditors. To increase your success on the exam, remember the standard of care required is **reasonable care**, not absolute assurance.

Due Care in Practice

The IIA provides guidance for the application of due care in Implementation Guide 1220, *Due Professional Care*:

- "[D]ue professional care requires conformance with The IIA's Code of Ethics and may entail conformance with the organization's code of conduct and any additional codes of conduct relevant to other professional designations attained."

- "[T]he internal audit activity's policies and procedures provide a systematic and disciplined approach to planning, executing, and documenting internal audit work. By following this systematic and disciplined approach, internal auditors essentially apply due professional care. However, what constitutes due professional care partially depends upon the complexities of the engagement."

- "Internal auditors demonstrate conformance with Attribute Standard 1220 through proper application of the IPPF's Mandatory Guidance, which would be reflected in their engagement plans, work programs, and workpapers."

The following Implementation Standards provide guidance for the application of due care during **assurance** engagements:

Implementation Standard 1220.A1

Internal auditors must exercise due professional care by considering the:

- Extent of work needed to achieve the engagement's objectives.

- Relative complexity, materiality, or significance of matters to which assurance procedures are applied.

- Adequacy and effectiveness of governance, risk management, and control processes.

- Probability of significant errors, fraud, or noncompliance.

- Cost of assurance in relation to potential benefits.

Implementation Standard 1220.A2

In exercising due professional care internal auditors must consider the use of technology-based audit and other data analysis techniques.

Implementation Standard 1220.A3

Internal auditors must be alert to the significant risks that might affect objectives, operations, or resources. However, assurance procedures alone, even when performed with due professional care, do not guarantee that all significant risks will be identified.

The following Implementation Standard provides guidance for the application of due care during **consulting** engagements:

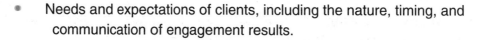

Implementation Standard 1220.C1

Internal auditors must exercise due professional care during a consulting engagement by considering the:

- Needs and expectations of clients, including the nature, timing, and communication of engagement results.

- Relative complexity and extent of work needed to achieve the engagement's objectives.

- Cost of the consulting engagement in relation to potential benefits.

Due professional care can be demonstrated if the auditor applied the care and skill of a **reasonably competent and prudent** internal auditor in the same or similar circumstances.

- In light of being reasonably competent and prudent, any unexpected results from analytical procedures should be investigated and adequately explained.

Continuing Professional Development

The IIA requires internal auditors to continue expanding their knowledge and abilities throughout their careers.

Attribute Standard 1230
Continuing Professional Development

Internal auditors must enhance their knowledge, skills, and other competencies through continuing professional development.

Implementation Guide 1230, *Continuing Professional Development*, gives specific advice regarding further education to enhance proficiency:

- "An individual internal auditor may use a self-assessment tool, such as the Competency Framework, as a basis for creating a professional development plan. The development plan may encompass on-the-job training, coaching, mentoring, and other internal and external training, volunteer, or certification opportunities."

- "Opportunities for professional development include participating in conferences, seminars, training programs, online courses and webinars, self-study programs, or classroom courses; conducting research projects; volunteering with professional organizations; and pursuing professional certifications . . ."

Certified internal auditors (CIAs) demonstrate their continuing professional development by completing **continuing professional education (CPE)**.

- Practicing and nonpracticing CIAs must complete 40 hours and 20 hours, respectively, of CPE annually (including at least 2 hours of ethics training).

- Qualifying CPE activities are those that contribute to internal audit competence. They include the following:
    - Educational programs (e.g., seminars, conferences, or technical sessions provided by auditing or accounting organizations and chapters; formal in-house training programs; college or university courses passed; or self-study programs relevant to internal auditing)
    - Passing examinations
    - Authoring or contributing to publications
    - Translating publications
    - Delivering oral presentations
    - Participating as a subject matter expert volunteer
    - Performing external quality assessments

You have completed the outline for this subunit.
Study multiple-choice questions 1 through 6 beginning on page 97.

STOP & REVIEW

3.2 QUALITY ASSURANCE AND IMPROVEMENT PROGRAM (QAIP)

Every internal audit department should have a QAIP that evaluates and helps the internal audit activity improve its efficiency and effectiveness.

Attribute Standard 1300

Quality Assurance and Improvement Program

The chief audit executive must develop and maintain a quality assurance and improvement program that covers all aspects of the internal audit activity.

Interpretation of Standard 1300

A quality assurance and improvement program is designed to enable an evaluation of the internal audit activity's conformance with the *Standards* and an evaluation of whether internal auditors apply the Code of Ethics. The program also assesses the efficiency and effectiveness of the internal audit activity and identifies opportunities for improvement. The chief audit executive should encourage board oversight in the quality assurance and improvement program.

Characteristics of a QAIP

"The QAIP should encompass all aspects of operating and managing the internal audit activity— including consulting engagements—as found in the mandatory elements of the [IPPF]."

"A well-developed QAIP ensures that the concept of **quality** is embedded in the internal audit activity and **all** of its operations."

"[I]t must include ongoing and periodic internal assessments as well as external assessments by a qualified independent assessor or assessment team . . ." (Implementation Guide 1300).

The QAIP consists of **five components**:

1. Internal assessments,
2. External assessments,
3. Communication of QAIP results,
4. Proper use of a conformance statement, and
5. Disclosure of nonconformance.

"[T]he QAIP also includes ongoing measurements and analyses of performance metrics such as accomplishment of the internal audit plan, cycle time, recommendations accepted, and customer satisfaction" (Implementation Guide 1310).

CAE Responsibilities for the QAIP

- "The CAE must have a thorough understanding of the mandatory elements of the IPPF, especially the *Standards* and Code of Ethics. Generally, the CAE meets with the board to gain an understanding of the expectations for the internal audit activity, to discuss the importance of the *Standards* and the QAIP, and to encourage the board's support of these" (Implementation Guide 1300).

- "The CAE periodically evaluates the QAIP and updates it as needed. For example, as the internal audit activity matures, or as conditions within the internal audit activity change, adjustments to the QAIP may become necessary to ensure that it continues to operate in an effective and efficient manner and to assure stakeholders that it adds value by improving the organization's operations" (Implementation Guide 1300).

Requirements of the QAIP

Attribute Standard 1310

Requirements of the Quality Assurance and Improvement Program

The quality assurance and improvement program must include both internal and external assessments.

The CAE is responsible for ensuring that the internal audit activity conducts internal assessments and external assessments. Further guidance is provided in Implementation Guide 1310:

"**Internal assessments** consist of ongoing monitoring and periodic self-assessments . . . , which evaluate the internal audit activity's conformance with the mandatory elements of the IPPF, the quality and supervision of audit work performed, the adequacy of internal audit policies and procedures, the value the internal audit activity adds to the organization, and the establishment and achievement of key performance indicators."

- "**Ongoing monitoring** is achieved primarily through continuous activities such as engagement planning and supervision, standardized work practices, workpaper procedures and signoffs, report reviews, as well as identification of any weaknesses or areas in need of improvement and action plans to address them."

- "**Periodic self-assessments** are conducted to validate that ongoing monitoring is operating effectively . . ."

"**External assessments** provide an opportunity for an **independent** assessor or assessment team to conclude as to the internal audit activity's conformance with the *Standards* and whether internal auditors apply the Code of Ethics, and to identify areas for improvement."

- "[T]he CAE is responsible for ensuring that the internal audit activity conducts an external assessment at least **once every five years** . . .

- "A self-assessment may be performed in lieu of a full external assessment, provided it is validated by a qualified, independent, competent, and professional external assessor" (Implementation Guide 1310).

Deming Cycle

The Deming Cycle can be used to establish the QAIP in a planned, methodical manner. The Deming Cycle (or Plan-Do-Check-Act Cycle) is a continuous improvement model popularized by W. Edwards Deming.

The Deming Cycle consists of four steps:

1. **Plan** establishes standards and expectations for operating a process to meet goals.
2. **Do** executes the process and collects data for further analysis in the later steps.
3. **Check** compares actual results with expected results and analyzes the difference.
4. **Act** provides feedback by identifying and implementing improvements to the process.

STOP & REVIEW

You have completed the outline for this subunit.
Study multiple-choice questions 7 through 11 beginning on page 99.

3.3 INTERNAL AND EXTERNAL ASSESSMENTS

A QAIP requires both internal assessments (or self-evaluations) and external assessments.

Internal Assessments

Attribute Standard 1311
Internal Assessments

Internal assessments must include:

- Ongoing monitoring of the performance of the internal audit activity.

- Periodic self-assessments or assessments by other persons within the organization with sufficient knowledge of internal audit practices.

Interpretation of Standard 1311

Ongoing monitoring is an integral part of the day-to-day supervision, review, and measurement of the internal audit activity. Ongoing monitoring is incorporated into the routine policies and practices used to manage the internal audit activity and uses processes, tools, and information considered necessary to evaluate conformance with the Code of Ethics and the *Standards*.

Periodic assessments are conducted to evaluate conformance with the Code of Ethics and the *Standards*.

Sufficient knowledge of internal audit practices requires at least an understanding of all elements of the International Professional Practices Framework.

Implementation Guide 1311, *Internal Assessments*, provides more extensive guidance.

- "The two interrelated parts of internal assessments—ongoing monitoring and periodic self-assessments—provide an effective structure for the internal audit activity to continuously assess its conformance with the *Standards* and whether internal auditors apply the Code of Ethics."

The chief audit executive (CAE) establishes a structure for reporting results of internal assessments that maintains appropriate credibility and objectivity. Generally, those assigned responsibility for conducting ongoing and periodic reviews report to the CAE while performing the reviews and communicate results directly to the CAE.

The CAE should report the results of internal assessments, necessary action plans, and their successful implementation to senior management and the board.

Ongoing Monitoring (of internal assessments)

"[O]ngoing monitoring is generally focused on reviews conducted at the **engagement level**."

- "Thus, ongoing monitoring helps the CAE determine whether internal audit processes are delivering quality on an **engagement-by-engagement basis**."

- Compared with periodic self-assessments, ongoing monitoring emphasizes evaluating conformance with the performance standards.

"Generally, ongoing monitoring occurs routinely throughout the year . . ."

"Ongoing monitoring is achieved **primarily** through **continuous activities** such as
- Engagement planning and supervision,
- Standardized work practices,
- Workpaper procedures and signoffs, [and]
- Report reviews . . ."

Additional mechanisms commonly used for ongoing monitoring include

- Checklists or automation tools,

- Feedback from internal audit clients and other stakeholders,

- Staff and engagement key performance indicators (e.g., the number of certified internal auditors on staff, their years of experience in internal auditing, the number of continuing professional development hours they earned during the year, timeliness of engagements, and stakeholder satisfaction).

Periodic Self-Assessments

Compared with ongoing monitoring, periodic self-assessments "generally provide a more holistic, comprehensive review of the *Standards* and the internal audit activity."

Periodic self-assessments are generally conducted by those with extensive internal auditing experience (e.g., senior internal auditors or certified internal auditors).

"The internal audit activity conducts periodic self-assessments to validate its continued conformance with the *Standards* and Code of Ethics and to evaluate

1. The quality and supervision of work performed.
2. The adequacy and appropriateness of internal audit policies and procedures.
3. The ways in which the internal audit activity adds value.
4. The achievement of key performance indicators.
5. The degree to which stakeholder expectations are met."

Adequate Supervision

"Adequate supervision is a fundamental element of any quality assurance and improvement program (QAIP). Supervision begins with planning and continues throughout the performance and communication phases of the engagement. Adequate supervision is ensured through expectation-setting, ongoing communications among internal auditors throughout the engagement, and workpaper review procedures, including timely sign-off by the individual responsible for supervising engagements."

External Assessments

Attribute Standard 1312
External Assessments

External assessments must be conducted at least once every five years by a qualified, independent assessor or assessment team from outside the organization. The chief audit executive must discuss with the board:

- The form and frequency of external assessments.

- The qualifications and independence of the external assessor or assessment team, including any potential conflict of interest.

External assessments provide an independent and objective evaluation of the internal audit activity's conformance with the *Standards* and Code of Ethics.

Relevant guidance is provided in Implementation Guide 1312, *External Assessments*:

- "External assessments may be accomplished using one of two approaches: a full external assessment, or a self-assessment with independent external validation (SAIV)."

- "A **full external assessment** would be conducted by a qualified, independent external assessor or assessment team. The team should be comprised of competent professionals and led by an experienced and professional project team leader. The **scope** of a full external assessment typically includes three core components:

  - The level of conformance with the *Standards* and Code of Ethics. This may be evaluated via a review of the internal audit activity's charter, plans, policies, procedures, and practices. In some cases, the review may also include applicable legislative and regulatory requirements.

  - The efficiency and effectiveness of the internal audit activity. This may be measured through an assessment of the internal audit activity's processes and infrastructure, including the QAIP, and an evaluation of the internal audit staff's knowledge, experience, and expertise.

  - The extent to which the internal audit activity meets expectations of the board, senior management, and operations management, and adds value to the organization."

- "The second approach to meeting the requirement for an external assessment is an SAIV [**self-assessment with independent external validation**]. This type of external assessment typically is conducted by the internal audit activity and then validated by a qualified, **independent** external assessor. The scope of [this assessment] typically consists of:

    1. A comprehensive and fully documented self-assessment process that emulates the full external assessment process, at least with respect to evaluating the internal audit activity's conformance with the *Standards* and Code of Ethics.
    2. Onsite validation by a qualified, independent external assessor.
    3. Limited attention to other areas such as benchmarking; review, consultation, and employment of leading practices; and interviews with senior and operations management."

- "[E]xternal assessors or assessment teams must be competent in two main areas:

    1. "[T]he professional practice of internal auditing (including current in-depth knowledge of the IPPF) and
    2. [T]he external quality assessment process."

External assessors must have no real or apparent **conflict of interest** due to current or past relationships with the organization.

- Matters relating to independence include conflicts of **former employees** or of **firms** providing (1) the financial statement audit, (2) significant consulting services, or (3) assistance to the internal audit activity.

- An individual in another part of the organization or in a related organization (e.g., a parent or an affiliate) is not independent.

- **Peer review** among three unrelated organizations (but not between two) may satisfy the independence requirement.

- Given concerns about independence, one or more **independent individuals** may provide separate validation.

SUCCESS TIP

The IIA has asked candidates to identify differences between a full external assessment and a self-assessment with independent external validation.

STOP & REVIEW

You have completed the outline for this subunit.
Study multiple-choice questions 12 through 16 beginning on page 101.

3.4 REPORTING ON QUALITY ASSURANCE

The results of the QAIP must be reported to senior management and the board.

Reporting Results

Senior management and the board must be kept informed about the degree to which the internal audit activity achieves the degree of professionalism required by The IIA.

Attribute Standard 1320
Reporting on the Quality Assurance and Improvement Program

The chief audit executive must communicate the results of the quality assurance and improvement program to senior management and the board. Disclosure should include:

- The scope and frequency of both the internal and external assessments.

- The qualifications and independence of the assessor(s) or assessment team, including potential conflicts of interest.

- Conclusions of assessors.

- Corrective action plans.

The IIA addresses the frequency of reporting on the QAIP in the following excerpt from the Interpretation of Standard 1320:

> *To demonstrate conformance with the Code of Ethics and the Standards, the results of external and periodic internal assessments are communicated **upon completion** of such assessments and the results of ongoing monitoring are communicated at least **annually**.*

The expression of an opinion or conclusion on the results of the **external assessment** is included in the external assessment report. The report typically includes an assessment for each standard and an overall assessment for each standard series (attribute and performance). These assessments are in addition to the overall conformance results. The following is an example of a rating scale that may be used to show the degree of conformance:

- **Generally conforms.** The top rating means that
    - An internal audit activity has a charter, policies, and processes, and
    - Their execution and results conform with the *Standards*.

- **Partially conforms.** Deficiencies in practice are judged to deviate from the *Standards*. But they do not preclude the internal audit activity from performing its responsibilities.

- **Does not conform.** Deficiencies in practice are judged to be so significant as to seriously impair, or preclude, the internal audit activity's ability to perform adequately in all or in significant areas of its responsibilities.

During an external assessment, the assessor may provide recommendations to address

- Areas that were not in conformance with the *Standards* and
- Opportunities for improvement.
    - The CAE may provide management action plans to address recommendations from the external assessment.
    - The CAE also may consider
        - Adding the recommendations and management action plans to the internal audit activity's existing monitoring of progress related to internal audit engagement findings and
        - Reporting on resolutions.
    - Verification that recommendations identified during the external assessment have been implemented is communicated to the board either
        - As part of the internal audit activity's monitoring of progress or
        - By following up separately through the next QAIP internal assessment.

Importance of Conforming with the Standards

The internal audit activity **cannot** claim to comply with the *Standards* unless it has a successfully functioning QAIP.

Attribute Standard 1321

Use of "Conforms with the *International Standards for the Professional Practice of Internal Auditing*"

Indicating that the internal audit activity conforms with the *International Standards for the Professional Practice of Internal Auditing* is appropriate only if supported by the results of the quality assurance and improvement program.

Importance of Reporting Nonconformance

The internal audit activity is a crucial part of the modern complex organization's governance processes. Senior management and the board must be informed when an assessment discovers a significant degree of nonconformance.

- Nonconformance of this type refers to the overall internal audit activity and not to specific engagements.

Attribute Standard 1322

Disclosure of Nonconformance

When nonconformance with the Code of Ethics or the *Standards* impacts the overall scope or operation of the internal audit activity, the chief audit executive must disclose the nonconformance and the impact to senior management and the board.

You have completed the outline for this subunit.
Study multiple-choice questions 17 through 20 beginning on page 103.

STOP & REVIEW

QUESTIONS

3.1 Due Professional Care and Continuing Professional Development

1. An internal auditor observes that a receivables clerk has physical access to and control of cash receipts. The auditor worked with the clerk several years before and has a high level of trust in the individual. Accordingly, the auditor notes in the engagement working papers that controls over receipts are adequate. Has the auditor exercised due professional care?

   A. Yes, reasonable care has been taken.

   B. No, irregularities were not noted.

   C. No, alertness to conditions most likely indicative of irregularities was not shown.

   D. Yes, the engagement working papers were annotated.

Answer (C) is correct.
   REQUIRED: The true statement as to whether the internal auditor has exercised due professional care.
   DISCUSSION: Internal auditors must be alert to those conditions and activities where irregularities are most likely to occur and must identify inadequate controls. Thus, the internal auditor did not exercise due professional care. Cash has a high degree of inherent risk and should therefore be subject to strict controls. Access to cash and the recordkeeping functions should be separated regardless of the personal qualities of the individuals involved. That the internal auditor trusts the clerk is irrelevant. Management still needs to be aware that internal control over receivables is inadequate.
   Answer (A) is incorrect. The auditor's engagement observation is inappropriate given the lack of segregation of functions. **Answer (B) is incorrect.** No indication is given that irregularities have occurred. **Answer (D) is incorrect.** Annotating the working papers does not indicate that the auditor exercised due professional care. Cash has a high inherent risk of irregularities, and professional judgment and alertness are necessary.

2. An internal auditor judged an item to be immaterial when planning an assurance engagement. However, the assurance engagement may still include the item if it is subsequently determined that

   A. Sufficient staff is available.

   B. Adverse effects related to the item are likely to occur.

   C. Related information is reliable.

   D. Miscellaneous income is affected.

Answer (B) is correct.
   REQUIRED: The basis for including an item in the engagement although it is immaterial.
   DISCUSSION: Internal auditors must exercise due professional care by considering the relative complexity, materiality, or significance of matters to which assurance procedures are applied (Impl. Std. 1220.A1). Materiality judgments are made in the light of all the circumstances and involve qualitative as well as quantitative considerations. Moreover, internal auditors also must consider the interplay of risk with materiality. Consequently, engagement effort may be required for a quantitatively immaterial item if adverse effects are likely to occur, for example, a material contingent liability arising from an illegal payment that is otherwise immaterial.
   Answer (A) is incorrect. In the absence of other considerations, devoting additional engagement effort to an immaterial item is inefficient. **Answer (C) is incorrect.** Additional engagement procedures might not be needed if related information is reliable. **Answer (D) is incorrect.** The item is more likely to be included if it affects recurring income items rather than miscellaneous income.

3. With regard to the exercise of due professional care, an internal auditor should

A. Consider the relative materiality or significance of matters to which assurance procedures are applied.

B. Emphasize the potential benefits of an engagement without regard to the cost.

C. Consider whether criteria have been established to determine whether goals are achieved, not whether those criteria are adequate.

D. Select procedures that are likely to provide absolute assurance that irregularities do not exist.

Answer (A) is correct.
    REQUIRED: The guidance prescribed by the *Standards* concerning due professional care.
    DISCUSSION: Exercising due professional care means applying the care and skill expected of a reasonably prudent and competent internal auditor (Attr. Std. 1220). Internal auditors must exercise due professional care by considering, among other things, the relative complexity, materiality, or significance of matters to which assurance procedures are applied (Impl. Std. 1220.A1).
    Answer (B) is incorrect. The internal auditor should consider the cost in relation to the potential benefits before beginning an engagement. **Answer (C) is incorrect.** Adequate criteria are needed to evaluate controls. If determined to be adequate, internal auditors must use such criteria in their evaluation. If inadequate, internal auditors must work with management to develop appropriate evaluation criteria. **Answer (D) is incorrect.** Internal auditors cannot give absolute assurance that noncompliance or irregularities do not exist.

4. A certified internal auditor performed an assurance engagement to review a department store's cash function. Which of the following actions will be deemed lacking in due professional care?

A. Organizational records were reviewed to determine whether all employees who handle cash receipts and disbursements were bonded.

B. A flowchart of the entire cash function was developed, but only a sample of transactions was tested.

C. The final engagement communication included a well-supported recommendation for the reduction in staff, although it was known that such a reduction would adversely affect morale.

D. Because of a highly developed system of internal control over the cash function, the final engagement communication assured senior management that no irregularities existed.

Answer (D) is correct.
    REQUIRED: The action deemed lacking in due professional care.
    DISCUSSION: Internal auditors cannot give absolute assurance that noncompliance or irregularities do not exist.
    Answer (A) is incorrect. Reviewing records to determine whether all employees who handle cash receipts and disbursements were bonded is a standard procedure. **Answer (B) is incorrect.** Sampling is permissible. Detailed reviews of all transactions are often not required or feasible. **Answer (C) is incorrect.** In exercising due professional care, internal auditors should be alert to inefficiency.

5. Due professional care calls for

A. Detailed reviews of all transactions related to a particular function.

B. Infallibility and extraordinary performance when the system of internal control is known to be weak.

C. Consideration of the possibility of material irregularities during every engagement.

D. Testing in sufficient detail to give absolute assurance that noncompliance does not exist.

Answer (C) is correct.
 REQUIRED: The implication of due care.
 DISCUSSION: Due care implies reasonable care and competence, not infallibility or extraordinary performance. Due care requires the internal auditor to conduct examinations and verifications to a reasonable extent, but does not require detailed reviews of all transactions. Accordingly, internal auditors cannot give absolute assurance that noncompliance or irregularities do not exist. Nevertheless, the possibility of material irregularities or noncompliance should be considered whenever an internal auditor undertakes an internal auditing assignment.
 Answer (A) is incorrect. Detailed reviews of all transactions are not required. **Answer (B) is incorrect.** Reasonable care and skill, not infallibility or extraordinary performance, are necessary. **Answer (D) is incorrect.** Only reasonable, not absolute, assurance can be given.

6. Internal auditors are responsible for continuing their education to maintain their proficiency. Which of the following is true regarding the continuing education requirements of the practicing internal auditor?

A. Practicing certified internal auditors are required to obtain 40 hours of continuing professional education every 2 years.

B. CIAs have formal requirements that must be met in order to continue as CIAs.

C. Attendance, as an officer or committee member, at formal IIA meetings does not meet the criteria of continuing professional development.

D. In-house programs meet continuing professional education requirements only if they have been preapproved by The IIA.

Answer (B) is correct.
 REQUIRED: The true statement about continuing education requirements.
 DISCUSSION: Internal auditors must enhance their knowledge, skills, and other competencies through continuing professional development (Attr. Std. 1230). To maintain the CIA designation, the CIA must commit to a formal program of continuing professional development and report to the Certification Department of The IIA.
 Answer (A) is incorrect. Practicing certified internal auditors are required to obtain 40 hours of CPE annually. **Answer (C) is incorrect.** Continuing education may be obtained by participation in professional organizations. **Answer (D) is incorrect.** Prior approval by The IIA is not necessary for CPE courses.

3.2 Quality Assurance and Improvement Program (QAIP)

7. The chief audit executive should develop and maintain a quality assurance and improvement program that covers all aspects of the internal audit activity and continuously monitors its effectiveness. All of the following are included in a quality program **except**

A. Annual appraisals of individual internal auditors' performance.

B. Periodic internal assessment.

C. Supervision.

D. Periodic external assessments.

Answer (A) is correct.
 REQUIRED: The element not part of a quality assurance program.
 DISCUSSION: Appraising each internal auditor's work at least annually is properly a function of the human resources program of the internal audit activity.
 Answer (B) is incorrect. Internal assessment is an element of a quality program. **Answer (C) is incorrect.** Supervision is an element of a quality program. Ongoing reviews are internal assessments that include engagement supervision. **Answer (D) is incorrect.** External assessment is an element of a quality program.

8. Assessment of a quality assurance and improvement program should include evaluation of all of the following **except**

    A. Adequacy of the oversight of the work of external auditors.

    B. Conformance with the *Standards* and Code of Ethics.

    C. Adequacy of the internal audit activity's charter.

    D. Contribution to the organization's governance processes.

Answer (A) is correct.
    REQUIRED: The element not required in the assessment of a QAIP.
    DISCUSSION: Oversight of the work of external auditors, including coordination with the internal audit activity, is the responsibility of the board. It is not within the scope of the process for monitoring and assessing the QAIP.
    Answer (B) is incorrect. Conformance with the *Standards* and Code of Ethics is an element of the assessment of a QAIP. **Answer (C) is incorrect.** Adequacy of the internal audit activity's charter, goals, objectives, policies, and procedures is an element of the assessment of a QAIP. **Answer (D) is incorrect.** Contribution to the organization's governance, risk management, and control processes is an element of the assessment of a QAIP.

9. The internal audit activity's quality assurance and improvement program is the responsibility of

    A. External auditors.

    B. The chief audit executive.

    C. The board.

    D. The audit committee.

Answer (B) is correct.
    REQUIRED: The individual(s) responsible for the quality assurance reviews of the internal audit activity.
    DISCUSSION: The chief audit executive must develop and maintain a quality assurance and improvement program that covers all aspects of the internal audit activity (Attr. Std. 1300).
    Answer (A) is incorrect. External auditors may perform an external assessment, but the CAE is responsible for it. **Answer (C) is incorrect.** The CAE may report results to the board, but the program is the CAE's responsibility. **Answer (D) is incorrect.** The CAE may report results to the audit committee, but the program is the CAE's responsibility.

10. What are the four key steps of the Deming Cycle?

    A. Perform, Design, Act, and Review.

    B. Examine, Act, Check, and Verify.

    C. Plan, Do, Check, and Act.

    D. Perform, Diagnose, Calculate, and Act.

Answer (C) is correct.
    REQUIRED: The key steps of the Deming Cycle.
    DISCUSSION: Plan, Do, Check, and Act are the four key steps of the Deming Cycle that operate in an interactive manner. The Deming Cycle can be used to establish an organization's quality assurance and improvement program (QAIP) in a planned and methodological manner. The steps are (1) Plan, establish standards and expectations for operating a process to meet goals; (2) Do, execute the process and collect data for further analysis in the latter steps; (3) Check, compare actual results with expected results and analyze the difference; and (4) Act, provide feedback by identifying and implementing improvements to the process.

11. According to The IIA's International Professional Practices Framework, when may a self-assessment be performed in lieu of a full external assessment?

A. When the self-assessment has been validated by a qualified, independent, competent, and professional external assessor.

B. When the internal audit activity has conducted an external assessment within the past two years.

C. When ongoing monitoring of the internal audit activity has not identified any weaknesses or areas in need of improvement.

D. A self-assessment may not be performed in lieu of a full external assessment of the internal audit activity's conformance with the *Standards*.

Answer (A) is correct.
      REQUIRED: The external assessment requirements of Standard 1310 *Requirements of the Quality Assurance and Improvement Program.*
      DISCUSSION: Implementation Guide 1310 states, "External assessments provide an opportunity for an independent assessor or assessment team to conclude as to the internal audit activity's conformance with the *Standards* and whether internal auditors apply the Code of Ethics and to identify areas for improvement. The CAE is responsible for ensuring that the internal audit activity conducts an external assessment at least once every five years. A self-assessment may be performed in lieu of a full external assessment, provided it is validated by a qualified, independent, competent, and professional external assessor."
      Answer (B) is incorrect. Completion of an external assessment within the past two years is not a criterion for performance of a self-assessment. **Answer (C) is incorrect.** Ongoing monitoring is an internal assessment and is achieved primarily through continuous activities such as engagement planning and supervision, standardized work practices, workpaper procedures and signoffs, report reviews, as well as identification of any weaknesses or areas in need of improvement and action plans to address them (Implementation Guide 1310). External assessments are still required even if the internal audit activity has not identified any weaknesses or areas in need of improvement. **Answer (D) is incorrect.** A self-assessment may be performed in lieu of a full external assessment when certain criteria are met.

3.3 Internal and External Assessments

12. An external assessment of an internal audit activity contains an expressed opinion. The opinion may apply

A. Only to the internal audit activity's conformance with the *Standards*.

B. Only to the effectiveness of the internal auditing coverage.

C. Only to the adequacy of internal control.

D. To conformance with the *Standards* and an assessment for each standard.

Answer (D) is correct.
      REQUIRED: The subject of the opinion expressed in a communication after an external assessment of a quality program.
      DISCUSSION: External assessments of an internal audit activity contain an expressed opinion or conclusion on overall conformance with the Code of Ethics and the *Standards* and possibly an assessment for each standard or series of standards. An external assessment also includes, as appropriate, recommendations (corrective action plans) for improvement.
      Answer (A) is incorrect. The opinion also addresses conformance with the Code of Ethics (Interp. Std. 1320). **Answer (B) is incorrect.** The scope of an external assessment extends to more than the effectiveness of the internal auditing coverage. **Answer (C) is incorrect.** An external assessment addresses the internal audit activity, not the adequacy of the organization's controls.

13. As a part of a quality program, internal assessment teams most likely will examine which of the following to evaluate the quality of engagement planning and documentation for individual engagements?

A. Measures of project budgets and audit plan completion.

B. Project assignment documentation.

C. Weekly status reports.

D. The long-range engagement work schedule.

Answer (A) is correct.
REQUIRED: The item(s) most likely examined to evaluate the quality of planning and documentation for individual engagements.
DISCUSSION: Internal assessments must include ongoing monitoring of the performance of the internal audit activity and periodic self-assessments or assessments by other persons within the organization with sufficient knowledge of internal auditing practices (Attr. Std. 1311). The processes and tools used in ongoing internal assessments include, among other things, measures of project budgets, timekeeping systems, and audit plan completion. These may help to determine whether the appropriate amount of time was spent on all parts of the engagement (IG 1311).
Answer (B) is incorrect. Project assignment documentation contains less relevant information for assessment purposes than work programs. **Answer (C) is incorrect.** Status reports do not bear directly on planning. **Answer (D) is incorrect.** The long-range engagement work schedule does not relate to planning and documentation for individual engagements.

14. Ordinarily, those conducting internal quality program assessments report to

A. The board.

B. The chief audit executive.

C. Senior management.

D. The internal audit staff.

Answer (B) is correct.
REQUIRED: The person(s) to whom those conducting internal quality program assessments report.
DISCUSSION: The CAE establishes a structure for reporting results of internal assessments that maintains appropriate credibility and objectivity. Generally, those assigned responsibility for conducting ongoing and periodic reviews report to the CAE while performing the reviews and communicate results directly to the CAE.
Answer (A) is incorrect. At least annually, the CAE reports the results of internal assessments to the board. **Answer (C) is incorrect.** The CAE shares information about internal assessments with appropriate persons outside the internal audit activity, such as senior management. **Answer (D) is incorrect.** Results ordinarily are communicated directly to the CAE. Given a self-assessment, reporting to the internal audit staff essentially involves having the staff report to itself.

15. Quality program assessments may be performed internally or externally. A distinguishing feature of an external assessment is its objective to

A. Identify tasks that can be performed better.

B. Determine whether internal audit services meet professional standards.

C. Set forth the recommendations for improvement.

D. Provide independent assurance.

Answer (D) is correct.
REQUIRED: The distinguishing feature of an external assessment.
DISCUSSION: External assessments must be conducted at least once every 5 years by a qualified, independent reviewer or review team from outside the organization (Attr. Std. 1312). Individuals who perform the external assessment are free of any obligation to, or interest in, the organization whose internal audit activity is assessed.
Answer (A) is incorrect. An internal assessment will identify tasks that can be performed better. **Answer (B) is incorrect.** An internal assessment will determine whether internal audit services meet professional standards. **Answer (C) is incorrect.** An internal assessment will set forth recommendations for improvement.

16. External assessment of an internal audit activity is **not** likely to evaluate

A. Adherence to the internal audit activity's charter.

B. Conformance with the *Standards*.

C. Detailed cost-benefit analysis of the internal audit activity.

D. The internal audit staff's expertise.

Answer (C) is correct.
    REQUIRED: The purpose not served by external assessment of an internal audit activity.
    DISCUSSION: The external assessment has a broad scope of coverage that includes (1) conformance with the Code of Ethics and the *Standards* evaluated by review of the internal audit activity's charter, plans, policies, procedures, practices, and applicable legislative and regulatory requirements; (2) the expectations of the internal audit activity expressed by the board, senior management, and operational managers; and (3) the efficiency and effectiveness of the internal audit activity (IG 1312). However, the costs and benefits of internal auditing are neither easily quantifiable nor the subject of an external assessment.
    Answer (A) is incorrect. Adherence to the internal audit activity's charter is within the broad scope of coverage of the external assessment. **Answer (B) is incorrect.** Conformance with the *Standards* is within the broad scope of coverage of the external assessment. **Answer (D) is incorrect.** The efficiency and effectiveness of the internal audit activity, including the internal auditors knowledge, experience, and expertise, are within the broad scope of coverage of the external assessment.

3.4 Reporting on Quality Assurance

17. At what minimal required frequency does the chief audit executive report the results of internal assessments in the form of ongoing monitoring to senior management and the board?

A. Monthly.

B. Quarterly.

C. Annually.

D. Biennially.

Answer (C) is correct.
    REQUIRED: The frequency of reporting by the CAE to the board and senior management.
    DISCUSSION: To demonstrate conformance with the mandatory IIA guidance, the results of external and periodic internal assessments are communicated upon completion of such assessments and the results of ongoing monitoring are communicated at least annually (Inter. Std. 1320).

18. Following an external assessment of the internal audit activity, who is (are) responsible for communicating the results to the board?

A. Internal auditors.

B. Audit committee.

C. Chief audit executive.

D. External auditors.

Answer (C) is correct.
    REQUIRED: The individual or group responsible for communicating the results of external assessments to the board.
    DISCUSSION: The chief audit executive must communicate the results of the QAIP to senior management and the board (Attr. Std. 1320).

19. Internal auditors may include in their audit report that their activities conform with The IIA *Standards*. They may use this statement only if

- A. It is supported by the results of the quality program.

- B. An independent external assessment of the internal audit activity is conducted annually.

- C. Senior management or the board is accountable for implementing a quality program.

- D. External assessments of the internal audit activity are made by external auditors.

Answer (A) is correct.
  REQUIRED: The condition permitting internal auditors to report that their activities conform with the *Standards*.
  DISCUSSION: The chief audit executive may state that the internal audit activity conforms with the *International Standards for the Professional Practice of Internal Auditing* only if the results of the quality assurance and improvement program support this statement (Attr. Std. 1321).
  Answer (B) is incorrect. An independent external assessment of the internal audit activity must be conducted at least once every 5 years. **Answer (C) is incorrect.** The CAE must develop and maintain a QAIP that covers all aspects of the internal audit activity. **Answer (D) is incorrect.** Assessments also may be made by others who are (1) independent, (2) qualified, and (3) from outside the organization.

20. When is initial use of the conformance phrase by internal auditors appropriate?

- A. After an internal review completed within the past 5 years.

- B. After an external review completed within the past 10 years.

- C. After an internal review completed within the past 10 years.

- D. After an external review completed within the past 5 years.

Answer (D) is correct.
  REQUIRED: The time when the use of the conformance phrase is appropriate.
  DISCUSSION: The chief audit executive may state that the internal audit activity conforms with the *International Standards for the Professional Practice of Internal Auditing* only if the results of the quality assurance and improvement program support this statement (Attr. Std. 1321). The internal audit activity conforms with mandatory guidance when it achieves the outcomes described in the Code of Ethics and the *Standards*. The results of the quality assurance and improvement program include the results of both internal and external assessments. All internal audit activities will have the results of internal assessments. Internal audit activities in existence for at least 5 years will also have the results of external assessments (Inter. Std. 1321; Attr. Std. 1312). Thus, to use the phrase, the chief audit executive of an internal audit activity in existence for at least 5 years must have the results of an external assessment within that period.
  Answer (A) is incorrect. An internal audit activity must have an external assessment every 5 years. **Answer (B) is incorrect.** Initial use of the conformance phrase requires the completion of an external assessment within the past 5 years. **Answer (C) is incorrect.** Initial use of the conformance phrase requires the completion of an external assessment within the past 5 years.

STUDY UNIT FOUR

GOVERNANCE

(20 pages of outline)

This study unit is the first of four covering **Domain V: Governance, Risk Management, and Control** from The IIA's CIA Exam Syllabus. This domain makes up 35% of Part 1 of the CIA exam and is tested at the **basic** and **proficient** cognitive levels. The four study units are

- **Study Unit 4: Governance**
- Study Unit 5: Risk Management
- Study Unit 6: Controls: Types and Frameworks
- Study Unit 7: Controls: Application

The **learning objectives** of Study Unit 4 are

- Describe the concept of organizational governance

- Recognize the impact of organizational culture on the overall control environment and individual engagement risks and controls

- Recognize and interpret the organization's ethics and compliance-related issues, alleged violations, and dispositions

- Describe corporate social responsibility

Governance is a combination of people, policies, procedures, and processes (including internal control). It helps ensure that an entity effectively and efficiently directs its activities toward meeting the objectives of its stakeholders. Governance can be influenced by internal or external sources.

SUCCESS TIP

The roles of the board, senior management, and internal auditors in organizational governance are frequently tested on the exam. A sound understanding of their unique roles in organizational governance will increase your success on the exam.

4.1 GOVERNANCE PRINCIPLES

Corporate Governance

Governance is "[t]he combination of processes and structures implemented by the board to inform, direct, manage, and monitor the activities of the organization toward the achievement of its objectives" (The IIA Glossary).

- "Corporate governance involves a set of relationships between a company's management, its board, its shareholders, and other stakeholders.

    - Corporate governance also provides the structure through which the objectives of the company are set, and the means of attaining those objectives and monitoring performance are determined" (Organization for Economic Co-operation and Development).

- Stakeholders are persons or entities who are affected by the activities of the entity. Among others, these include shareholders, employees, suppliers, customers, neighbors of the entity's facilities, and government regulators.

Corporate governance can be influenced by internal or external mechanisms.

- Internal mechanisms include corporate charters and bylaws, boards of directors, and internal audit functions.

- External mechanisms include laws, regulations, and the government regulators who enforce them.

Governance Principles

Governance does not exist independently of risk management and control. Rather, governance, risk management, and control (collectively referred to as GRC) are interrelated.

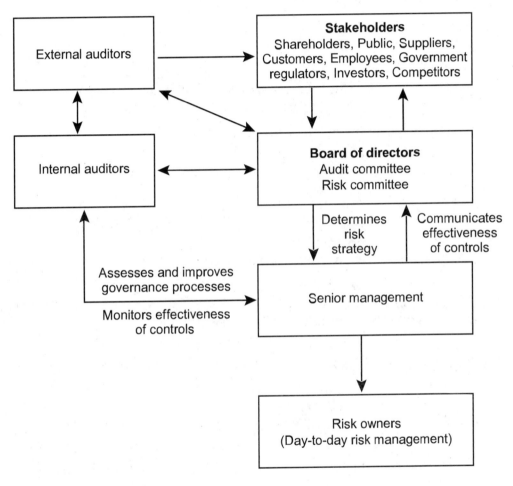

Figure 4-1

- Effective governance considers risk when setting strategy, and risk management relies on effective governance (e.g., tone at the top, risk appetite and tolerance, risk culture, and the oversight of risk management).

- Effective governance relies on controls to manage risks and on communication of their effectiveness to the board.

The following is a summary of governance principles:

- An independent and objective board with sufficient expertise, experience, authority, and resources to conduct independent inquiries

- An understanding by senior management and the board of the operating structure, including structures that impede transparency

- An organizational strategy used to measure organizational and individual performance

- An organizational structure that supports accomplishing strategic objectives

- A governing policy for the operation of key activities

- Clear, enforced lines of responsibility and accountability

- Effective interaction among the board, management, and assurance providers

- Appropriate oversight by management, including strong controls

- Compensation policies—especially for senior management—that encourage appropriate behavior consistent with the organization's values, objectives, strategy, and internal control

- Reinforcement of an ethical culture, including employee feedback without fear of retaliation

- Effective use of internal and external auditors, ensuring their independence, the adequacy of their resources and scope of activities, and the effectiveness of operations

- Clear definition and implementation of risk management policies and processes

- Transparent disclosure of key information to stakeholders

- Comparison of governance processes with national codes or best practices

- Oversight of related party transactions and conflicts of interest

Governance Process and Roles

CIA candidates should understand governance components and how internal audit's role fits into the governance process.

Governance has two major components: **strategic direction** and **oversight**.

1. **Strategic direction** determines

    ▪ The business model,
    ▪ Overall objectives,
    ▪ The approach to risk taking (including the risk appetite), and
    ▪ The limits of organizational conduct.

2. **Oversight** is the governance component with which internal auditing is most concerned. It is also the component to which risk management and control activities are most likely to be applied. The elements of oversight are

    ▪ Risk management activities performed by senior management and risk owners and
    ▪ Internal and external assurance activities.

The **board** is defined by The IIA as the highest level governing body (for instance, a board of directors, a supervisory board, or a board of governors or trustees) charged with the responsibility to direct and/or oversee the organization's activities and hold senior management accountable.

● Although governance arrangements vary among jurisdictions and sectors, typically the board includes members who are not part of management. If a board does not exist, the word "board" refers to a group or person charged with governance of the organization.

● Furthermore, "board" may refer to a committee or another body to which the governing body has delegated certain functions (for example, an audit committee). Thus, the board is the source of overall direction to, and the authority of, management. It also has the **ultimate responsibility for oversight**.

    ▪ Another responsibility is to identify stakeholders, whether directly involved with the business (employees, customers, and suppliers), indirectly involved (investors), or having influence over the business (regulators and competitors).

    ▪ The board must determine the expectations of stakeholders and the outcomes that are unacceptable.

- The board has the following duties:
  - Selection and removal of officers
  - Decisions about capital structure (mix of debt and equity, consideration to be received for shares, etc.)
  - Adding, amending, or repealing bylaws (unless this authority is reserved to the shareholders)
  - Initiation of fundamental changes (mergers, acquisitions, etc.)
  - Decisions to declare and distribute dividends
  - Setting of management compensation (sometimes performed by a subcommittee called the compensation committee)
  - Coordinating audit activities (most often performed by a subcommittee called the audit committee)
  - Evaluating and managing risk (sometimes performed by a subcommittee called the risk committee)
- A **risk committee** may be created that
  - Identifies key risks,
  - Connects them to risk management processes,
  - Delegates them to risk owners, and
  - Considers whether tolerance levels delegated to risk owners are consistent with the organization's risk appetite.

Management performs day-to-day governance functions. Senior management carries out board directives (within specified tolerances for unacceptable outcomes) to achieve objectives.

- Senior management determines
  - Where specific risks are to be managed,
  - Who will be **risk owners** (managers responsible for specific day-to-day risks), and
  - How specific risks will be managed.

- Senior management establishes reporting requirements for risk owners related to their risk management activities.

- Governance expectations, including tolerance levels, must be periodically reevaluated by the board and senior management. The result may be changes in risk management activities.

The **internal audit activity** is responsible for assessing and improving governance processes. (The internal audit activity's responsibilities are discussed later in this subunit and Subunit 4.2.)

Risk owners are responsible for

- Evaluating the adequacy of the design of risk management activities and the organization's ability to carry them out as designed;

- Determining whether risk management activities are operating as designed;

- Establishing monitoring activities; and

- Ensuring that information to be reported to senior management and the board is accurate, timely, and available.

Governance Practices

Governance applies to all organizational activities. Governance practices reflect the organization's unique culture and largely depend on it for effectiveness.

- **Culture** consists of the attitudes, behaviors, and understanding about risk, both positive and negative, that influence the decisions of management and personnel and reflect the mission, vision, and core values of the organization.

- Accordingly, **organizational culture** is reflected in
  - Setting values, objectives, and strategies;
  - Defining roles and behaviors;
  - Measuring performance;
  - Specifying accountability; and
  - Complying with corporate social responsibilities.

- Organizational culture affects the overall **control environment** and individual engagement risks and controls. (The control environment is defined in Appendix A.)

EXAMPLE 4-1	Organizational Culture and the Control Environment

If an organization's culture is risk aggressive, then the organization is more likely to have low regard for the importance of internal control, and the internal audit team is more likely to underestimate engagement risks.

Conversely, if an organization's culture is risk averse, then the organization is more likely to have high regard for the importance of internal control, and the internal audit team is more likely to overestimate engagement risks.

- **Senior management** is primarily responsible for establishing and maintaining an organizational culture.

Governance practices may use various legal forms, structures, strategies, and procedures. They ensure that the organization

   ✓   Complies with society's legal and regulatory rules;

   ✓   Satisfies the generally accepted business norms, ethical principles, and social expectations of society;

   ✓   Provides overall benefit to society and enhances the interests of the specific stakeholders in both the long and short term; and

   ✓   Reports fully and truthfully to its stakeholders, including the public, to ensure accountability for its decisions, actions, and performances.

Ethical Culture

The ethical culture is an important component of the organizational culture and is crucial to the effectiveness of governance practices. Because decision making is complex and dispersed in most organizations, each person should be an ethics advocate, whether officially or informally.

Codes of conduct and vision statements are issued to state

- The organization's values and objectives;

- The behavior expected; and

- The strategies for maintaining a culture consistent with legal, ethical, and societal responsibilities.

The **board** oversees the organization's ethical climate.

Senior management has ultimate responsibility for promoting and setting the example of ethical behavior (i.e., setting the tone at the top).

- Senior management is also responsible for establishing and maintaining sound ethics-related objectives and programs.

Organizations may designate a chief ethics officer.

Internal auditors may have an active role in support of the organization's ethical culture. Roles may include chief ethics officer, member of an ethics council, or assessor of the ethical climate.

- In some circumstances, the role of chief ethics officer may conflict with the independence attribute of the internal audit activity.
  - The organizational independence of the internal audit activity is necessary because it performs internal assurance services.

The internal audit activity periodically assesses the elements of the ethical climate of the organization and its effectiveness in achieving legal and ethical compliance. Internal auditors therefore evaluate the effectiveness of the following:

- A formal code of conduct and related statements and policies (including procedures covering fraud and corruption)

- Frequent demonstrations of ethical attitudes and behavior by influential leaders

- Explicit strategies to support the ethical culture

- Confidential reporting of alleged misconduct

- Regular declarations by employees, suppliers, and customers about the requirements of ethical behavior

- Clear delegation of responsibilities for providing counsel, investigation, and reporting

- Easy access to learning opportunities

- Personnel practices that encourage contributions by employees

- Regular surveys of employees, suppliers, and customers to determine the state of the ethical climate

- Regular reviews of the processes that undermine the ethical culture

- Regular reference and background checks

Governance System Maturity

The role of the internal audit activity and the advice given by it depend on the maturity of the governance system.

- In a **less mature** system, the internal audit activity emphasizes compliance with policies, procedures, laws, etc. It also addresses the basic risks to the organization.

- In a **more mature** governance system, the internal audit activity's emphasis is on optimizing structure and practices.

- As the internal audit activity becomes more sophisticated, it transitions from only auditing to auditing **and** adding value to the company by suggesting how to optimize the company's operations.

The responsibility of the internal audit activity in an assurance engagement for ethics-related matters is described in the following standard:

Implementation Standard 2110.A1

The internal audit activity must evaluate the design, implementation, and effectiveness of the organization's ethics-related objectives, programs, and activities.

You have completed the outline for this subunit.
Study multiple-choice questions 1 through 14 beginning on page 125.

STOP & REVIEW

4.2 ROLES OF INTERNAL AUTITORS IN GOVERNANCE

Governance is one of the three basic processes identified in the Definition of Internal Auditing.

The board and management are responsible for the design and implementation of governance processes.

SUCCESS TIP

The IIA tests the performance standard below in two ways.

1. The IIA may ask straightforward questions about how the internal audit activity should make appropriate recommendations for the improvement of the organization's governance processes. In such questions, candidates must recall the correct processes to identify the correct answer choice.

2. The IIA may also test candidates at a higher level of understanding by combining the concept of governance with other concepts. In these questions, candidates can eliminate incorrect answer choices by knowing the performance standard below.

Performance Standard 2110
Governance

The internal audit activity must assess and make appropriate recommendations to improve the organization's governance processes for:

- Making strategic and operational decisions.

- Overseeing risk management and control.

- Promoting appropriate ethics and values within the organization.

- Ensuring effective organizational performance management and accountability.

- Communicating risk and control information to appropriate areas of the organization.

- Coordinating the activities of, and communicating information among, the board, external and internal auditors, other assurance providers, and management.

Implementation Standard 2110.A2

The internal audit activity must assess whether the information technology governance of the organization supports the organization's strategies and objectives.

Understanding the role of the internal audit activity begins with understanding the nature of governance in a specific organization.

Governance has a range of definitions depending on the circumstances.

- The CAE should work with the board and senior management to determine how governance should be defined for audit purposes.

Governance models generally treat governance as a process or system that is not static.

- The approach in the *Standards* emphasizes the board and its governance activities.

Governance requirements vary by entity type and regulatory jurisdiction. Examples include publicly traded companies, not-for-profits, governments, private companies, and stock exchanges.

The design and practice of effective governance vary with

- The size, complexity, and life-cycle maturity of the organization;
- Its stakeholder structure; and
- Legal and cultural requirements.

The internal audit activity's **ultimate responsibility** is to evaluate and improve governance.

The unique position of internal auditors in the organization enables them to observe and formally assess governance processes while remaining independent.

The definition of governance should be agreed upon with the board and senior management. The internal auditors should understand governance processes and the relationships among governance, risk, and control.

Internal auditors assess the design and operating effectiveness of governance processes. They also provide advice on improving those processes.

- Internal auditors may facilitate board self-assessments of governance.

The audit plan should be based on an assessment of risks that considers governance processes and related controls. The plan should include the higher-risk governance processes.

- Moreover, inclusion of an assessment of processes or risk areas should be considered if the board or senior management has requested that work be performed.

The plan

- Defines the nature of the work;
- Determines the governance processes; and
- Specifies the nature of the assessments, such as consideration of specific

  - Risks,
  - Processes, and
  - Activities to reduce risks.

The CAE should consider the following in planning assessments of governance:

- An audit should address controls in governance processes that are designed to prevent or detect events that could have a negative effect on the organization.

- Controls within governance processes often are significant in managing multiple risks. For example, controls related to the code of conduct may be relied upon to manage compliance and fraud risks.

- If other audits assess controls in governance processes, the auditor should consider relying on their results.

Assessments of governance are likely to be based on numerous audits. The internal auditor should consider

- Audits of specific processes,
- Governance issues arising from audits not focused on governance,
- The results of other assurance providers' work, and
- Such other information as adverse incidents indicating an opportunity to improve governance.

When control issues are known or the governance process is not mature, the CAE may consider different methods for improving control or governance through consulting services.

During the planning, evaluating, and reporting phases, the internal auditor should be sensitive to the consequences of the results and ensure appropriate communications with the board and senior management.

- The internal auditor should consider consulting legal counsel both before the audit and before issuing the final report.

Other roles of internal auditors in governance include the following:

- Obtain the board's approval of the internal audit charter.

- Communicate the plan of engagements.

- Report significant audit issues.

- Communicate key performance indicators to the board on a regular basis.

- Discuss areas of significant risk.

- Support the board in enterprise-wide risk assessment.

- Review the positioning of the internal audit activity within the risk management framework within the organization.

- Monitor compliance with the corporate code of conduct/business practices.

- Report on the effectiveness of the control framework.

- Assess the ethical climate of the board and the organization.

- Conduct a follow-up and report on management's response to regulatory body reviews.

- Conduct a follow-up and report on management's response to external audit.

- Assess the adequacy of the performance measurement system and achievement of organizational objectives.

- Support a culture of fraud awareness and encourage the reporting of improprieties.

STOP & REVIEW

You have completed the outline for this subunit.
Study multiple-choice questions 15 through 18 beginning on page 131.

4.3 CORPORATE SOCIAL RESPONSIBILITY (CSR)

Characteristics of CSR

Stakeholders increasingly expect organizations to accept responsibility and implement strategies and controls that

- Manage their effects on the environment and society,
- Engage stakeholders in their efforts, and
- Report results to the public.

CSR is a response to stakeholder expectations.

- CSR refers to social responsibility, sustainable development, and corporate citizenship.

- CSR is defined, in part, as "the willingness of an organization to incorporate social and environmental considerations in its decision making and be accountable for the impacts of its decisions and activities on society and the environment" (International Organization for Standardization).

- Similarly, an IIA Practice Guide defines CSR as "the way firms integrate social, environmental, and economic concerns into their values, culture, decision-making, strategy and operations in a transparent and accountable manner and thereby establish better practices within the firm, create wealth, and improve society."

A.B. Caroll identified four responsibilities that an organization must fulfill to be called socially responsible:

1. Economic responsibility to be profitable, or to do what is required by capitalism

2. Legal responsibility to obey the law, or to do what is required by stakeholders

3. Ethical responsibility to be ethical in its practices, given local and global standards, or to do what is expected by stakeholders

4. Philanthropic responsibility to be a good corporate citizen, or to do what is desired by stakeholders

Despite increasing pressure from stakeholders for organizations to be more socially and environmentally responsible, CSR is largely a **voluntary** practice.

- In the U.S.A., public companies are not required to disclose their CSR performance.

- Furthermore, organizations exercise significant discretion in deciding what to disclose about their CSR performance.

CSR Frameworks

Two major frameworks exist that provide guidance on CSR implementation.

1.   The Global Reporting Initiative (GRI) has developed a sustainability **reporting** framework that provides specific guidance on measuring CSR performance against predefined criteria.

2.   While GRI guidance emphasizes reporting, ISO 26000 emphasizes how to **implement and manage a CSR initiative**.

ISO 14000 standards are a set of criteria for certification of an environmental management system.

-   According to ISO, the benefits of using ISO 14000 can include the following:
    -   Reduced cost of waste management
    -   Savings in consumption of energy and materials
    -   Lower distribution costs
    -   Improved corporate image among regulators, customers, and the public

Responsibility for CSR

The board is responsible for overseeing CSR and the effectiveness of governance, risk management, and internal control processes related to CSR.

Management is responsible for establishing CSR objectives, assessing and managing risks, measuring performance, and monitoring and reporting activities.

The internal auditor is responsible for evaluating whether controls over CSR are adequate to achieve CSR objectives.

All employees are responsible for the success of CSR initiatives.

CSR Strategies

The following are four alternative strategies for responding to CSR initiatives:

1. **Reaction.** The organization denies responsibility and tries to maintain the status quo.

2. **Defense.** The organization uses legal action or public relations efforts to avoid additional responsibilities.

3. **Accommodation.** The organization assumes additional responsibilities only when pressured.

4. **Proaction.** The organization takes the initiative in implementing a CSR program that serves as an example for the industry.

Risks

The risks of failing to implement an effective CSR program include the following, among others:

*   **Loss of reputation.** The organization's brand or reputation could be damaged.

*   **Noncompliance.** The organization may fail to comply with regulations or contractual obligations.

*   **Lawsuits.** The organization may be held liable for alleged harms.

*   **Operational failures.** Operational pressure points (e.g., environmental effects of processes or products) may indicate risks. Risks also result from, for example, not achieving CSR objectives because of inappropriate CSR strategies or over-emphasis on CSR strategies.

*   **Stock market.** The organization may lose investors.

*   **Employment market.** Employees may leave the organization, or attracting new employees may be difficult.

*   **Sales decline.** Customers may boycott services or products.

CSR Business Activities

CSR business activities generally include the following:

- Establishing and communicating policies and procedures

- Setting objectives, performance goals, and strategies

- Communicating and integrating CSR principles and controls into the business decision-making processes

- Monitoring, evaluating results, and benchmarking

- Engaging stakeholders (e.g., through satisfaction surveys, focus groups, and complaint management processes)

- Auditing (e.g., public disclosures, internal controls, and contractual compliance with CSR terms and conditions)

- External and internal reporting of results

Evaluating and Auditing CSR

The internal audit activity must maintain its independence and objectivity while performing CSR audits.

- The internal audit activity's independence and objectivity is not impaired if it
    - Provides advice on the design and implementation of CSR programs or
    - Facilitates a management self-assessment of CSR controls and results.

Any internal audit activity that collectively lacks the appropriate skill and knowledge should not perform CSR audits.

The chief audit executive (CAE) considers CSR risks, and the internal audit activity evaluates whether the organization has adequate controls to achieve its CSR objectives.

- Evaluation criteria may include compliance with internal control frameworks (e.g., COSO), quality frameworks (e.g., ISO), or contractual obligations.

CSR Maturity Model

The CAE compares the organization's CSR maturity level [using a 5-level maturity scale (level 1 is "initial" and level 5 is "optimizing")] at the time of the internal audit with the level the organization desires to achieve.

Two common approaches to auditing CSR are auditing by **element** and by **stakeholder group**.

Element

Separate audits of each element are performed. The following are typical CSR elements with example audit questions:

- Governance (Do board members have sufficient and relevant information to fulfill their roles and responsibilities?)

- Community investment (What philanthropic practices are in place, and how are decisions made?)

- Environment (Are social and environmental impact assessments performed?)

- Ethics (Is an anti-corruption culture included in the organization's risk assessment, code of conduct, and policies?)

- Health, safety, and security (Are incidents reported, communicated, managed, and resolved appropriately?)

- Transparency (Does the organization follow appropriate accounting standards?)

- Working conditions and human rights (Is compensation based on fair pay, living wages, and job opportunities?)

Stakeholder Group

Separate audits of CSR programs related to each significant stakeholder group are performed that consider compliance with laws, regulations, and contracts. The following are typical stakeholder groups with example audit questions:

- Customers (Does the organization have product safety and recall processes?)
- Employees and their families (Does the organization prohibit discrimination and harassment?)
- Environment (Are social and environmental impact assessments performed?)
- Neighboring communities (Does the organization give to local economic support programs?)
- Shareholders (Does the organization abide by shareholder rights?)
- Suppliers (Are rates and payment terms fair?)

Reporting CSR

Every organization must make a business decision about

- The **cost or benefit** of producing a CSR report and
- What information to include in the report.

Many organizations use **verification and assurance processes** for all or parts of the report to increase accountability and reduce the likelihood that the report will appear to be a marketing tool.

Reporting methods include the following:

- Providing a standalone CSR report
- Integrating the CSR report with the annual financial report
- Providing CSR information booklets on special topics

Distribution formats include the following:

- Web pages
- Booklets
- Press releases
- Regulatory filings

STOP & REVIEW

You have completed the outline for this subunit.
Study multiple-choice questions 19 and 20 on page 133.

QUESTIONS

4.1 Governance Principles

1. The internal audit activity most directly contributes to an organization's governance process by

A. Identifying significant exposures to risk.

B. Evaluating the effectiveness of internal control over financial reporting.

C. Promoting continuous improvement of controls.

D. Evaluating the design of ethics-related activities.

Answer (D) is correct.

REQUIRED: The way in which internal audit activity most directly contributes to an organization's governance process.

DISCUSSION: Performance Standard 2110 states, "The internal audit activity must assess and make appropriate recommendations to improve the organization's governance processes for:

- Making strategic and operational decisions.
- Overseeing risk management and control.
- Promoting appropriate ethics and values within the organization.
- Ensuring effective organizational performance management and accountability.
- Communicating risk and control information to appropriate areas of the organization.
- Coordinating the activities of, and communicating information among, the board, external and internal auditors, other assurance providers, and management."

Thus, in an assurance engagement, the internal audit activity must evaluate the design, implementation, and effectiveness of the organization's ethics-related objectives, programs, and activities.

Answer (A) is incorrect. Identifying significant exposures to risk most directly relates to risk management rather than to governance. **Answer (B) is incorrect.** Evaluating the effectiveness of internal control over financial reporting more directly relates to risk management rather than to governance. **Answer (C) is incorrect.** Promoting continuous improvement of controls relates to controls rather than to governance.

2. Which of the following is **not** a goal of corporate governance?

A. Complying with society's legal and regulatory rules.

B. Providing an overall benefit to society.

C. Reporting fully and truthfully to stakeholders.

D. Maximizing executive compensation.

Answer (D) is correct.

REQUIRED: The item not a goal of corporate governance.

DISCUSSION: Governance practices may use various legal forms, structures, strategies, and procedures. They ensure that the organization (1) complies with society's legal and regulatory rules; (2) satisfies the generally accepted business norms, ethical principles, and social expectations of society; (3) provides overall benefit to society and enhances the interests of the specific stakeholders in both the long- and short-term; and (4) reports fully and truthfully to its stakeholders, including the public, to ensure accountability for its decisions, actions, and performances. But maximizing executive compensation is not a goal of corporate governance.

Answer (A) is incorrect. Ensuring compliance with society's legal and regulatory rules is a goal of corporate governance. **Answer (B) is incorrect.** Proving an overall benefit to society is a goal of corporate governance. **Answer (C) is incorrect.** Reporting fully and truthfully to stakeholders is a goal of corporate governance.

3. The role of the internal audit activity in the ethical culture of an organization is to

    A. Assess its effectiveness in achieving legal compliance.

    B. Avoid involvement in the ethical culture because of loss of objectivity.

    C. Become a member of an ethics council.

    D. Assume responsibility for the governance process.

Answer (A) is correct.
    REQUIRED: The role of the internal audit activity in the ethical culture of an organization.
    DISCUSSION: The internal audit activity periodically assesses the elements of the ethical climate of the organization and its effectiveness in achieving legal and ethical compliance. Internal auditors therefore evaluate the effectiveness of, among other things, a formal code of conduct and related statements and policies.
    Answer (B) is incorrect. Internal auditors must be active ethics advocates. However, assuming the role of, for example, chief ethics officer may, in some circumstances, impair individual objectivity and the internal audit activity's independence. **Answer (C) is incorrect.** The internal auditor's basic role is to be the assessor of the ethical culture. However, an internal auditor may become chief ethics officer or a member of an ethics council, although the first role may, in some circumstances, impair individual objectivity and the internal audit activity's independence. **Answer (D) is incorrect.** The organization's board and its senior management are responsible for the effectiveness of the governance process.

4. Which of the following is a **false** statement about the role of internal auditors in an organization's ethical culture?

    A. Roles may include chief ethics officer.

    B. The role of chief ethics officer sometimes conflicts with the independence of the internal audit activity.

    C. In a more mature system, the internal audit activity emphasizes compliance.

    D. In a more mature governance system, the internal audit activity's emphasis is on optimizing structure and practices.

Answer (C) is correct.
    REQUIRED: The false statement about the role of internal auditors in an organization's ethical culture.
    DISCUSSION: The role of the internal audit activity depends on the maturity of the governance system. In a less mature system, the internal audit activity emphasizes compliance with policies, procedures, laws, etc. It also addresses the basic risks to the organization.
    Answer (A) is incorrect. Internal auditors' roles may include chief ethics officer. **Answer (B) is incorrect.** In some circumstances, the role of chief ethics officer may conflict with the independence attribute of the internal audit activity. **Answer (D) is incorrect.** In a more mature governance system, the internal audit activity's emphasis is on optimizing structure and practices.

5. Senior management is primarily responsible for

    A. Implementing and monitoring controls designed by the board of directors.

    B. Ensuring that external auditors oversee risk management and control processes.

    C. Evaluating the controls over the reliability and integrity of financial and operational information.

    D. Determining who will be risk owners.

Answer (D) is correct.
    REQUIRED: The best description of senior management's responsibility.
    DISCUSSION: Senior management determines (1) where specific risks are to be managed, (2) who will be risk owners (managers responsible for specific day-to-day risks), and (3) how specific risks will be managed.
    Answer (A) is incorrect. The board has oversight responsibilities but ordinarily does not become involved in the details of operations. **Answer (B) is incorrect.** Management ensures that sound risk management processes are in place and are adequate and effective. **Answer (C) is incorrect.** Internal auditors are responsible for evaluating the adequacy and effectiveness of controls, including those relating to the reliability and integrity of financial and operational information.

6. Which of the following correctly classifies the corporate governance functions as internal or external?

	Internal	External
A.	Corporate charter	Bylaws
B.	Laws	Board of directors
C.	Internal audit function	Corporate charter
D.	Bylaws	Government regulation

Answer (D) is correct.
    REQUIRED: The correct classification of the corporate governance functions.
    DISCUSSION: Bylaws are an example of internal corporate governance, and laws, regulations, and the government regulators who enforce them are examples of external governance.
    Answer (A) is incorrect. Bylaws are an example of internal corporate governance. **Answer (B) is incorrect.** Laws provide external corporate governance. **Answer (C) is incorrect.** A corporate charter is an example of internal corporate governance.

7. Ensuring effective organizational performance management and accountability is most directly the proper function of

    A. Control.

    B. Governance.

    C. Risk management.

    D. A quality assurance program.

Answer (B) is correct.
    REQUIRED: The process responsible for ensuring effective organizational performance management and accountability.
    DISCUSSION: Organizational performance is measured by achieving objectives. The IIA Glossary defines governance as the combination of processes and structures implemented by the board to inform, direct, manage, and monitor the activities of the organization toward the achievement of its objectives. Thus, ensuring effective organizational performance management and accountability is most directly the proper function of governance.
    Answer (A) is incorrect. Governance (not control) is directly responsible for ensuring effective organizational performance management and accountability. **Answer (C) is incorrect.** Governance (not risk management) is directly responsible for ensuring effective organizational performance management and accountability. **Answer (D) is incorrect.** A quality assurance program normally is implemented for an organizational unit, e.g., the internal audit activity.

8. Which of the following should be stated in an organization's code of conduct?

1. The organization's values and objectives

2. The behavior expected

3. The strategies for maintaining a culture inconsistent with legal, ethical, and societal responsibilities

    A. 1 and 2 only.

    B. 1 and 3 only.

    C. 2 and 3 only.

    D. 1, 2, and 3.

Answer (A) is correct.
    REQUIRED: The most likely content of an organization's code of conduct.
    DISCUSSION: Codes of conduct and vision statements are issued to state

- The organization's values and objectives;
- The behavior expected; and
- The strategies for maintaining a culture consistent with legal, ethical, and societal responsibilities.

9. The role of the internal audit activity in the ethical culture of an organization is to

A. Avoid active support of the ethical culture because of possible loss of independence.

B. Evaluate the effectiveness of the organization's formal code of conduct.

C. Assume accountability for the effectiveness of the governance process.

D. Become the chief ethics officer.

Answer (B) is correct.
   REQUIRED: The minimum role of the internal audit activity in the ethical culture of an organization.
   DISCUSSION: The internal audit activity periodically assesses the elements of the ethical climate of the organization and its effectiveness in achieving legal and ethical compliance. Internal auditors therefore evaluate the effectiveness of, among other things, a formal code of conduct and related statements and policies.
   Answer (A) is incorrect. Internal auditors must be active ethics advocates. However, assuming the role of, for example, chief ethics officer may, in some circumstances, impair individual objectivity and the internal audit activity's independence. **Answer (C) is incorrect.** The organization's board and its senior management are responsible for the effectiveness of the governance process. **Answer (D) is incorrect.** The internal auditor's basic role is to be the assessor of the ethical culture. However, an internal auditor may become chief ethics officer or a member of an ethics council, although the first role may, in some circumstances, impair individual objectivity and the internal audit activity's independence.

10. Which of the following correctly classifies governance functions as internal or external?

	Internal	External
A.	Internal audit function	Government regulation
B.	Senior management	Corporate charter
C.	Privacy laws	External auditors
D.	Corporate charter	Ethical culture

Answer (A) is correct.
   REQUIRED: The correct classification of the corporate governance functions.
   DISCUSSION: The internal audit function is an example of internal corporate governance, and laws, regulations, and the government regulators who enforce them are examples of external governance.
   Answer (B) is incorrect. A corporate charter is an example of internal corporate governance. **Answer (C) is incorrect.** Laws provide external corporate governance. **Answer (D) is incorrect.** An ethical culture is an example of internal corporate governance.

11. Which of the following is most likely an internal audit role in a less structured governance process?

A. Designing specific governance processes.

B. Playing a consulting role in optimizing governance practices and structure.

C. Providing advice about basic risks to the organization.

D. Evaluating the effectiveness of specific governance processes.

Answer (C) is correct.
    REQUIRED: The internal audit activity's likely role in a less structured governance process.
    DISCUSSION: A less mature governance system will emphasize the requirements for compliance with policies, procedures, plans, laws, regulations, and contracts. It will also address the basic risks to the organization. Thus, the internal audit activity will provide advice about such matters. As the governance process becomes more structured, the internal audit activity's emphasis will shift to optimizing the governance structure and practices.
    Answer (A) is incorrect. Internal auditors impair their objectivity by designing processes. However, evaluating the design and effectiveness of specific processes is a typical internal audit role. **Answer (B) is incorrect.** Playing a consulting role in optimizing governance practices and structure is typical of a more structured internal auditing governance maturity model. The emphasis shifts to considering best practices and adapting them to the specific organization. **Answer (D) is incorrect.** Evaluating the effectiveness of specific governance processes is typical of a more structured internal auditing governance maturity model.

12. Which of the following is a situation in which an internal auditor's role of chief ethics officer conflicts with the independence attribute of the internal audit activity?

A. The chief ethics officer requests that the internal auditors assess whether the organization as a whole is not complying with the organization's code of conduct.

B. The chief ethics officer informs the board of recommendations made by the internal audit activity regarding the organization's compliance with the code of conduct.

C. The chief ethics officer proposes and implements a new whistleblower program for the organization.

D. The internal audit activity informs the chief ethics officer that the organization is in compliance with all laws and regulations.

Answer (C) is correct.
    REQUIRED: The situation in which the internal auditor's role is inconsistent with the independence attribute.
    DISCUSSION: Proposing and implementing a new whistleblower program conflicts with the independence attribute of the internal audit activity. Implementation is a management function and is therefore inconsistent with the organizational independence of the internal audit activity.

13. The internal and external auditors report directly to an audit committee composed of independent directors. This practice is directly related to which of the following governance principles?

1. Effective use of internal and external auditors.

2. Effective interaction among the board, management, and assurance providers.

3. An organizational structure that supports accomplishing strategic objectives.

4. An organizational structure used to measure organizational and individual performance.

    A. 1 and 2 only.

    B. 2 and 3 only.

    C. 3 and 4 only.

    D. 1, 2, 3, and 4.

Answer (A) is correct.
    REQUIRED: The principles directly related to the reporting relationship of auditors.
    DISCUSSION: Internal and external auditors should be used effectively to ensure (1) their independence, (2) the adequacy of their resources and the scope of their activities, and (3) the effectiveness of operations. Moreover, an entity should have an independent and objective board with sufficient expertise, experience, authority, and resources to conduct independent inquiries.
    Answer (B) is incorrect. An organizational structure that supports accomplishing strategic objectives is not directly related. **Answer (C) is incorrect.** An organizational structure that supports accomplishing strategic objectives and an organizational structure used to measure organizational and individual performance are not directly related. **Answer (D) is incorrect.** An organizational structure that supports accomplishing strategic objectives and an organizational structure used to measure organizational and individual performance are not directly related.

14. Governance should help ensure that the objectives of an entity's stakeholders are met. Stakeholders include

1. Employees
2. Regulators
3. Suppliers
4. Customers

    A. 1 and 4 only.

    B. 2 and 3 only.

    C. 2, 3, and 4 only.

    D. 1, 2, 3, and 4.

Answer (D) is correct.
    REQUIRED: The most likely stakeholders.
    DISCUSSION: Stakeholders are persons or entities who are affected by the activities of the entity. Among others, these include (1) shareholders, (2) employees, (3) suppliers, (4) customers, (5) neighbors of the entity's facilities, and (6) government regulators.
    Answer (A) is incorrect. Regulators and suppliers are stakeholders. **Answer (B) is incorrect.** Employees and customers are stakeholders. **Answer (C) is incorrect.** Employees are stakeholders.

4.2 Roles of Internal Auditors in Governance

15. Which of the following should be defined in the internal audit plan for an assessment of governance?

1. The nature of the work
2. The governance process
3. The nature of the assessments

   A. 1 and 2 only.

   B. 2 and 3 only.

   C. 1 and 3 only.

   D. 1, 2, and 3.

Answer (D) is correct.
   REQUIRED: The items that should be defined in the internal audit plan for an assessment of governance.
   DISCUSSION: The audit plan should include higher-risk governance processes. It should define (1) the nature of the work; (2) the governance processes; and (3) the nature of the assessments, e.g., consideration of specific risks, processes, or activities.

16. In the governance process, the internal audit activity most likely should

   A. Coordinate the activities of the external and internal auditors and management.

   B. Communicate risk and control information.

   C. Evaluate the process for performance management.

   D. Promote ethics and values.

Answer (C) is correct.
   REQUIRED: The internal audit activity's function in the governance process.
   DISCUSSION: The internal audit activity must assess and make appropriate recommendations to improve the organization's governance processes for

- Making strategic and operational decisions;
- Overseeing risk management and control;
- Promoting appropriate ethics and values within the organization;
- Ensuring effective organizational performance management and accountability;
- Communicating risk and control information to appropriate areas of the organization; and
- Coordinating the activities of, and communicating information among, the board, external and internal auditors, other assurance providers, and management (Perf. Std. 2110).

   Answer (A) is incorrect. The internal audit activity evaluates the processes by which activities of the external and internal auditors and management are coordinated. **Answer (B) is incorrect.** The internal audit activity evaluates the processes by which risk and control information is communicated. **Answer (D) is incorrect.** The internal audit activity evaluates the processes by which ethics and values are promoted.

17. A basic principle of governance is

    A. Assessment of the governance process by an independent internal audit activity.

    B. Holding the board, senior management, and the internal audit activity accountable for its effectiveness.

    C. Exclusive use of external auditors to provide assurance about the governance process.

    D. Separation of the governance process from promoting an ethical culture in the organization.

Answer (A) is correct.
    REQUIRED: The basic principle of governance.
    DISCUSSION: The internal audit activity must assess and make appropriate recommendations for improving the governance process.
    Answer (B) is incorrect. The internal audit activity is an assessor of the governance process. It is not accountable for that process. **Answer (C) is incorrect.** External parties and internal auditors may provide assurance about the governance process. **Answer (D) is incorrect.** The internal audit activity must assess and make appropriate recommendations for improving the governance process in its promotion of appropriate ethics and values within the organization.

18. Which of the following should an internal auditor consider when assessing governance?

1. Audits of specific processes

2. Governance issues arising from audits not focused on governance

3. The results of other assurance providers' work

4. Information such as adverse incidents indicating an opportunity to improve governance

    A. 1 and 3 only.

    B. 2 and 4 only.

    C. 1, 2, and 3 only.

    D. 1, 2, 3, and 4.

Answer (D) is correct.
    REQUIRED: The items that an internal auditor should consider when assessing governance.
    DISCUSSION: Assessments of governance are likely to be based on numerous audits. The internal auditor should consider

- Audits of specific processes,
- Governance issues arising from audits not focused on governance,
- The results of other assurance providers' work, and
- Other information such as adverse incidents indicating an opportunity to improve governance.

    Answer (A) is incorrect. Internal auditors should also consider governance issues arising from audits not focused on governance and other information such as adverse incidents indicating an opportunity to improve governance. **Answer (B) is incorrect.** Internal auditors should also consider audits of specific processes and the results of other assurance providers' work. **Answer (C) is incorrect.** Internal auditors should also consider other information such as adverse incidents indicating an opportunity to improve governance.

4.3 Corporate Social Responsibility (CSR)

19. Examples of CSR include all of the following **except**

    A. A pharmaceutical company that produces potentially addictive pain medication donates to addiction treatment facilities.

    B. A tobacco company donates money to stop-smoking initiatives as a result of the settlement to a lawsuit.

    C. A professional services firm pays its employees a bonus each year for providing services as volunteers to local not-for-profit organizations.

    D. A delivery company uses its distribution network to deliver supplies for free to areas affected by natural disasters.

Answer (B) is correct.
    REQUIRED: The item that is not an example of CSR.
    DISCUSSION: The donation is not an example of CSR because it is not voluntary. Socially responsible actions that are required in response to corporate misdeeds or in response to a lawsuit are more akin to punishment than to CSR.
    Answer (A) is incorrect. The donation is voluntary and intended to benefit groups other than shareholders. **Answer (C) is incorrect.** The bonus is voluntary and benefits groups other than shareholders. CSR does not only apply to corporate entities, despite its title. **Answer (D) is incorrect.** The delivery is voluntary and benefits groups other than shareholders.

20. Which of the following is **not** a benefit of implementing ISO 14000?

    A. Increased cost of waste management.

    B. Savings in consumption of energy.

    C. Lower distribution costs.

    D. Improved corporate image.

Answer (A) is correct.
    REQUIRED: The item that is not a benefit of implementing ISO 14000.
    DISCUSSION: Using ISO 14000 can (1) decrease, not increase, the cost of waste management; (2) provide savings in consumption of energy and materials; (3) lower distribution costs; and (4) improve corporate image among regulators, customers, and the public.
    Answer (B) is incorrect. Using ISO 14000 should result in savings in consumption of energy and materials. **Answer (C) is incorrect.** Using ISO 14000 should lower distribution costs. **Answer (D) is incorrect.** Using ISO 14000 should improve corporate image among regulators, customers, and the public.

GLEIM

GO TO ONLINE COURSE

Access the **Gleim CIA Premium Review System** featuring our SmartAdapt technology from your Gleim Personal Classroom to continue your studies. You will experience a personalized study environment with exam-emulating multiple-choice questions.

STUDY UNIT FIVE

RISK MANAGEMENT

(25 pages of outline)

This study unit is the second of four covering **Domain V: Governance, Risk Management, and Control** from The IIA's CIA Exam Syllabus. This domain makes up 35% of Part 1 of the CIA exam and is tested at the **basic** and **proficient** cognitive levels. The four study units are

- Study Unit 4: Governance
- **Study Unit 5: Risk Management**
- Study Unit 6: Controls: Types and Frameworks
- Study Unit 7: Controls: Application

The **learning objectives** of Study Unit 5 are

- Interpret fundamental concepts of risk and the risk management process

- Describe globally accepted risk management frameworks appropriate to the organization

- Examine the effectiveness of risk management within processes and functions

- Recognize the appropriateness of the internal audit activity's role in the organization's risk management process

Risk management assesses and controls these risks to achieve an organization's goals. Management must focus on risks at all levels of the entity and take the necessary action to manage them. All risks that could affect achievement of objectives must be considered.

5.1 RISK MANAGEMENT PROCESSES

Risk is "[t]he possibility of an event occurring that will have an impact on the achievement of objectives. Risk is measured in terms of impact and likelihood" (The IIA Glossary).

- Risk management is "a process to identify, assess, manage, and control potential events or situations to provide **reasonable assurance** regarding the achievement of the organization's objectives" (The IIA Glossary).

  - It is one of the three processes specifically addressed in the Definition of Internal Auditing.

Performance Standard 2120
Risk Management

The internal audit activity must evaluate the effectiveness and contribute to the improvement of risk management processes.

The Risk Management Process

Management must focus on risks at all levels of the entity and take the necessary action to manage them. All risks that could affect achievement of objectives must be considered.

Step 1 Identification of Context	Step 2 Risk Identification

• A precondition to risk identification is identifying the significant contexts within which risks should be managed.
 	
• Contexts include the following:
 	
   ■ Laws and regulations
   ■ Capital projects
   ■ Business processes
   ■ Technology
   ■ Organizations
   ■ Market risk
 	
      ▸ Interest rates, foreign exchange rates, etc.
	• Risk identification should be performed at every level of the entity (entity-level, division, business unit) relevant to the identified context(s).
	
	• Some occurrences may be inconsequential at the entity level but disastrous for an individual unit.
	
	• Past events and future possibilities must be considered.
	
	• SWOT analysis, workshops, and scenario analysis can be used to identify risks.

Step 3 Risk Assessment and Prioritization	Step 4 Risk Response

• The risk assessment process may be formal or informal.
 	
• The three-part process involves
 	
  1. Assessing the significance of an event,
  2. Assessing the event's likelihood, and
  3. Considering the means of managing the risk.
 	
• The results of assessing the likelihood and impact of the risk events identified are used to prioritize risks and produce decision-making information.
 	
• Risk assessment methods may be qualitative or quantitative.
 	
   ■ Risk ranking, risk maps, and risk modeling
	• Risk responses are the means by which an organization elects to manage individual risks.
	
	• Each organization selects risk responses that align risks with the organizations risk appetite, or
	
	   ■ The level of risk the organization is willing to accept.
	
	• **Controls** are actions taken by management to manage risk and ensure risk responses are carried out.
	
	• **Residual risk** is the risk that remains after risk responses are executed.
	
	• **Control risk** is the risk that controls fail to effectively manage controllable risk.

Step 5 Risk Monitoring

• Risk monitoring is a four-step continuous process that includes aspects of prior steps.

• The **two** most important sources of information for ongoing assessments of the adequacy of risk responses and the changing nature of the risks are

  1. **Those closest to the activities**, such as the manager of an operating unit.

     ▸ However, because they design the strategy to mitigate risks, they are not always objective.

  2. **The audit function.**

     ▸ Analyzing risks and responses are among the normal responsibilities of internal auditors, who should be objective.

Track identified risks → Evaluate current risk response plans → Monitor residual risks → Identify new risks

Responsibility for Aspects of Organizational Risk Management

Risk management is a key responsibility of senior management and the board.

- **Boards** have an oversight function. They determine that risk management processes are in place, adequate, and effective.

- **Management** ensures that sound risk management processes are functioning.

- The **internal audit activity** may be directed to examine, evaluate, report, or recommend improvements.

  - It also has a consulting role in identifying, evaluating, and implementing risk management methods and controls.

Risk management processes may be formal or informal, quantitative or subjective, or embedded in business units or centralized. They are designed to fit the organization's culture, management style, and objectives. For example, a small entity may use an informal risk committee.

The CAE must understand management's and the board's expectations of the internal audit activity in risk management. The understanding is codified in the charters of the internal audit activity and the board.

- If the organization has no formal risk management processes, the CAE has formal discussions with management and the board about their obligations for understanding, managing, and monitoring risks.

Internal Audit's Role in Risk Management

The IIA issued the following Interpretation to clarify internal audit's role:

Interpretation of Standard 2120

Determining whether risk management processes are effective is a judgment resulting from the internal auditor's assessment that:

- Organizational objectives support and align with the organization's mission;

- Significant risks are identified and assessed;

- Appropriate risk responses are selected that align risks with the organization's risk appetite; and

- Relevant risk information is captured and communicated in a timely manner across the organization, enabling staff, management, and the board to carry out their responsibilities.

The internal audit activity may gather the information to support this assessment during multiple engagements. The results of these engagements, when viewed together, provide an understanding of the organization's risk management processes and their effectiveness.

Risk management processes are monitored through ongoing management activities, separate evaluations, or both.

Two Implementation Standards for assurance engagements link the assessment of risk to specific risk areas.

Implementation Standard 2120.A1

The internal audit activity must evaluate risk exposures relating to the organization's governance, operations, and information systems regarding the:

- Achievement of the organization's strategic objectives;
- Reliability and integrity of financial and operational information;
- Effectiveness and efficiency of operations and programs;
- Safeguarding of assets; and
- Compliance with laws, regulations, policies, procedures, and contracts.

Implementation Standard 2120.A2

The internal audit activity must evaluate the potential for the occurrence of fraud and how the organization manages fraud risk.

Implementing Standard 2120

To put the previous standards into practice, the CAE and internal auditors should obtain a clear **understanding** of the organization's

- Risk appetite

- Business missions and objectives

- Business strategies

- Risks identified by management

    - Risks may be financial, operational, legal or regulatory, or strategic.

- Current risk management environment and prior corrective actions

- Means of identifying, assessing, and overseeing risks

The CAE should speak with the board and senior management about risk appetite, risk tolerance, and risk management.

- After reviewing the strategic plan, business plan, and policies, the CAE may determine whether strategic objectives align with the mission, vision, and risk appetite. Mid-level managers may give insight into alignment at the business-unit level.

The internal audit activity

- Alerts management to new risks or inadequately mitigated risks
- Provides recommendations and action plans for risk responses
- Evaluates risk management processes

Internal auditors review risk assessments by senior management, external auditors, and regulators. The purpose is to learn how the organization identifies, addresses, and determines the acceptability of risks.

- The responsibilities and risk processes of the board and key managers also are evaluated.

The internal audit actively performs its own risk assessments.

- The discussions with the board and management permit alignment of recommended risk responses with the risk appetite.

- An established framework (e.g., COSO or ISO 31000) may be used for risk identification.

- (1) New developments in the industry and (2) processes for monitoring, assessing, and responding to risks (or opportunities) may be researched.

The internal audit activity also should

- Ensure management of its risks (e.g., audit failure, false assurance, and damage to reputation) and

- Monitor all corrective actions.

Conformance with Standard 2120

To demonstrate compliance, the internal audit charter and audit plan are relevant documents.

Also relevant are minutes of meetings in which the elements of the standard (e.g., recommendations by the internal auditors) were discussed with the board, senior management, task forces, and committees.

Internal audit risk assessments and action plans demonstrate evaluation and improvement.

Risk Management Considerations for Consulting Engagements

Three Implementation Standards address the risk management responsibilities of internal auditors when performing consulting engagements.

Implementation Standard 2120.C1

During consulting engagements, internal auditors must address risk consistent with the engagement's objectives and be alert to the existence of other significant risks.

Implementation Standard 2120.C2

Internal auditors must incorporate knowledge of risks gained from consulting engagements into their evaluation of the organization's risk management processes.

Implementation Standard 2120.C3

When assisting management in establishing or improving risk management processes, internal auditors must refrain from assuming any management responsibility by actually managing risks.

STOP & REVIEW

You have completed the outline for this subunit.
Study multiple-choice questions 1 through 9 beginning on page 160.

5.2 COSO FRAMEWORK -- ENTERPRISE RISK MANAGEMENT (ERM) OVERVIEW

COSO Risk Management Framework

Enterprise Risk Management – Integrating with Strategy and Performance (COSO ERM framework) is a framework that complements, and incorporates some concepts of, the COSO internal control framework.

The COSO ERM framework provides a basis for coordinating and integrating all of an organization's risk management activities. Effective integration

- Improves **decision making** and
- Enhances **performance**.

Effective enterprise risk management can

- Increase the range of opportunities
- Identify and manage risk entity wide
- Increase positive outcomes
- Reduce performance variability
- Improve resource deployment
- Enhance enterprise resilience

ERM Definition and Concepts

ERM is based on the premise that every organization exists to provide **value** for its stakeholders. Accordingly, ERM is defined as

> *The culture, capabilities, and practices, integrated with strategy-setting and performance, that organizations rely on to* ***manage risk*** *in creating, preserving, and realizing* ***value***.

Key Concepts

Culture consists of "[t]he attitudes, behaviors, and understanding **about risk**, both positive and negative, that influence the decisions of management and personnel and reflect the mission, vision, and core values of the organization."

- **Mission** is the organization's core purpose.

- **Vision** is the organization's aspirations for what it intends to achieve over time.

- **Core values** are the organization's essential beliefs about what is acceptable or unacceptable.

Capabilities are the skills needed to carry out the entity's mission and vision.

Practices are the collective methods used to manage risk.

Integrating Strategy Setting and Performance

Risk must be considered in setting strategy, business objectives, performance targets, and tolerance.

- **Strategy** communicates how the organization will achieve its mission and vision and apply its core values. ERM enhances strategy selection.

- **Business objectives** are the steps taken to achieve the strategy.

- **Tolerance** is the range of acceptable variation in performance results. (This term is identical to "risk tolerance" in the COSO internal control framework.)

The organization considers the effect of strategy on its risk profile and portfolio view.

- **Risk profile** is a composite view of the types, severity, and interdependencies of **risks** related to a specific strategy or business objective and their effect on **performance**.

    - A risk profile may be created at any level (e.g., entity, division, operating unit, or function) or aspect (e.g., product, service, or geography) of the organization.

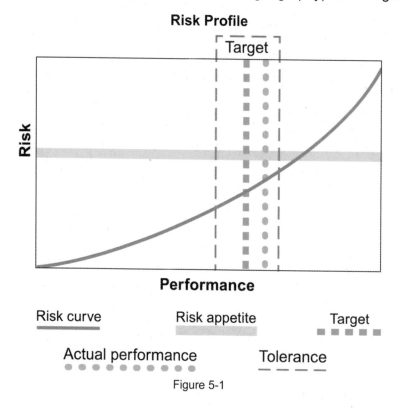

Figure 5-1

- **Portfolio view** is similar to a risk profile.

    - The difference is that it is a composite view of the risks related to **entity-wide** strategy and business objectives and their effects on **entity** performance.

Managing Risk

Risk is "[t]he possibility that events will occur and affect the achievement of strategy and business objectives."

Risk inventory consists of all identified risks that affect strategy and business objectives.

Risk capacity is the maximum amount of risk the organization can assume.

Risk appetite consists of the amount and types of risk the organization is willing to accept in pursuit of value.

Actual residual risk is the risk remaining after taking management actions to alter its severity. Actual residual risk should be equal to or less than target residual risk.

Inherent risk is the risk in the absence of management actions to alter its severity.

- Actual residual risk remains after management actions to alter its severity.

Risk response is an action taken to bring identified risks within the organization's risk appetite.

- A **residual risk profile** includes risk responses.

Target residual risk is the risk the entity prefers to assume knowing that management has acted or will act to alter its severity.

ERM Roles and Responsibilities

The **board** provides risk oversight of ERM culture, capabilities, and practices. However, the board can delegate to the following specialized committees:

- An **audit** committee (often required by regulators),
- A **risk** committee that directly oversees ERM, and
- An **executive compensation** committee.

Management has **overall responsibility** for ERM and is generally responsible for the **day-to-day** managing of risk, including the implementation and development of the COSO ERM framework.

- Within management, the **CEO** has **ultimate responsibility** for ERM and achievement of strategy and business objectives.

An organization may designate a **risk officer** as a centralized coordinating point to facilitate risk management across the entire enterprise.

STOP & REVIEW

You have completed the outline for this subunit.
Study multiple-choice questions 10 through 12 on page 163.

5.3 COSO FRAMEWORK -- ERM COMPONENTS AND LIMITATIONS

ERM Components

The COSO ERM framework consists of **five interrelated components**. Twenty principles are distributed among the components.

Enterprise Risk Management

Governance and Culture	Strategy and Objective Setting	Performance	Review and Revision	Information, Communication, and Reporting
Sets tone and establishes responsibilities.	Strategy must support the organization's mission, vision, and core values.	ERM practices that support the organization's decisions in pursuit of value.	The organization reviews and revises its current ERM capabilities and practices based on changes in strategy and business objectives.	The organization must capture, process, manage, and communicate timely and relevant information to identify risks that could affect strategy and business objectives.
1. Exercises Board Risk Oversight 2. Establishes Operating Structures 3. Defines Desired Culture 4. Demonstrates Commitment to Core Values 5. Attracts, Develops, and Retains Capable Individuals	6. Analyzes Business Context 7. Defines Risk Appetite 8. Evaluates Alternative Strategies 9. Formulates Business Objectives	10. Identifies Risk 11. Assesses Severity of Risk 12. Prioritizes Risk 13. Implements Risk Responses 14. Develops Portfolio View	15. Assesses Substantial Change 16. Reviews Risk and Performance 17. Pursues Improvement in Enterprise Risk Management	18. Leverages Information and Technology 19. Communicates Risk Information 20. Reports on Risk, Culture, and Performance

▨ Supporting aspect   ▨ Common process

Figure 5-2

Governance and Culture

Governance sets the organization's tone and establishes responsibilities for ERM. Culture relates to the desired behaviors, values, and overall understanding about risk held by personnel within the organization. **Five principles** relate to governance and culture.

1. The **board** exercises risk **oversight**.

    ■ The full board ordinarily is responsible for risk oversight. However, the board may delegate risk oversight to a board committee, such as a **risk committee**.

    ▶ **Management** generally has day-to-day responsibility for managing performance and risks taken to achieve strategy and business objectives.

2. The organization establishes **operating structures**.

    ■ They describe how the entity is organized and carries out its day-to-day operations.
    ■ They generally are aligned with the entity's legal structure and management structure.

    ▶ The **legal structure** determines how the entity operates (e.g., as a single legal entity or as multiple, distinct legal entities).

    ▶ The **management structure** establishes reporting lines (e.g., direct reporting versus secondary reporting), roles, and responsibilities. Management is responsible for clearly defining roles and responsibilities.

3. The organization defines the desired **culture**.

    ■ The board and management are responsible for defining culture.
    ■ Culture is shaped by internal and external factors.

    ▶ **Internal** factors include (1) the level of judgment and autonomy allowed to personnel, (2) standards and rules, and (3) the reward system in place.

    ▶ **External** factors include (1) legal requirements and (2) expectations of stakeholders (e.g., customers and investors).

    ■ Culture is not static and will change over time.

4. The organization demonstrates commitment to **core values**.

5. The organization **attracts**, **develops**, and **retains** capable individuals.

Strategy and Objective Setting

Strategy must support the organization's mission, vision, and core values. The integration of ERM with strategy setting helps to understand the risk profile related to strategy and business objectives. **Four principles** relate to strategy and objective setting.

1. The organization analyzes **business context** and its effect on the risk profile.

    ▪   Business context pertains to the relationships, events, trends, and other factors that influence the organization's strategy and business objectives. Accordingly, business context includes the organization's internal and external environments.

    ▪   Business context may be

        ▸   **Dynamic.** New, emerging, and changing risks can appear at any time (e.g., low barriers of entry allow new competitors to emerge).

        ▸   **Complex.** A context may have many interdependencies and interconnections (e.g., a transnational company has several operating units around the world, each with unique external environmental factors).

        ▸   **Unpredictable.** Change occurs rapidly and in unanticipated ways (e.g., currency fluctuations).

    ▪   The effect of business context on the risk profile may be analyzed based on past, present, and future performance.

2. The organization defines **risk appetite** (the amount of risk it is willing to accept in pursuit of value).

    ▪   The organization considers its mission, vision, culture, prior strategies, and risk capacity (the maximum risk it can assume) to set its risk appetite.

    ▪   In setting risk appetite, the optimal balance of opportunity and risk is sought.

        ▸   Risk appetite is rarely set above risk capacity.

    ▪   Risk appetite may be expressed **qualitatively** (e.g., low, moderate, high) or **quantitatively** (e.g., as a percentage of a financial amount).

    ▪   The board approves the risk appetite, and management communicates it throughout the organization.

3. The organization evaluates **alternative strategies** and their effects on the risk profile.

    ▪   Approaches to evaluating strategy include SWOT (Strengths-Weaknesses-Opportunities-Threats) analysis, competitor analysis, and scenario analysis.

4. The organization establishes **business objectives** that align with and support strategy.

Performance

Performance relates to ERM practices that support the organization's decisions in pursuit of value. Those practices consist of identifying, assessing, prioritizing, responding to, and developing a portfolio view of risk. **Five principles** relate to performance.

1. The organization **identifies risks** that affect the performance of strategy and business objectives.

    ■ The organization should identify risks that disrupt operations and affect the **reasonable expectation** of achieving strategy and business objectives.

    ■ **New**, **emerging**, and **changing** risks are identified. Examples are risks resulting from changes in business objectives or the business context.

    ■ Risk identification **methods** and **approaches** include

    ▶ Day-to-day activities (e.g., budgeting, business planning, or reviewing customer complaints),

    ▶ Simple questionnaires,

    ▶ Facilitated workshops,

    ▶ Interviews, and

    ▶ Data tracking.

    ■ The **risk inventory** consists of all risks that could affect the entity.

2. The organization assesses the **severity of risk**. Severity is a measure of such considerations as impact, likelihood, and the time to recover from events.

    ■ Common measures of severity include combinations of impact and likelihood.

    ▶ **Impact** is the result or effect of the risk. Impact may be positive or negative.

    ▶ **Likelihood** is the possibility that an event will occur. Likelihood may be expressed qualitatively (e.g., a remote probability), quantitatively (e.g., a 75% probability), or in terms of frequency (e.g., once every 6 months).

    ■ The **time horizon** to assess risk should be identical to that of the related strategy and business objective. For example, the risk affecting a strategy that takes 2 years to achieve should be assessed over the same period.

    ■ Risk is assessed at **multiple levels** (e.g., entity, division, operating unit, and function) of the organization and linked to the related strategy and business objective.

    ■ Qualitative and quantitative methods may be used to assess risk.

    ▶ **Qualitative** methods are more efficient and less costly than quantitative methods. Examples are interviews, surveys, and benchmarking.

    ▶ **Quantitative** methods are more precise than qualitative methods. Examples are decision trees, modeling (probabilistic and nonprobabilistic), and Monte Carlo simulation.

3. **Risk modeling** is a method of risk assessment and prioritization.
    - Risk factors may be weighted based on professional judgments to determine their relative significance, but the weights need not be quantified.

EXAMPLE 5-1	Risk Modeling

A chief audit executive is reviewing the following enterprise-wide **risk map**:

IMPACT	LIKELIHOOD		
	Remote	Possible	Likely
Critical	Risk A	Risk B	
Major			Risk D
Minor		Risk C	

To establish priorities for the use of limited internal audit resources, the CAE makes the following analysis:

- Risk D clearly takes precedence over Risk C because D has both a higher likelihood and a greater impact.

- Risk B also clearly has a higher priority than Risk A because B has a higher likelihood and the same impact.

Choosing the higher priority between Risk D and Risk B is a matter of professional judgment based on the organizational risk assessment and the stated priorities of senior management and the board.

- If the more likely threat is considered the greater risk, Risk D will rank higher in the internal audit work plan.

- Likewise, if the threat with the greater possible impact causes senior management and the board more concern, the internal audit activity will place a higher priority on Risk B.

4. The organization identifies and selects **risk responses**, recognizing that risk may be managed but not eliminated. Risks should be managed within the business context and objectives, performance targets, and risk appetite.

SUCCESS TIP

Risk response is a frequently tested risk management topic. Having a sound knowledge and understanding of the risk response strategies (listed below) and examples for each will increase your success on the exam.

- The following are the five categories of risk responses:

    1. **Acceptance (retention).** No action is taken to alter the severity of the risk. Acceptance is appropriate when the risk is within the risk appetite. This term is synonymous with self-insurance.

    2. **Avoidance.** Action is taken to remove the risk. Avoidance typically suggests no response would reduce the risk to an acceptable level. For example, the risk of pipeline sabotage can be avoided by selling the pipeline.

    3. **Pursuit.** Action is taken to accept increased risk to improve performance without exceeding acceptable tolerance.

    4. **Reduction (mitigation).** Action is taken to reduce the severity of the risk so that it is within the target residual risk profile and risk appetite. For example, the risk of systems penetration can be reduced by maintaining an effective information security function within the entity.

    5. **Sharing (transfer).** Action is taken to reduce the severity of the risk by transferring a portion of the risk to another party. Examples are insurance; hedging; joint ventures; outsourcing; and contractual agreements with customers, vendors, or other business partners.

- The following are the **factors** considered in selecting and implementing risk responses:

    ▸ They should be chosen for, or adapted to, the **business context**.

    ▸ **Costs and benefits** should be proportionate to the severity of the risk and its priority.

    ▸ They should further **compliance** with obligations and achievement of **expectations**.

    ▸ They should bring risk within **risk appetite** and result in performance outcomes within **tolerance**.

    ▸ Risk response should reflect risk severity.

5.   The organization develops and evaluates its **portfolio view of risk**.

■   The culmination of risk identification, assessment, prioritization, and response is the full portfolio view of risk.

■   Using a portfolio view of risk, management determines whether the entity's **residual risk profile** (risk profile inclusive of risk responses) aligns with overall **risk appetite**.

■   The following four risk views have different levels of risk integration:

1.   **Risk view (minimal integration).** Risks are identified and assessed. Emphasis is on the event, not the business objective. For example, the risk of a breach may impact the entity's compliance with local regulations.

2.   **Risk category view (limited integration).** Identified and assessed risks are categorized, e.g., based on operating structures. For example, the accounting department will have responsibilities for helping the organization manage its risks related to potential accounting rule changes.

3.   **Risk profile view (partial integration).** Risks are linked to the business objectives they affect, and any dependencies between objectives are identified and assessed. For example, an objective of increased sales may depend on an objective to introduce a new product line.

4.   **Portfolio view (full integration).** This composite view of risks relates to **entity-wide** strategy and business objectives and their effect on **entity** performance. At the top level, greater emphasis is on strategy. Thus, responsibility for business objectives and specific risks **cascades** through the entity.

Review and Revision

The organization reviews and revises its current ERM capabilities and practices based on changes in strategy and business objectives. **Three principles** relate to review and revision.

1.   The organization identifies and assesses **changes** that may substantially affect strategy and business objectives.

■   Changes in the organization's **business context** and **culture** are most likely to substantially affect strategy and business objectives.

■   Such changes may result from changes in the organization's internal or external environment.

2. The organization reviews **entity performance** results and considers **risk**.

    ■   Performance results that deviate from target performance or tolerance may indicate

        ▶   Unidentified risks,
        ▶   Improperly assessed risks,
        ▶   New risks,
        ▶   Opportunities to accept more risk, or
        ▶   The need to revise target performance or tolerance.

    ■   In reviewing performance, the organization seeks to answer questions such as

        ▶   Has the entity performed as expected and achieved its target?
        ▶   What risks are occurring that may be affecting performance?
        ▶   Was the entity taking enough risks to attain its target?
        ▶   Was the estimate of the amount of risk accurate?

3. The organization pursues **improvement** of ERM.

    ■   The organization must continually improve ERM at all levels, even if actual performance aligns with target performance or tolerance.

Information, Communication, and Reporting

The organization must capture, process, manage (organize and store), and communicate timely and relevant information to **identify risks** that could affect strategy and business objectives. **Three principles** relate to information, communication, and reporting.

1. The organization leverages its **information systems** to support ERM.

    ■   **Data** are raw facts collectible for analysis, use, or reference. **Information** is processed, organized, and structured data about a fact or circumstance. Information systems transform data (e.g., risk data) into relevant information (e.g., risk information).

        ▶   **Knowledge** is data transformed into information.

        ▶   Information is **relevant** if it helps the organization be more agile in decision making, giving it a competitive advantage.

    ■   Information systems must be **adaptable to change**. As the organization adapts its strategy and business objectives in response to changes in the business context, its information systems also must change.

2. The organization uses **communication channels** to support ERM.

    ■   Management communicates the organization's strategy and business objectives to internal (e.g., personnel and the board) and external (e.g., shareholders) stakeholders.

    ■   Communications between management and the board should include continual discussions about **risk appetite** and adjust strategy and business objectives accordingly.

    ■   Communication **methods** include written documents (e.g., policies and procedures), electronic messages, public events or forums (e.g., town hall meetings), and informal or spoken communications (e.g., one-on-one discussions).

3. The organization **reports** on risk, culture, and performance at multiple levels and across the entity.

    ■   The purpose of reporting is to **support** personnel in their

        ▸   Understanding of the relationships among risk, culture, and performance.

        ▸   Decision making related to setting strategy and objectives, governance, and day-to-day operations.

Assessing ERM

The COSO ERM framework provides criteria for assessing whether the organization's ERM culture, capabilities, and practices together effectively manage risks to strategy and business objectives.

When the **components**, **principles**, and supporting **controls** are present and functioning, ERM is **reasonably expected** to manage risks effectively and to help create, preserve, and realize **value**.

ERM Limitations

Limitations of ERM result from the possibility of

-   Faulty human judgment,
-   Cost-benefit considerations,
-   Simple errors or mistakes,
-   Collusion, and
-   Management override of ERM practices.

STOP & REVIEW

You have completed the outline for this subunit.
Study multiple-choice questions 13 through 19 beginning on page 164.

5.4 ISO 31000 RISK MANAGEMENT FRAMEWORK

SUCCESS TIP

The ISO 31000 risk management framework is a frequently tested risk management topic. Accordingly, mastery of this framework will increase your success on the exam.

ISO 31000 – Principles, Framework, and Process

ISO 31000 is a **principles-based** approach to risk management. Its principles are the foundation for risk management. They also communicate the characteristics, value, and purpose of effective and efficient risk management.

Principles

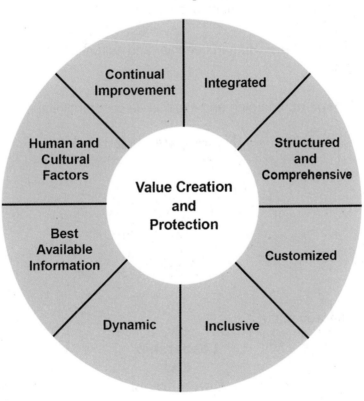

Figure 5-3

Value creation and protection are the purposes of risk management. The principles are described below:

- **Integrated.** Risk management is integrated into all organizational activities.

- **Structured and comprehensive.** The risk management approach needs to be structured and comprehensive.

- **Customized.** The risk management framework and process should be customized to the organizational objectives.

- **Inclusive.** Appropriate involvement of stakeholders enables informed risk management.

- **Dynamic.** Risk management foresees, recognizes, and reacts to changing risks.

- **Best available information.** Risk management considers past, current, and future information and any related limitations of such information.

- **Human and cultural factors.** Human behavior and culture affect all facets and each level of risk management.

- **Continual improvement.** Learning and experience constantly improve risk management.

Framework

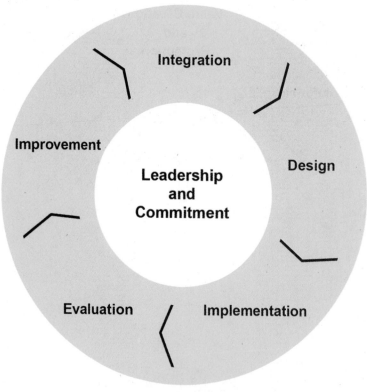

Figure 5-4

The board and senior management demonstrate **leadership and commitment** by implementing the framework's components; adopting a policy that establishes a risk management plan or approach; committing resources to risk management; and assigning accountability, authority, and responsibility at each organizational level.

The **integration** of the framework into all facets of an organization, including its objectives, structure, governance, and culture, is a dynamic process. All personnel in the organization are responsible for managing risks.

The **design** of the framework involves the following:

- Understanding the organization and its context

- Articulating commitment to risk management

- Assigning and communicating authorities, responsibilities, and accountabilities for risk management roles at all levels

- Allocating resources (e.g., people, experience, processes, and information systems) to support risk management while recognizing the limitations of existing resources

- Establishing communication and consultation

The **implementation** of the framework can be achieved by developing a plan; identifying decision-making processes; modifying decision-making processes as change occurs; and ensuring stakeholders' understanding of, and engagement with, the organization's risk management arrangement.

The **evaluation** of the framework's effectiveness involves measuring performance against expectations.

The **improvement** of the framework is through monitoring and updating the framework in response to changes, thereby enhancing organization performance.

Process

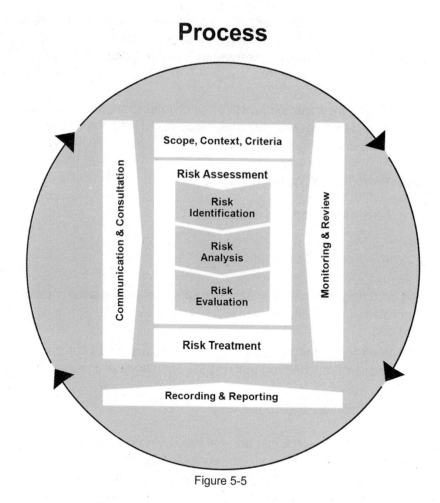

Figure 5-5

To improve understanding of risks and decisions made, **communication** to raise awareness and **consultation** to obtain feedback and information require ongoing, structured coordination with stakeholders.

The **scope, context, and criteria** should be established to customize risk management. This element includes defining the scope of the risk management process, understanding its external and internal context, and defining risk criteria.

- The context of the risk management process derives from the understanding of the specific external and internal environment of the organization.

Risk assessment is the process of identifying, analyzing, and evaluating risk.

- **Risk identification** finds risks that can contribute to or prevent achieving organizational objectives. For example, it considers risk sources, changes in context, threats and opportunities, emerging risk indicators, and consequences and their effects on objectives.

- **Risk analysis** examines the nature, characteristics, and level of risk. It considers such factors as likelihood of events and consequences, control effectiveness, and confidence level.

- **Risk evaluation** supports decision making by comparing the defined risk criteria with the risk analysis outcome and determining whether any action is required.

Risk treatment is a repetitive process of selecting risk treatments (e.g., accept, avoid, reduce, share, or pursue), implementing the treatment, assessing the treatment's effectiveness, determining whether the residual risk is acceptable, and adopting another treatment if the first was unacceptable.

Monitoring and review should occur in all phases of the risk management process to improve its quality and effectiveness.

Recording and reporting of the risk management process and its results should be facilitated to communicate and improve risk management activities, support decisions, and enhance communications with stakeholders.

Responsibilities for Risk Management

The **board** is responsible for overseeing risk management and has overall responsibility for ensuring that risks are managed and the risk management system is effective.

Management is responsible for setting the organization's **risk attitude**, which is defined by ISO as an "organization's approach to assess and eventually pursue, retain, take, or turn away from risk." Management also identifies and manages risks.

The **internal audit activity** is responsible for providing assurance regarding the entire risk management system.

Assurance Approaches

ISO 31000 describes three approaches to providing assurance on the risk management process:

1. The **key principles** approach evaluates whether the risk management principles are in practice.

2. The **process element** approach evaluates whether the risk management elements have been put into practice.

3. The **maturity model** approach is based on the principle that effective risk management processes develop and improve with time as value is added at each phase in the maturation process. The basic principle is that risk management must add value.

    ■   Accordingly, this approach determines where the risk management process is on the maturity curve and evaluates whether it (1) is progressing as expected, (2) adds value, and (3) meets organizational needs.

You have completed the outline for this subunit.
Study multiple-choice questions 20 through 22 beginning on page 166.

STOP & REVIEW

QUESTIONS

5.1 Risk Management Processes

1. Which of the following is **not** an activity undertaken as part of risk management?

- A. Risk identification.
- B. Risk analysis.
- C. Risk exposure.
- D. Risk response.

Answer (C) is correct.
REQUIRED: The activity that is not part of risk management.
DISCUSSION: Risk exposure is a condition, not an activity.

2. When the executive management of an organization decided to form a team to investigate the adoption of an activity-based costing (ABC) system, an internal auditor was assigned to the team. The best reason for including an internal auditor is the internal auditor's knowledge of

- A. Activities and cost drivers.
- B. Information processing procedures.
- C. Current product cost structures.
- D. Risk management processes.

Answer (D) is correct.
REQUIRED: The best reason for including an internal auditor in a team investigating an ABC system.
DISCUSSION: The internal audit activity's scope of work extends to evaluating the organization's risk management processes. The internal audit activity should assist the organization by identifying and evaluating significant exposures to risk and contributing to the improvement of risk management and control systems.
Answer (A) is incorrect. An engineer has more knowledge than an internal auditor about activities and cost drivers. **Answer (B) is incorrect.** An information systems expert has more knowledge than an internal auditor about information needs and information processing procedures. **Answer (C) is incorrect.** A management accountant has more knowledge than an internal auditor about a company's current product cost.

3. Internal auditors should review the means of physically safeguarding assets from losses arising from

- A. Misapplication of accounting principles.
- B. Procedures that are not cost justified.
- C. Exposure to the elements.
- D. Underusage of physical facilities.

Answer (C) is correct.
REQUIRED: The cause of losses resulting in physical safeguards that should be reviewed by the auditor.
DISCUSSION: The internal audit activity must evaluate risk exposures relating to governance, operations, and information systems regarding the safeguarding of assets (Impl. Std. 2120.A1). For example, internal auditors evaluate risk exposure arising from theft, fire, improper or illegal activities, and exposure to the elements.
Answer (A) is incorrect. Misapplication of accounting principles relates to the reliability of information and not physical safeguards. **Answer (B) is incorrect.** Procedures that are not cost justified relate to efficiency, not effectiveness, of operations. **Answer (D) is incorrect.** Underusage of facilities relates to efficiency of operations.

4. Which of the following activities is outside the scope of internal auditing?

A. Evaluating risk exposures regarding compliance with policies, procedures, and contracts.

B. Safeguarding of assets.

C. Evaluating risk exposures regarding compliance with laws and regulations.

D. Ascertaining the extent to which management has established criteria to determine whether objectives have been accomplished.

Answer (B) is correct.
REQUIRED: The activity outside the scope of internal auditing.
DISCUSSION: Safeguarding assets is an operational activity and is therefore beyond the scope of the internal audit activity. However, the internal audit activity's assurance function evaluates the adequacy and effectiveness of controls related to the organization's governance, operations, and information systems regarding safeguarding of assets (Perf. Std. 2130).
Answer (A) is incorrect. Internal auditors must evaluate risk exposures relating to, among other things, the organization's compliance with laws, regulations, policies, procedures, and contracts. **Answer (C) is incorrect.** The internal audit activity must evaluate risk exposures relating to, among other things, the organization's compliance with laws, regulations, policies, procedures, and contracts. **Answer (D) is incorrect.** Ascertaining the extent to which management has established adequate criteria to determine whether objectives have been accomplished is within the scope of internal auditing.

5. Standard 2120 states that the internal audit activity must evaluate the effectiveness and contribute to the improvement of risk management processes. Conformance with Standard 2120 is best demonstrated by

A. The work programs for formal consulting engagements.

B. The business continuity plan.

C. The charter of the internal audit activity.

D. Review by the internal auditors immediately following a disaster.

Answer (C) is correct.
REQUIRED: The best demonstration of conformance with Standard 2120.
DISCUSSION: Documents demonstrating conformance with Standard 2120 include the internal audit charter. It describes the internal audit activity's roles and responsibilities regarding risk management. Other documents include (1) the internal audit plan, (2) minutes of meetings in which internal audit recommendations were discussed, (3) internal audit risk assessments, and (4) internal audit action plans addressing risks.
Answer (A) is incorrect. A work program is a listing of specific procedures. **Answer (B) is incorrect.** Business continuity planning is just one element of risk management. **Answer (D) is incorrect.** The internal audit activity's role needs to be understood before a crisis.

6. In the risk management process, management's view of the internal audit activity's role is likely to be determined by all of the following factors **except**

A. Organizational culture.

B. Preferences of the independent auditor.

C. Ability of the internal audit staff.

D. Local conditions and customs of the country.

Answer (B) is correct.
REQUIRED: The factor not influencing management's view of the role of internal auditing.
DISCUSSION: Ultimately, the role of internal auditing in the risk management process is determined by senior management and the board. Their view on internal auditing's role is likely to be determined by factors such as the culture of the organization, ability of the internal audit staff, and local conditions and customs.
Answer (A) is incorrect. Organizational culture is a factor that influences management's view of the role of internal auditing. **Answer (C) is incorrect.** The ability of the internal audit staff is a factor that influences management's view of the role of internal auditing. **Answer (D) is incorrect.** Local conditions and customs of the country influence management's view of the role of internal auditing.

7. Which of the following is the most accurate term for a process to identify, assess, manage, and control potential events or situations to provide reasonable assurance regarding the achievement of the organization's objectives?

    A. The internal audit activity.

    B. Control process.

    C. Risk management.

    D. Consulting service.

Answer (C) is correct.
    REQUIRED: The process to identify, assess, manage, and control potential events or situations.
    DISCUSSION: Risk management is "a process to identify, assess, manage, and control potential events or situations to provide reasonable assurance regarding the achievement of the organization's objectives" (The IIA Glossary).
    Answer (A) is incorrect. The internal audit activity assists in risk management; it is not the same thing as risk management. **Answer (B) is incorrect.** Control processes are "the policies, procedures, and activities that are part of a control framework designed to ensure that risks are contained within the risk tolerances established by the risk management process" (The IIA Glossary). **Answer (D) is incorrect.** Consulting services are "advisory and related client service activities, the nature and scope of which are agreed with the client" (The IIA Glossary).

8. The internal audit activity must evaluate the effectiveness and contribute to the improvement of risk management processes. With respect to evaluating the adequacy of risk management processes, internal auditors most likely should

    A. Recognize that organizations should use similar techniques for managing risk.

    B. Determine that the key objectives of risk management processes are being met.

    C. Determine the level of risks acceptable to the organization.

    D. Treat the evaluation of risk management processes in the same manner as the risk analysis used to plan engagements.

Answer (B) is correct.
    REQUIRED: The responsibility of internal auditors for assessing the adequacy of risk management processes.
    DISCUSSION: Internal auditors need to obtain sufficient and appropriate evidence to determine that key objectives of the risk management processes are being met to form an opinion on the adequacy of risk management processes.
    Answer (A) is incorrect. Risk management processes vary with the size and complexity of an organization's business activities. **Answer (C) is incorrect.** Management and the board determine the level of acceptable organizational risks. **Answer (D) is incorrect.** Evaluating management's risk processes differs from the internal auditors' risk assessment used to plan an engagement, but information from a comprehensive risk management process is useful in such planning.

9. Which of the following is the correct order of steps in the risk management process?

1. Identify risks
2. Monitor risk responses
3. Formulate risk responses
4. Assess and prioritize risks
5. Identify context

    A. 5, 1, 4, 3, 2.

    B. 1, 4, 3, 2, 5.

    C. 1, 3, 5, 4, 2.

    D. 1, 5, 4, 3, 2.

Answer (A) is correct.
    REQUIRED: The order of steps in the risk management process.
    DISCUSSION: The correct order of steps in the risk management process is as follows: identify context, identify risks, assess and prioritize risks, formulate risk responses, and monitor risk responses.
    Answer (B) is incorrect. Identifying context occurs before identifying risks. **Answer (C) is incorrect.** Identifying context occurs before identifying risks; assessing and prioritizing risks occurs before formulating risk responses. **Answer (D) is incorrect.** Identifying context occurs before identifying risks.

5.2 COSO Framework -- Enterprise Risk Management (ERM) Overview

10. Which of the following members of an organization has ultimate ownership responsibility of the enterprise risk management, provides leadership and direction to senior managers, and monitors the entity's overall risk activities in relation to its risk appetite?

- A. Chief risk officer.
- B. Chief executive officer.
- C. Internal auditors.
- D. Chief financial officer.

Answer (B) is correct.
   REQUIRED: The member of the organization with the stated responsibilities.
   DISCUSSION: The chief executive officer (CEO) sets the tone at the top of the organization and has ultimate responsibility for ownership of the ERM. The CEO will influence the composition and conduct of the board, provide leadership and direction to senior managers, and monitor the entity's overall risk activities in relation to its risk appetite. If any problems arise with the organization's risk appetite, the CEO will also take any measures to adjust the alignment to better suit the organization.
   Answer (A) is incorrect. The risk officer works in assigned areas of responsibility in a staff function. The work of a risk officer often extends beyond one specific area because the officer will have the necessary resources to work across many segments or divisions. **Answer (C) is incorrect.** The internal auditors evaluate the ERM and may provide recommendations. **Answer (D) is incorrect.** The CFO is subordinate to the CEO.

11. Company management completes event identification and assesses the severity of risk. Management then acts to alter the severity of risk. According to COSO's ERM framework, the risk remaining after management's actions is

- A. Inherent risk.
- B. Actual residual risk.
- C. Event risk.
- D. Target residual risk.

Answer (B) is correct.
   REQUIRED: The type of risk that exists after management acts to alter its severity.
   DISCUSSION: Actual residual risk is the risk that remains after management acts to alter its severity. It should not exceed target residual risk.
   Answer (A) is incorrect. Inherent risk is the risk that exists in the absence of management actions to alter its severity, that is, a risk response in the form of acceptance or pursuit. **Answer (C) is incorrect.** COSO defines an event as an occurrence or set of occurrences. It defines risk as the possibility that events will occur and affect the achievement of strategy and business objectives. **Answer (D) is incorrect.** Target residual risk is the risk the entity prefers to assume knowing that management has acted or will act to alter its severity.

12. Which of the following is closely related to traditional risk management instead of enterprise risk management (ERM)?

- A. Rapid response to opportunities.
- B. Organization-level view of risk.
- C. Emphasis on specific functions.
- D. Achieving financial goals.

Answer (C) is correct.
   REQUIRED: The difference between traditional risk management and ERM.
   DISCUSSION: The enterprise risk management approach set forth by the Committee of Sponsoring Organizations of the Treadway Commission (COSO) attempts to approach an organization as a whole instead of focusing on any specific area or risk.
   Answer (A) is incorrect. Rapid response to opportunities is a characteristic of ERM, which tries to offset potential risks with opportunities. **Answer (B) is incorrect.** ERM tries to view risk as it affects every level of an organization. **Answer (D) is incorrect.** Financial goals are an example of the methods ERM uses to achieve objectives in one or more separate but overlapping categories.

5.3 COSO Framework -- ERM Components and Limitations

13. According to COSO's ERM framework, which view of risk is fully integrated?

A. Portfolio view.

B. Risk view.

C. Risk profile view.

D. Risk category view.

Answer (A) is correct.
 REQUIRED: The fully integrated view of risk.
 DISCUSSION: A portfolio view is fully integrated. It is a composite view of the risks related to entity-wide strategy and business objectives and their effect on entity performance.
 Answer (B) is incorrect. A risk view is minimally integrated. Risks are identified and assessed.
 Answer (C) is incorrect. A risk profile view is partially integrated. It is a composite view of the types, severity, and interdependencies of risks related to a specific strategy or business objective and their effect on performance. **Answer (D) is incorrect.** A risk category results from limited integration. The risks identified and assessed in the risk view (minimal integration) are categorized.

14. Which of the following is a **false** statement about risk responses?

A. Each organization must assess the relationship between the likelihood and significance of risks.

B. Identified risks cannot simply be accepted.

C. Some risks require the creation of elaborate control structures.

D. There is no direct correlation between the severity of a risk and the cost of the response to that risk.

Answer (B) is correct.
 REQUIRED: The statement about risk responses that is false.
 DISCUSSION: While some risks require the creation of elaborate control structures, others may simply be accepted.
 Answer (A) is incorrect. Each organization must assess the relationship between the likelihood and significance of risks and must design the appropriate controls. **Answer (C) is incorrect.** This is a true statement about risk responses. For example, although the total physical destruction of a data center may be highly unlikely, if it were to occur, the ability of the entity to function may be questionable. Therefore, a contingency plan for such an occurrence is almost a necessity. **Answer (D) is incorrect.** There is no direct correlation between the severity of a risk and the cost of the response to that risk.

15. Management considers risk appetite for all of the following reasons **except**

- A. Aligning with development of strategy.
- B. Aligning with business objectives.
- C. Implementing risk responses.
- D. Setting risk capacity.

Answer (D) is correct.
   REQUIRED: The item not a reason for considering risk appetite.
   DISCUSSION: Risk appetite consists of the types and amount of risk the entity is willing to accept in pursuit of value. Among other things, risk appetite should be considered in

1. Aligning with development of strategy.
2. Aligning with business objectives.
3. Prioritizing risks.
4. Implementing risk responses.

Risk capacity is the maximum amount of risk an entity is able to bear and remain solvent. The organization considers its mission, vision, culture, prior strategies, and risk capacity to set its risk appetite. In setting risk appetite, the optimal balance of opportunity and risk is sought. Risk appetite is rarely set above risk capacity.
   Answer (A) is incorrect. Management considers risk appetite when evaluating strategic options. **Answer (B) is incorrect.** Management considers risk appetite when setting objectives. **Answer (C) is incorrect.** Management considers risk appetite when implementing risk responses.

16. Each of the following is a limitation of enterprise risk management (ERM), **except**

- A. ERM deals with risk, which relates to the future and is inherently uncertain.
- B. ERM operates at different levels with respect to different objectives.
- C. ERM can provide absolute assurance with respect to objective categories.
- D. ERM is as effective as the people responsible for its functioning.

Answer (C) is correct.
   REQUIRED: The item that is not a limitation of ERM.
   DISCUSSION: ERM cannot provide absolute assurance with respect to different objectives. However, if it could, it would be an advantage, not a limitation.
   Answer (A) is incorrect. ERM is limited because some matters are beyond management's ability to predict and control. **Answer (B) is incorrect.** A limitation of ERM is that different objectives concern different needs, and the ERM attention devoted to them varies. **Answer (D) is incorrect.** Limitations of ERM arise from the possibility of faulty human judgment, simple errors or mistakes, collusion, and management override.

17. According to COSO, which component of enterprise risk management (ERM) addresses an entity's operating structures and core values?

- A. Review and revision.
- B. Governance and culture.
- C. Strategy and objective-setting.
- D. Information, communication, and reporting.

Answer (B) is correct.
   REQUIRED: The component of ERM that addresses an entity's operating structures and core values.
   DISCUSSION: The governance and culture component addresses board responsibilities, operating structures, and core values, among others.
   Answer (A) is incorrect. The review and revision component addresses the review of, and changes in, strategy, performance targets and tolerance, and ERM practices. **Answer (C) is incorrect.** The strategy and objective-setting component addresses business context, risk appetite, strategy selection, and business objectives. **Answer (D) is incorrect.** The information, communication, and reporting component addresses information systems, communication channels, and reporting (on risk, culture, and performance).

18. Which of the following is a factor affecting risk?

   A. New personnel.

   B. New or revamped information systems.

   C. Rapid growth.

   D. All of the answers are correct.

Answer (D) is correct.
   REQUIRED: The item that is a factor affecting risk.
   DISCUSSION: New personnel, new or revamped information systems, and rapid growth are all factors that affect risk.

19. According to the COSO ERM framework, the organization establishes business objectives that align with and support strategy. Which of the following may relate to business objectives?

1. Operational excellence
2. Financial performance
3. Compliance obligations

   A. 1 and 2 only.

   B. 2 and 3 only.

   C. 1 and 3 only.

   D. 1, 2, and 3.

Answer (D) is correct.
   REQUIRED: The business objectives which align with and support strategy.
   DISCUSSION: According to COSO ERM framework, business objectives may relate to, among others, financial performance, operational excellence, or compliance obligations.
   Answer (A) is incorrect. Compliance obligations may also relate to business objectives. **Answer (B) is incorrect.** Operational excellence may also relate to business objectives. **Answer (C) is incorrect.** Financial performance may also relate to business objectives.

5.4 ISO 31000 Risk Management Framework

20. Which of the following approaches to providing assurance on the risk management process is based on the principle that effective risk management processes develop as value is added at each stage of maturation?

   A. The process element approach.

   B. The key principles approach.

   C. The maturity model approach.

   D. None of the answers are correct.

Answer (C) is correct.
   REQUIRED: The risk management approach that adds value.
   DISCUSSION: The maturity model approach is based on the principle that effective risk management processes develop as value is added at each stage of maturation. Accordingly, this approach determines where risk management is on the maturity curve and whether it (1) is progressing as expected, (2) adds value, and (3) meets organizational needs.
   Answer (A) is incorrect. The process element approach determines whether certain elements (i.e., formal risk identification, formal risk analysis, risk evaluation, etc.) have been implemented. **Answer (B) is incorrect.** The key principles approach determines whether the risk management principles are in place (e.g., integrated, structured, comprehensive, and customized). **Answer (D) is incorrect.** One of the answers is correct.

21. Which of the following is **not** a component of the risk management framework of the ISO 31000 model?

- A. Evaluation.
- B. Improvement.
- C. Human and cultural factor.
- D. Design.

Answer (C) is correct.
    REQUIRED: The item that is not a component of ISO 31000.
    DISCUSSION: The "human and cultural factor" is a principle, not a component, of the framework of risk management in the ISO 31000 model.
    Answer (A) is incorrect. Evaluation is a component of the framework of the ISO 31000 model. **Answer (B) is incorrect.** Improvement is a component of the framework of the ISO 31000 model. **Answer (D) is incorrect.** Design is a component of the framework of the ISO 31000 model.

22. According to ISO 31000, the design of a risk management framework involves all of the following **except**

- A. Deciding on an appropriate risk response.
- B. Understanding the organization and its context.
- C. Allocating the necessary resources.
- D. Establishing communication and consultation.

Answer (A) is correct.
    REQUIRED: The design of a risk management framework according to ISO 31000.
    DISCUSSION: Deciding on an appropriate risk response is not involved in the design of a risk management framework according to ISO 31000. The design of the framework involves (1) understanding the organization and its context; (2) articulating commitment to risk management; (3) assigning and communicating authorities, responsibilities, and accountabilities for risk management roles at all levels; (4) allocating resources (e.g., people, experience, processes, and information systems) to support risk management while recognizing the limitations of existing resources; and (5) establishing communication and consultation.

Access the **Gleim CIA Premium Review System** featuring our SmartAdapt technology from your Gleim Personal Classroom to continue your studies. You will experience a personalized study environment with exam-emulating multiple-choice questions.

STUDY UNIT SIX

CONTROLS: TYPES AND FRAMEWORKS

(31 pages of outline)

This study unit is the third of four covering **Domain V: Governance, Risk Management, and Control** from The IIA's CIA Exam Syllabus. This domain makes up 35% of Part 1 of the CIA exam and is tested at the **basic** and **proficient** cognitive levels. The four study units are

- Study Unit 4: Governance
- Study Unit 5: Risk Management
- **Study Unit 6: Controls: Types and Frameworks**
- Study Unit 7: Controls: Application

The **learning objectives** of Study Unit 6 are

- Interpret internal control concepts and types of controls

- Apply globally accepted internal control frameworks appropriate to the organization (COSO, etc.)

- Examine the effectiveness and efficiency of internal controls

Control activities are the policies and procedures that help ensure that management directives are carried out. Whether automated or manual, they have various objectives and are applied at various levels. Relevant controls ordinarily address the entity's objectives related to the preparation of fairly presented financial statements, including management of risks of material misstatements.

Effective controls assist with, but are not limited to, the safeguarding of assets, reliability of financial reporting, effectiveness and efficiency of operations, and compliance with applicable laws and regulations.

6.1 OVERVIEW OF CONTROL

SUCCESS TIP

Many questions on the CIA exam address controls. Few such questions are answerable based on memorization. Moreover, no study aid can feasibly present comprehensive lists of procedures. Thus, candidates must be able to apply reasoning processes and knowledge of auditing concepts to unfamiliar situations involving controls. By answering our questions, you will be able to synthesize, understand, and apply internal control theory to scenarios on the CIA exam.

Control Definitions from The IIA Glossary

Control is "any action taken by management, the board, and other parties to manage risk and increase the likelihood that established objectives and goals will be achieved. Management plans, organizes, and directs the performance of sufficient actions to provide reasonable assurance that objectives and goals will be achieved."

Control processes are "the policies, procedures (both manual and automated), and activities that are part of a control framework, designed and operated to ensure that risks are contained within the level that an organization is willing to accept."

Control environment is "[t]he attitude and actions of the board and management regarding the importance of control within the organization. The control environment provides the discipline and structure for the achievement of the primary objectives of the system of internal control. The control environment includes the following elements:

- Integrity and ethical values
- Management's philosophy and operating style
- Organizational structure
- Assignment of authority and responsibility
- Human resource policies and practices
- Competence of personnel"

The Control Process

Control requires feedback on the results of organizational activities for the purposes of measurement and correction.

The control process includes the following:

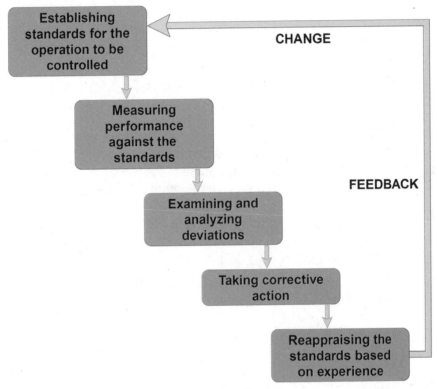

Figure 6-1

An evaluation-reward system should be implemented to encourage compliance with the control system.

Internal control only provides reasonable assurance of achieving objectives. It cannot provide absolute assurance because any system of internal control has the following inherent limitations:

- **Human judgment** is faulty, and controls may fail because of simple errors or mistakes.

- **Management** may inappropriately override internal controls, e.g., to fraudulently achieve revenue projections or hide liabilities.

- Manual or automated controls can be circumvented by **collusion**.

- The **cost** of internal control must not be greater than its **benefits**.

Characteristics of Automated Processing

The use of computers in business information systems has fundamental effects on the nature of business transacted, the procedures followed, the risks incurred, and the methods of mitigating those risks.

- These effects result from the characteristics that distinguish computer-based from manual processing.

Audit Trails

An audit trail is a record by which accounting measurements, details of a trade, or other financial data can be traced back to its source. Audit trails can be used to verify and track transactions. For example, a transaction processing system can trace a purchase back to a copy of the purchase order to see when the items were ordered and who authorized the order.

- A complete trail useful for audit and other purposes might exist for only a short time or only in computer-readable form.

- The nature of the trail is often dependent on the transaction processing mode. For example, transactions may be batched prior to processing or processed immediately as they happen.

Uniform Processing of Transactions

Computer processing uniformly subjects similar transactions to the same processing instructions and thus virtually eliminates clerical error.

- But programming errors (or other similar systematic errors in either the hardware or software) will result in all similar transactions being processed incorrectly when they are processed under the same conditions.

Segregation of Duties

For any given transaction, certain functions should be performed by separate individuals in different parts of the organization.

The internal control system is designed to detect fraud by one person but not fraud by collusion or management override.

Segregation of Functions: Computer-Based Systems

Many controls once performed by separate individuals may be concentrated in computer systems. Thus, an individual who has access to the computer may perform incompatible functions.

- As a result, other controls may be necessary to achieve the control objectives ordinarily accomplished by segregation of functions.

EXAMPLE 6-1 Computer-Generated Documents

Receiving cash, issuing a receipt to a payor, preparing a deposit slip, and preparing a journal entry may once have been performed by separate individuals. In a computer-based system, the receipt, deposit slip, and journal entry may be automatically generated by the computer. If the same employee who receives the cash is also responsible for entering the relevant data into the system, the potential for fraud or error is increased. To mitigate this concern, other controls are added to lower the risk of error or fraud resulting in a similar overall risk that was prevalent before the switch to computer-based systems.

Potential for Errors and Fraud

The potential for individuals, including those performing control procedures, to gain unauthorized access to data, to alter data without visible evidence, or to gain access (direct or indirect) to assets may be greater in computer systems.

Decreased human involvement in handling transactions can reduce the potential for errors and fraud resulting from human observation. On the other hand, errors or fraud in the design or changing of application programs can remain undetected for a long time.

EXAMPLE 6-2 Purchase Orders in an Electronic Data Interchange (EDI) System

EDI is the communication of electronic documents directly from a computer in one entity to a computer in another entity. EDI eliminates the paper documents, both internal and external, that are the traditional basis for many audit procedures.

An enterprise resource planning system at a manufacturing company may automatically generate a purchase order when materials inventory reaches a certain level. If the company shares an EDI system with the vendor, the purchase order may be sent to the vendor electronically without any human intervention.

Potential for Increased Management Supervision

Computer systems offer management many analytical tools for review and supervision of operations. These additional controls may enhance internal control.

- Traditional comparisons of actual and budgeted operating ratios and reconciliations of accounts are often available for review on a more timely basis.

- Furthermore, some programmed applications provide statistics regarding computer operations that may be used to monitor actual processing.

Initiation or Subsequent Execution of Transactions by Computer

Certain transactions may be automatically initiated or certain procedures required to execute a transaction may be automatically performed by a computer system.

- The authorization of these transactions or procedures may not be documented in the same way as those in a manual system. Accordingly, management's authorization may be implicit in its acceptance of the design of the system.

Dependence of Controls in Other Areas on Controls over Computer Processing

Computer processing may produce reports and other output that are used in performing manual control procedures.

- The effectiveness of these controls can be dependent on the effectiveness of controls over the completeness and accuracy of computer processing. The effectiveness of a manual review of a computer-produced exception listing is dependent on the controls over the production of the listing.

Manual Controls (Human Action) vs. Automated Controls (Electronic Action)

Manual controls (such as bank reconciliations or sign-offs on hard copy or electronic documents) may be more suitable where judgment and discretion are required, such as

- For large, unusual, or nonrecurring transactions;

- For circumstances where misstatements are difficult to define, anticipate, or predict;

- In changing circumstances that require a control response outside the scope of an existing automated control; and

- In monitoring the effectiveness of automated controls.

Automated controls are suitable for

- High-volume transactions that require additional calculations.
- Routine errors that can be predicted and corrected.
- Circumstances that require a high degree of accuracy.

Roles of Internal Auditors in Control

Performance Standard 2130
Control

The internal audit activity must assist the organization in maintaining effective controls by evaluating their effectiveness and efficiency and by promoting continuous improvement.

Implementation Standard 2130.A1

The internal audit activity must evaluate the adequacy and effectiveness of controls in responding to risks within the organization's governance, operations, and information systems regarding the:

- Achievement of the organization's strategic objectives.
- Reliability and integrity of financial and operational information.
- Effectiveness and efficiency of operations and programs.
- Safeguarding of assets.
- Compliance with laws, regulations, policies, procedures, and contracts.

Implementation Standard 2130.C1

Internal auditors must incorporate knowledge of controls gained from consulting engagements into evaluation of the organization's control processes.

Implementation Standard 2210.A3

Adequate criteria are needed to evaluate governance, risk management, and controls. Internal auditors must ascertain the extent to which management and/or the board has established adequate criteria to determine whether objectives and goals have been accomplished. If adequate, internal auditors must use such criteria in their evaluation. If inadequate, internal auditors must identify appropriate evaluation criteria through discussion with management and/or the board.

Controls **mitigate risks** at the entity, activity, and transaction levels. The roles and responsibilities are as follows:

- **Senior management** oversees the establishment, administration, and assessment of the system of controls.

- **Managers** assess controls within their responsibilities.

- The **internal auditors** provide assurance about the effectiveness of existing controls.

In fulfilling their responsibilities, internal auditors should
- Clearly understand control and typical control processes
- Consider risk appetite, risk tolerance, and risk culture
- Understand the critical risks that could prevent reaching objectives
- Understand the controls that mitigate risks
- Understand the control framework(s) used
- Have a process for planning, auditing, and reporting control problems

Evaluating the Effectiveness of Controls

Controls should be assessed relative to risks at each level. A **risk and control matrix** (Figure 6-2 in Subunit 6.2 on page 189) may be useful to

- Identify objectives and related risks.

- Determine the significance of risks (impact and likelihood).

- Determine responses to the significant risks (for example, accept, pursue, transfer, mitigate, or avoid).

- Determine key management controls.

- Evaluate the adequacy of control design.

- Test adequately designed controls to ascertain whether they have been implemented and are operating effectively.

Evaluating the Efficiency of Controls

The internal auditors consider whether management monitors the **costs and benefits** of control. The issue is whether resources used exceed the benefits and controls create significant issues (for example, error, delay, or duplication of effort).

The level of a control should be appropriate to the relevant risk.

Promoting Continuous Improvement

The CAE may recommend a **control framework** if none exists. The internal audit activity also may recommend improvements in the **control environment** (for example, the tone at the top should promote an ethical culture and not tolerate noncompliance).

Continuous improvement of controls involves

- Training and ongoing self-monitoring
- Control (or risk and control) assessment meetings with managers
- A logical structure for documentation, analysis, and assessment of design and operation
- Identification, evaluation, and correction of control weaknesses
- Informing managers about new issues, laws, and regulations
- Monitoring relevant technical developments (Implementation Guide 2130)

STOP & REVIEW

You have completed the outline for this subunit.
Study multiple-choice questions 1 through 7 beginning on page 200.

6.2 TYPES OF CONTROLS

Primary Controls

Preventive controls deter the occurrence of unwanted events.

- Storing petty cash in a locked safe and segregating duties, e.g., using a lockbox system, are examples.

- IT examples include

    - Designing a database so that users cannot enter a letter in the field that stores a Social Security number and
    - Requiring the number of invoices in a batch to be entered before processing begins.

Detective controls alert the proper people after an unwanted event. They are effective when detection occurs before material harm occurs.

EXAMPLE 6-3   Detective Controls
A batch of invoices submitted for processing may be rejected by the computer system if it includes identical payments to a single vendor. A detective control provides for automatic reporting of all rejected batches to the accounts payable department.   A burglar alarm is another example.

Corrective controls correct the negative effects of unwanted events.

- An example is a requirement that all cost variances over a certain amount be justified.

Directive controls cause or encourage the occurrence of a desirable event. These include the following:

- Policy and procedure manuals
- Employee training
- Job descriptions

Secondary Controls

A secondary control offsets the absence of a key control and acts as a fallback control.

Compensating (mitigative) controls are likely to be established when segregation of duties is not maintained and/or primary controls are ineffective. Compensating controls may include (1) more supervision or (2) owner involvement in the process.

- Compensating controls do not, by themselves, reduce risk to an acceptable level.

EXAMPLE 6-4	Compensating Controls in a Cash Sale Environment

The cash sales process often lacks the segregation of duties necessary for the proper framework of control. For example, the sales clerk often

- Authorizes the sale (e.g., acceptance of a check),
- Records the sale (i.e., enters it on the sales terminal), and
- Has custody of the assets related to the sale (i.e., cash and inventory).

Compensating controls include

- Use of a cash register or sales terminal to record the sale. The terminal makes a permanent record of the event that the clerk cannot erase.

- Assignment of one clerk to be responsible for sales recording and cash receipts during a work period. The cash drawer can be reconciled with the record of sales and accountability assigned to the clerk.

- Increased supervision. For example, cameras may be positioned to observe the clerks' sales recording and cash collection activities.

- Customer audit of the transaction. Displaying the recorded transaction and providing a receipt to the customer provides some assurance that the recording process was accomplished appropriately by the clerk.

- Bonding of employees responsible for handling cash. Because the bonding company investigates employees before providing the bond, some assurance is provided concerning their integrity. Also, the bond provides insurance against losses.

Complementary controls work with other controls to reduce risk to an acceptable level. In other words, their synergy is more effective than either control by itself.

- For example, separating the functions of accounting for and custody of cash receipts is complemented by obtaining deposit slips validated by the bank.

Two Basic Processing Modes

Batch Processing

In this mode, transactions are accumulated and submitted to the computer as a single batch. In the early days of computers, this was the only way a job could be processed.

In batch processing, the user cannot influence the process once the job has begun (except to ask that it be aborted completely). (S)he must wait until the job is finished running to see whether any transactions were rejected and failed to post.

Despite huge advances in computer technology, this accumulation of transactions for processing on a delayed basis is still widely used. It is very efficient for such applications as payroll because large numbers of routine transactions must be processed on a regular schedule.

Memo posting is used by banks for financial transactions when batch processing is used. It posts temporary credit or debit transactions to an account if the complete posting to update the balance will be done as part of the end-of-day batch processing. Information can be viewed immediately after updating.

- Memo posting is an intermediate step between batch processing and real-time processing.

Online, Real-Time Processing

In some systems, having the latest information available at all times is crucial to the proper functioning of the system. An airline reservation system is a common example.

In an online, real-time system, the database is updated immediately upon entry of the transaction by the operator. Such systems are referred to as **online transaction processing**, or **OLTP**, systems.

Entity-Level, Process-Level, and Transaction-Level Controls

Entity-level controls are designed to achieve organizational objectives and to address entity-wide risks. They include governance controls and management oversight controls.

- Entity-level **governance controls** are established by the board of directors at the highest level (governance level). They include organizational policies and procedures that define the entity's culture and communicate its expectations. Examples include IT policies, the code of conduct, oversight of controls, and setting the risk appetite.

- Entity-level **management oversight controls** are implemented by management at the business unit level to achieve business unit objectives and address business unit risks.

    - For example, supervisors approve employee overtime hours before they are worked, and supervisors confirm the employees worked only the authorized hours.

Process-level controls are designed to achieve process objectives and to address process risks. Examples include physical inventory counts, performance assessment, and review of revenue center reports.

Transaction-level controls are designed to achieve transaction objectives and to address risks specific to transactions. Examples include application controls, exception reports, and segregation of duties.

IT General Controls

General controls are approved by management and are the umbrella under which the IT function operates. They affect the organization's entire processing environment and commonly include controls over

- Data center and network operations;
- Systems software acquisition, change, and maintenance;
- Access security; and
- Application system acquisition, development, and maintenance.

The objectives of IT general controls are to ensure the appropriate development and implementation of applications, as well as the integrity of program and data files and of computer operations.

The following are the most common IT general controls:

- Logical access controls (e.g., passwords) over infrastructure, applications, and data limit access in accordance with the principle that all persons should have access only to those elements of the organization's information systems that are necessary to perform their job duties. Logical controls have a double focus: authentication and authorization.

- System development life cycle controls and program change management controls ensure that operating systems, utilities, and database management systems are acquired and changed only under close supervision and that vendor updates are routinely installed.

- Physical security controls over the data center limit physical access and environmental damage to computer equipment, data, and important documents.

- System and data backup and recovery controls ensure that access to data (e.g., hardware, software, and records), communications, work areas, and other business processes can be restored.

Application Controls

Application controls are built into each application (payroll, accounts payable, inventory management, etc.) and are designed to ensure that only correct, authorized data enter the system and that the data are processed and reported properly.

Application controls include input, processing, and output controls.

General controls apply to all computerized systems or applications. They include a mixture of software, hardware, and manual procedures that shape an overall control environment. In contrast, **application controls** are specific controls that differ with each computerized application.

Application controls are those that pertain to the scope of individual business processes or application systems. The objective of application controls is to ensure that

- Input data is accurate, complete, authorized, and correct.
    - These controls vary depending on whether input is entered in online or batch mode.

- Data is processed as intended in an acceptable time period.
    - Reasonable assurance must be provided that
        - All data submitted for processing are processed and
        - Only approved data are processed.

- Data stored is accurate and complete.

- Outputs are accurate and complete.
    - Assurance must be provided that the processing results (such as account listings or displays, reports, files, invoices, or disbursement checks) are accurate and that only authorized personnel receive the output.

- A record is maintained to track the process of data from input to storage and to the eventual output.

When designing data **input controls**, primary consideration should be given to authorization, validation, and error notification.

The most economical point for correcting input errors in an application is the time at which the data are entered into the system.

- For this reason, input controls are a primary focus of an internal auditor's assessment of application controls. Batch input and online input processing modes have their own controls.

Batch Input Controls

Financial totals summarize monetary amounts in an information field in a group of records. The total produced by the system after the batch has been processed is compared to the total produced manually beforehand.

Record counts track the number of records processed by the system for comparison to the number the user expected to be processed.

Hash totals are control totals without a defined meaning, such as the total of vendor numbers or invoice numbers, that are used to verify the completeness of the data.

EXAMPLE 6-5	Batch Input Controls

A company has the following invoices in a batch:

Invoice Number	Product	Quantity	Unit Price
303	G7	100	$15
305	A48	200	5
353	L30	125	10
359	Z26	150	20

The hash total is a control total without a defined meaning, such as the total of employee numbers or invoice totals, that is used to verify the completeness of data. Using invoice numbers, the hash total would be 1320.

Online (Real-Time) Input Controls

Preformatting of data entry screens, i.e., to make them imitate the layout of a printed form, can aid the operator in keying to the correct fields.

Field/format checks are tests of the characters in a field to verify that they are of an appropriate type for that field. For example, the system is programmed to reject alphabetic characters entered in the field for Social Security number.

Validity checks compare the data entered in a given field with a table of valid values for that field. For example, the vendor number on a request to cut a check must match the table of current vendors, and the invoice number must match the approved invoice table.

Limit (reasonableness) and range checks are based on known limits for given information. For example, hours worked per week must be between 0 and 100, with anything above that range requiring management authorization.

Check digits are an extra reference number that follows an identification code and bears a mathematical relationship to the other digits. This extra digit is input with the data. The identification code can be subjected to an algorithm and compared to the check digit.

Sequence checks are based on the logic that processing efficiency is greatly increased when files are sorted on some designated field, called the "key," before operations such as matching. If the system discovers a record out of order, it may indicate that the files were not properly prepared for processing.

Zero balance checks will reject any transaction or batch thereof in which the sum of all debits and credits does not equal zero.

Processing Controls

Processing controls ensure that data are complete and accurate during updating.

Concurrency controls manage situations where two or more users attempt to access or update a file or database simultaneously. These controls ensure the correct results are generated while getting those results as quickly as possible.

- For example, four customers access an airline's online reservation system at the same time to purchase eight tickets for the same flight (only six tickets are available) and the flight reservation system prevents the flight from being oversold.

Output Controls

Output controls ensure that processing results are complete, accurate, and properly distributed.

- An important output control is user review. Users should be able to determine when output is incomplete or not reasonable, particularly when the user prepared the input. Thus, users as well as computer personnel have a quality assurance function.

Integrity Controls

Integrity controls monitor data being processed and in storage to ensure it remains consistent and correct.

- For example, a system may reject a formula for a spreadsheet cell representing currency if a calculation involving multiple cells results in a cell containing data other than a number.

- Concerning internal memory of computer systems, failure of a defined data block to align with another value may be identified via integrity controls, indicating an error in processing.

Time-Based Controls

Feedback controls report information about completed activities. They permit improvement in future performance by learning from past mistakes.

- For example, the inspection of completed goods followed by performing variance analysis procedures helps identify deviations from what was expected. Thus, inspection and the analysis of variance provide feedback on how well the completion of goods meets expectations.

Concurrent controls adjust ongoing processes. These real-time controls monitor activities in the present to prevent them from deviating too far from standards. An example is close supervision of production-line workers.

Feedforward controls anticipate and prevent problems. These controls require a long-term perspective. Organizational policies and procedures are examples.

Financial vs. Operating Controls

Financial controls should be based on relevant established accounting principles.

- Objectives of financial controls may include
  - Proper authorization;
  - Appropriate recordkeeping;
  - Safeguarding of assets; and
  - Compliance with laws, regulations, and contracts.

Operating controls apply to production and support activities.

- Because they may lack established criteria or standards, they should be based on management principles and methods. They also should be designed with regard to the management functions of planning, organizing, directing, and controlling.

- The appropriate allocation of research and development costs to new products, product maintenance, and cost reduction programs based on an approved budget is an example of an operating control.

People-Based vs. System-Based Controls

People-based controls are dependent on the intervention of humans for their proper operation, for example, regular performance of bank reconciliations.

- Checklists, such as lists of required procedures for month-end closing, can be valuable to ensure that people-based controls are executed when needed.

System-based controls are executed whenever needed with no human intervention.

- An example is code in a computerized purchasing system that prevents any purchase order over a certain monetary threshold from being submitted to the vendor without managerial approval.

Use of a Control Matrix

Controls do not necessarily match risks one-to-one. Certain controls may address more than one risk, and more than one control may be needed to adequately address a single risk.

EXAMPLE 6-6   Control Matrix

Assume all petty cash custodians must present expense vouchers periodically. This control helps ensure that

- Petty cash accounts are maintained at the established level and
- Petty cash expenditures are reviewed for appropriateness.

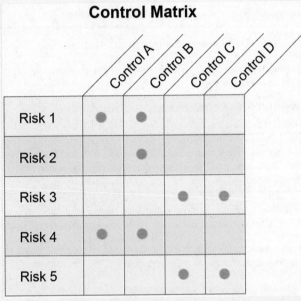

Control Matrix

	Control A	Control B	Control C	Control D
Risk 1	●	●		
Risk 2		●		
Risk 3			●	●
Risk 4	●	●		
Risk 5			●	●

Risk 1	Risk 2	Risk 3	Risk 4	Risk 5
Petty cash account is not maintained at the established level.	Petty cash funded is not appropriately secured.	Disbursements are not appropriately supported.	Empty petty cash fund.	Petty cash expenditures are not reviewed for appropriateness.

Control A	Control B	Control C	Control D
Establish maximum petty cash account balance and replenishment level.	Store petty cash in a locked safe.	Use petty cash disbursements receipts for disbursement approval.	Require purchase receipts for expenses to be approved for reimbursement.

Figure 6-2

You have completed the outline for this subunit.
Study multiple-choice questions 8 through 14 beginning on page 202.

STOP & REVIEW

Control Types Quick Study Guide	
Control Type and Description	**Control Type Examples**
Primary Controls (Key Controls)	
Preventive — Deter the occurrence of unwanted events.	Formal security policy
Detective — Alert the proper people after an unwanted event.	Physical inventory counts
Corrective — Remedy the negative effects of unwanted events.	Maintaining clean backup
Directive — Cause or encourage the occurrence of a desirable event.	Employee training
Secondary Controls — Offset the absence of a key control and act as a fallback control.	
Compensating (mitigative) — Type of secondary control that reduces risk (with the assistance of other controls) to an acceptable level.	Additional or more in-depth review
Complementary — Work with other controls to reduce risk to an acceptable level.	Encrypted financial data and security monitoring
IT General Controls — Apply to all computerized systems or applications. They include a mixture of software, hardware, and manual procedures that shape an overall control environment.	Program change management
IT Application Controls — In contrast with IT general controls, application controls are specific controls that differ with each business process or computerized application.	
Input — Provide reasonable assurance that data submitted for processing are (1) authorized, (2) complete, and (3) accurate.	Examples provided in batch input and online input below
Batch input — Used when data are grouped for processing.	Financial totals
Online input — Used when data are keyed into an input screen.	Preformatting
Processing — Ensure data are complete and accurate during updating.	Limit checks
Concurrency — Manage attempts by two or more users to access or update a file or database simultaneously and ensure results remain accurate.	Data accuracy
Output — Ensure that processing results are complete, accurate, and properly distributed.	Audit trails
Integrity — Monitor data being processed and in storage to ensure consistency and accuracy.	Backup and recovery
Entity-Level Controls — Designed to achieve organizational objectives and address entity-wide risks.	
Governance — Established by the board of directors at the highest level.	Code of conduct and policies
Management oversight — Implemented at the business-unit level to achieve its objectives and address its risks.	Period-end controls
-- Continued on next page --	

Control Types Quick Study Guide (Continued)		
Control Type and Description		**Control Type Examples**
Process-Level Controls	Designed to achieve process objectives and address process risks.	Revenue and cost center reports
Transaction-Level Controls	Designed to achieve transaction objectives and address risks specific to transactions.	Segregation of duties
Time-Based Controls		
Feedback	Permit improvement in future performance by learning from past mistakes.	Inspection of completed goods
Concurrent	Monitor and adjust ongoing processes in the present to prevent them from deviating too far from standards.	Supervision of assembly personnel
Feedforward	Require long-term perspective to anticipate and prevent problems.	Temperature regulation via coordination of outside and inside thermostats
Financial Controls	Based on relevant established accounting principles.	Compliance with laws, regulations, and contracts
Operating Controls	Based on management principles and methods and applied to production and support activities.	Planning, organizing, and directing
People-Based Controls	Dependent on the intervention of humans for their proper operation.	Month-end closing checklists
System-Based Controls	Executed whenever needed with no human intervention.	Automatic purchase order quantity or monetary threshold

General Controls and Application Controls Quick Study Guide

General controls apply to all computerized systems or applications. They include a mixture of software, hardware, and manual procedures that shape an overall control environment. In contrast, **application controls** are specific controls that differ with each computerized application.

Control Categories*	Control Type(s)
General (embedded in IT processes and services)	
Segregation of Duties	Corrective, preventive
Software and Hardware Controls	
Acquired under close supervision	Corrective, preventive
Vendor updates are routinely installed	Corrective, preventive
Parity checks	Preventive, detective, corrective
Echo checks	Preventive, detective, corrective
Change management controls	Corrective, preventive
Physical Controls	
Access Controls	
Passwords or ID numbers	Preventive
Device authorization table	Preventive
Encryption	Preventive
Biometric technologies	Preventive
System access logs	Detective
Environmental Controls	
Cooling and heating systems	Corrective, preventive
Fire-suppression system	Corrective, preventive
Logical Controls	
Authentication	Preventive
Authorization	Preventive
Firewall	
Network	Preventive
Application	Preventive
Antivirus Software	Preventive

-- Continued on next page --

General Controls and Application Controls Quick Study Guide (Continued)	
Control Categories*	**Control Type(s)**

Application (embedded in business process applications)

Input

Financial totals	Preventive
Record counts	Preventive
Hash totals	Detective
Validity checks	Preventive
Check digits	Preventive
Preformatting	Preventive
Closed-loop verification	Preventive

Processing

Concurrency	Preventive
Validation	Preventive
Completeness	Preventive
Key integrity	Preventive
Some controls duplicate input controls	
Limit checks	Preventive
Batch controls such as hash and record counts	Detective, preventive

Output

Error listings	Detective
Transaction logs	Detective
Some controls duplicate input controls and processing controls	
Batch controls such as hash and record counts	Detective
Processing controls such as run-to-run control totals	Detective

*Control descriptions provided are not all-inclusive

6.3 CONTROL FRAMEWORKS -- COSO AND COBIT 19

Accepted Control Frameworks

Several bodies have published control frameworks that provide a comprehensive means of ensuring that the organization has considered all relevant aspects of internal control.

- The use of a particular model or control design may be specified by regulatory or legal requirements.

- Some of the better-known frameworks are described below and on the following pages.

COSO Framework

COSO Definition of Internal Control

Internal control is a process, effected by an entity's board of directors, management, and other personnel, designed to provide reasonable assurance regarding the achievement of objectives relating to operations, reporting, and compliance.

Thus, internal control is

- Intended to achieve three classes of objectives

- An ongoing process

- Effected by people at all organizational levels, e.g., the board, management, and all other employees

- Able to provide reasonable, but not absolute, assurance

- Adaptable to an entity's structure

Objectives

The three classes of objectives direct organizations to the different (but overlapping) elements of control.

1. **Operations**
   - Operations objectives relate to achieving the entity's mission. Appropriate objectives include improving
     - Financial performance,
     - Productivity,
     - Quality,
     - Innovation, and
     - Customer satisfaction.
   - Operations objectives also include **safeguarding of assets**.
     - Objectives related to protecting and preserving assets assist in risk assessment and development of mitigating controls.
     - Avoidance of waste, inefficiency, and bad business decisions relates to broader objectives than safeguarding of assets.

2. **Reporting**
   - To make sound decisions, stakeholders must have reliable, timely, and transparent financial information.
   - Reports may be prepared for use by the organization and stakeholders.
   - Objectives may relate to
     - Financial and nonfinancial reporting
     - Internal or external reporting

3. **Compliance**
   - Entities are subject to laws, rules, and regulations that set minimum standards of conduct.
     - Examples include taxation, environmental protection, and employee relations.
     - Compliance with internal policies and procedures is an operational matter.

Achievement of Objectives

An internal control system is more likely to provide reasonable assurance of achieving the reporting and compliance objectives than the operational objectives.

Reporting and compliance objectives are responses to standards established by external parties, such as regulators.

- Thus, achieving these objectives depends on actions almost entirely within the entity's control.

However, operational effectiveness may not be within the entity's control because it is affected by human judgment and many external factors.

Components of Internal Control

Supporting the organization in its efforts to achieve objectives are the following five components of internal control:

1. **C**ontrol activities
2. **R**isk assessment
3. **I**nformation and communication
4. **M**onitoring
5. Control **e**nvironment

A useful memory aid for the COSO components of internal control is "Controls stop **CRIME**."

C	Control activities
R	Risk assessment
I	Information and communication
M	Monitoring
E	Control environment

Control Activities

Control activities are the policies and procedures established to support the mitigation of risks to the achievement of objectives.

Control activities may

- Be **preventive** or **detective**,
- Be **automated** or **manual**, and
- Cover activities such as

    - Authorizations and approvals,
    - Verifications,
    - Reconciliations, and
    - Reviews of business performance.

Control activities should be designed to incorporate **segregation of duties**; however, where this is not feasible, alternative control activities will need to be adopted. Control activities include general controls over the use of technology.

Risk Assessment

Risks are possible events, from both internal and external sources, that can affect an organization's achievement of its objectives.

Effective risk assessment allows an organization to

- **Identify** risks to the achievement of the organization's objectives, such as the potential for fraud;

- Determine how identified risks should be **managed**; and

- Consider the impact of any **changes**, both internal and external, that could impair the effectiveness of internal controls.

Clear specification of organizational **objectives** is a precondition for effective risk identification and assessment.

Information and Communication

Information enables an organization to execute the internal control activities developed as a result of the control environment and risk assessment components.

Information must be relevant and may arise internally or externally.

The information then needs to be communicated to the appropriate parties in order to comply with or execute control activities. Senior management communicates information to (1) maintain accountability and (2) measure and review performance. Communication of objectives and responsibilities for internal control is necessary to support the control environment.

Monitoring Activities

Monitoring is a process that evaluates whether the five components of the control framework are present and functioning. Criteria established by regulators, standard-setting bodies, or management and the board of directors will be used to evaluate the findings from the monitoring activities. Deficiencies that arise from the comparison need to be assessed and addressed appropriately.

Control Environment

The control environment comprises the standards, processes, and structures through which internal control is exercised across the organization.

By stressing the importance of internal controls and setting the expected standards of conduct, the board of directors and senior management establish the **tone at the top**. At various levels within the organization, management reinforces expectations and demonstrates the organizational commitment to integrity and ethical values.

The control environment is the means through which the board of directors exercises oversight of the development and performance of internal control while demonstrating independence from management. Subject to board oversight, management establishes the appropriate structures and reporting lines; creates the processes to recruit, develop, and remunerate competent personnel; and delegates the authorities and responsibilities required to achieve business objectives.

Individuals are held accountable for their internal control responsibilities. The control environment established has a **pervasive impact on the overall system of internal control**. If the control environment is not robust, the ability of the other components of the internal control framework to produce an effective system of internal control is impaired.

Integration

Components are identified separately but work together to support the achievement of the objectives across and within the various levels in the organization. The control environment provides organizational commitment to and structure of the control framework.

This commitment leads to a robust assessment of the undesirable events that could occur, which in turn leads to the identification of controls that are expected to either prevent or detect these undesirable events. The nature and content of the mandated control activities should be documented and communicated to the appropriate parties.

Adherence to these controls is monitored through self-assessments and internal audits. Adverse findings are then fed back to the control environment component.

Deviations from the prescribed control activities may indicate a need for the board of directors and senior management to reinforce and strengthen the message they convey through the tone at the top. This will require additional efforts from the information and communication and monitoring activities components.

COBIT 19 -- A Framework for IT Governance and Management

COBIT 19 is an internationally accepted IT governance system. It is the best-known control and governance framework that addresses information technology.

- In its original version, COBIT (Control Objectives for Information and Related Technology) was focused on controls for specific IT processes.

- Over the years, information technology has gradually pervaded every facet of the organization's operations. IT can no longer be viewed as a function distinct from other aspects of the organization.

  - The evolution of COBIT has reflected this change in the nature of IT within the organization.

COBIT 19 Governance Principles

Six Governance System Principles

A governance system is the rules, practices, and processes that direct and regulate an entity. A governance system must

1. Provide stakeholder value

2. Utilize a holistic approach that creates synergies among interconnected components

3. Respond dynamically to changes in design factors

4. Be distinct from management

5. Be tailored to enterprise needs and include design factors such as threat landscape

6. Encompass not only the IT function but all information, processes, and technology that contribute to organizational goal achievement

Three Governance Framework Principles

A governance framework is the structure upon which the governance system is built. A governance framework is

1. Based on a conceptual model to achieve consistency and automation by identifying components and their relationships

2. Open and flexible to permit inclusion of new content and issues without loss of consistency and integrity

3. Aligned with major standards, regulations, frameworks, and best practices

STOP & REVIEW

You have completed the outline for this subunit.
Study multiple-choice questions 15 through 18 beginning on page 204.

QUESTIONS

6.1 Overview of Control

1. Specific airline ticket information, including fare, class, purchase date, and lowest available fare options, as prescribed in the organization's travel policy, is obtained and reported to department management when employees purchase airline tickets from the organization's authorized travel agency. Such a report provides information for

- A. Quality of performance in relation to the organization's travel policy.
- B. Identifying costs necessary to process employee business expense report data.
- C. Departmental budget-to-actual comparisons.
- D. Supporting employer's business expense deductions.

Answer (A) is correct.
   REQUIRED: The information provided by reporting employee airline ticket information.
   DISCUSSION: Comparison of actual performance against a standard provides information for assessing quality of performance.
   Answer (B) is incorrect. This ticket information is preliminary; employees may change tickets and routings prior to their trip. **Answer (C) is incorrect.** Departmental budget-to-actual comparisons do not necessarily reflect the actual costs ultimately incurred. **Answer (D) is incorrect.** Supporting expense deductions may not necessarily reflect actual costs.

2. According to The IIA Glossary appended to the *Standards*, which of the following are most directly designed to ensure that risks are contained?

- A. Risk management processes.
- B. Internal audit activities.
- C. Control processes.
- D. Governance processes.

Answer (C) is correct.
   REQUIRED: The item most directly designed to ensure that risks are contained.
   DISCUSSION: Control processes are the policies, procedures, and activities that are part of a control framework, designed to ensure that risks are contained within the risk tolerances established by the risk management process.
   Answer (A) is incorrect. Risk management is a process to identify, assess, manage, and control potential events or situations to provide reasonable assurance regarding the achievement of the organization's objectives. **Answer (B) is incorrect.** An internal audit activity is a department, division, team of consultants, or other practitioner(s) that provides independent, objective assurance and consulting services designed to add value and improve an organization's operations. **Answer (D) is incorrect.** Governance is the combination of processes and structures implemented by the board to inform, direct, manage, and monitor the activities of the organization toward the achievement of its objectives.

3. The actions taken to manage risk and increase the likelihood that established objectives and goals will be achieved are best described as

A. Supervision.

B. Quality assurance.

C. Control.

D. Compliance.

Answer (C) is correct.
REQUIRED: The term for actions taken to manage risk and increase the likelihood that established objectives and goals will be achieved.
DISCUSSION: Control is "any action taken by management, the board, and other parties to manage risk and increase the likelihood that established objectives and goals will be achieved" (The IIA Glossary).
Answer (A) is incorrect. Supervision is just one means of achieving control. **Answer (B) is incorrect.** Quality assurance relates to just one set of objectives and goals. It does not pertain to achievement of all established organizational objectives and goals. **Answer (D) is incorrect.** Compliance is "adherence to policies, plans, procedures, laws, regulations, contracts, or other requirements" (The IIA Glossary).

4. Which of the following is **not** implied by the definition of control?

A. Measurement of progress toward goals.

B. Uncovering of deviations from plans.

C. Assignment of responsibility for deviations.

D. Indication of the need for corrective action.

Answer (C) is correct.
REQUIRED: The item not implied by the definition of control.
DISCUSSION: The elements of control include (1) establishing standards for the operation to be controlled, (2) measuring performance against the standards, (3) examining and analyzing deviations, (4) taking corrective action, and (5) reappraising the standards based on experience. Thus, assigning responsibility for deviations found is not part of the control function.
Answer (A) is incorrect. Measurement of progress toward goals is implied by the definition of control. **Answer (B) is incorrect.** The uncovering of deviations from plans is implied by the definition of control. **Answer (D) is incorrect.** Indication of the need for corrective action is implied by the definition of control.

5. An internal auditor is examining inventory control in a merchandising division with annual sales of $3,000,000 and a 40% gross profit rate. Tests show that 2% of the monetary amount of purchases do not reach inventory because of breakage and employee theft. Adding certain controls costing $35,000 annually could reduce these losses to .5% of purchases. Should the controls be recommended?

A. Yes, because the projected saving exceeds the cost of the added controls.

B. No, because the cost of the added controls exceeds the projected savings.

C. Yes, because the ideal system of internal control is the most extensive one.

D. Yes, regardless of cost-benefit considerations, because the situation involves employee theft.

Answer (B) is correct.
REQUIRED: The correct decision regarding whether to add inventory controls and the reason.
DISCUSSION: Controls must be subject to the cost-benefit criterion. The annual cost of these inventory controls is $35,000, but the cost savings is only $27,000 {(2.0% − 0.5%) × [$3,000,000 sales × (1.0 − 0.4 gross profit rate)]}. Hence, the cost exceeds the benefit, and the controls should not be recommended.
Answer (A) is incorrect. The cost exceeds the benefit. **Answer (C) is incorrect.** The ideal system is subject to the cost-benefit criterion. The most extensive system of internal controls may not be cost effective. **Answer (D) is incorrect.** Cost-benefit considerations apply even to employee theft.

6. Which of the following statements best describes the relationship between planning and controlling?

- A. Planning looks to the future; controlling is concerned with the past.
- B. Planning and controlling are completely independent of each other.
- C. Planning prevents problems; controlling is initiated by problems that have occurred.
- D. Controlling cannot operate effectively without the tools provided by planning.

Answer (D) is correct.
REQUIRED: The best description of the relationship between planning and controlling.
DISCUSSION: Control is the process of making certain that plans are achieving the desired objectives. The elements of control include (1) establishing standards for the operation to be controlled, (2) measuring performance against the standards, (3) examining and analyzing deviations, (4) taking corrective action, and (5) reappraising the standards based on experience. Planning provides needed tools for the control process by establishing standards, i.e., the first step.
Answer (A) is incorrect. A control system looks to the future when it provides for corrective action and review and revision of standards. **Answer (B) is incorrect.** Planning and controlling overlap. **Answer (C) is incorrect.** Comprehensive planning includes creation of controls.

7. Which of the following control procedures does an internal auditor expect to find during an engagement to evaluate risk management and insurance?

- A. Periodic internal review of the in-force list to evaluate the adequacy of insurance coverage.
- B. Required approval of all new insurance policies by the organization's CEO.
- C. Policy of repetitive standard journal entries to record insurance expense.
- D. Cutoff procedures with regard to insurance expense reporting.

Answer (A) is correct.
REQUIRED: The control that should be found in an audit of risk management and insurance.
DISCUSSION: Obtaining insurance and periodically reviewing its adequacy are among management's responses to the findings of a risk assessment. Insurance coverage should be sufficient to ensure that the relevant assessed risks are managed in accordance with the organization's risk appetite.
Answer (B) is incorrect. CEO approval is an operational decision ordinarily delegated to a lower level manager. **Answer (C) is incorrect.** A policy concerning standard journal entries is an accounting control, not a risk management and insurance control. **Answer (D) is incorrect.** Cutoff procedures with regard to insurance expense reporting are an accounting control, not a risk management and insurance control.

6.2 Types of Controls

8. The requirement that purchases be made from suppliers on an approved vendor list is an example of a

- A. Preventive control.
- B. Detective control.
- C. Corrective control.
- D. Monitoring control.

Answer (A) is correct.
REQUIRED: The type of control requiring that purchases be made from suppliers on an approved vendor list.
DISCUSSION: Preventive controls are actions taken prior to the occurrence of transactions with the intent of stopping errors from occurring. Use of an approved vendor list is a control to prevent the use of unacceptable suppliers.
Answer (B) is incorrect. A detective control identifies errors after they have occurred. **Answer (C) is incorrect.** Corrective controls correct the problems identified by detective controls. **Answer (D) is incorrect.** Monitoring controls are designed to ensure the quality of the control system's performance over time.

9. Controls that are designed to provide management with assurance of the realization of specified minimum gross margins on sales are

   A. Directive controls.

   B. Preventive controls.

   C. Detective controls.

   D. Output controls.

Answer (A) is correct.
   REQUIRED: The controls that provide assurance of the realization of specified minimum gross margins on sales.
   DISCUSSION: The objective of directive controls is to cause or encourage desirable events to occur, e.g., providing management with assurance of the realization of specified minimum gross margins on sales.
   Answer (B) is incorrect. Preventive controls deter undesirable events from occurring. **Answer (C) is incorrect.** Detective controls uncover and correct undesirable events that have occurred. **Answer (D) is incorrect.** Output controls relate to the accuracy and reasonableness of information processed by a system, not to operating controls.

10. Managerial control can be divided into feedforward, concurrent, and feedback controls. Which of the following is an example of a feedback control?

   A. Quality control training.

   B. Budgeting.

   C. Forecasting inventory needs.

   D. Variance analysis.

Answer (D) is correct.
   REQUIRED: The example of a feedback control.
   DISCUSSION: A feedback control measures actual performance, i.e., something that has already occurred, to ensure that a desired future state is attained. It is used to evaluate past activity to improve future performance. A variance is a deviation from a standard. Thus, variance analysis is a feedback control.
   Answer (A) is incorrect. Quality control training is a feedforward, or future-directed, control. **Answer (B) is incorrect.** Budgeting is a feedforward, or future-directed, control. **Answer (C) is incorrect.** Forecasting inventory needs is a feedforward, or future-directed, control.

11. Which of the following is **not** a type of control?

   A. Preventive.

   B. Reactive.

   C. Detective.

   D. Directive.

Answer (B) is correct.
   REQUIRED: The types of controls.
   DISCUSSION: Controls may be preventive (to deter undesirable events from occurring), detective (to detect and correct undesirable events which have occurred), or directive (to cause or encourage a desirable event to occur). "Reactive" is not a specified type of control. However, controls may be reactive in the sense that they detect an undesirable event and react to it or correct it.

12. The operations manager of a company notified the chief financial officer of that organization 60 days in advance that a new, expensive piece of machinery was going to be purchased. This notification allowed the chief financial officer to make an orderly liquidation of some of the company's investment portfolio on favorable terms. What type of control was involved?

   A. Feedback.

   B. Strategic.

   C. Concurrent.

   D. Feedforward.

Answer (D) is correct.
   REQUIRED: The type of control exemplified by advance notice of a purchase.
   DISCUSSION: Feedforward controls provide for the active anticipation of problems so that they can be avoided or resolved in a timely manner. Another example is the quality control inspection of raw materials and work-in-process to avoid defective finished goods.
   Answer (A) is incorrect. Feedback controls apply to decision making based on evaluations of past performance. **Answer (B) is incorrect.** Strategic controls are broad-based and affect an organization over a long period. They apply to such long-term variables as quality and R&D. **Answer (C) is incorrect.** Concurrent controls adjust ongoing processes.

13. Which of the following is a feedback control?

A. Preventive maintenance.

B. Inspection of completed goods.

C. Close supervision of production-line workers.

D. Measuring performance against a standard.

Answer (B) is correct.
    REQUIRED: The example of a feedback control.
    DISCUSSION: Feedback controls obtain information about completed activities. They permit improvement in future performance by learning from past mistakes. Thus, corrective action occurs after the fact. Inspection of completed goods is an example of a feedback control.
    Answer (A) is incorrect. Preventive maintenance is a feedforward control. It attempts to anticipate and prevent problems. **Answer (C) is incorrect.** The close supervision of production-line workers is a concurrent control. It adjusts an ongoing process. **Answer (D) is incorrect.** Measuring performance against a standard is a general aspect of control.

14. Which of the following is an operating control for a research and development department?

A. Research and development personnel are hired by the payroll department.

B. Research and development expenditures are reviewed by an independent person.

C. All research and development costs are charged to expense in accordance with the applicable accounting principles.

D. The research and development budget is properly allocated between new products, product maintenance, and cost reduction programs.

Answer (D) is correct.
    REQUIRED: The operating control for a research and development department.
    DISCUSSION: Operating controls are those applicable to production and support activities. Because they may lack established criteria or standards, they should be based on management principles and methods. The appropriate allocation of R&D costs to new products, product maintenance, and cost reduction programs is an example. This is in contrast to the expensing of R&D costs, which is required by the rules of external financial reporting.
    Answer (A) is incorrect. Only the human resources department should be responsible for hiring. A department responsible for recordkeeping (e.g., payroll) should not authorize transactions. **Answer (B) is incorrect.** Reviewing monetary amounts is a financial control. **Answer (C) is incorrect.** Expensing R&D costs is an accounting treatment rather than a control.

6.3 Control Frameworks -- COSO and COBIT 19

15. Which of the following are included in the control environment described in the COSO internal control framework?

A. Organizational structure, management philosophy, and planning.

B. Integrity and ethical values, assignment of authority, and human resource policies.

C. Competence of personnel, backup facilities, laws, and regulations.

D. Risk assessment, assignment of responsibility, and human resource practices.

Answer (B) is correct.
    REQUIRED: The elements of the control environment.
    DISCUSSION: The control environment is a set of standards, processes, and structures that includes

1.   Integrity and ethical values
2.   Commitment to competence
3.   Board of directors or audit committee
4.   Management's philosophy and operating style
5.   Organizational structure
6.   Assignment of authority and responsibility
7.   Human resource policies and practices

    Answer (A) is incorrect. Planning is not an element of the control environment. **Answer (C) is incorrect.** Backup facilities, laws, and regulations are not elements of the control environment. **Answer (D) is incorrect.** Risk assessment is part of planning the internal audit activity and specific engagements.

16. Which of the following are elements of the control environment?

    A. Management's philosophy and operating style.

    B. Organizational structure.

    C. Human resource policies and practices.

    D. All of the answers are correct.

Answer (D) is correct.
    REQUIRED: The elements of the control environment.
    DISCUSSION: The control environment is a set of standards, processes, and structures that includes

1. Integrity and ethical values
2. Commitment to competence
3. Board of directors or audit committee
4. Management's philosophy and operating style
5. Organizational structure
6. Assignment of authority and responsibility
7. Human resource policies and practices

    Answer (A) is incorrect. Organizational structure and human resource policies and practices are also part of the control environment. **Answer (B) is incorrect.** Management's philosophy and operating style and human resource policies and practices are also part of the control environment. **Answer (C) is incorrect.** Management's philosophy and operating style and organizational structure are also part of the control environment.

17. An organization's directors, management, external auditors, and internal auditors all play important roles in creating a proper control environment. Senior management is primarily responsible for

    A. Establishing a proper organizational culture and specifying a system of internal control.

    B. Designing and operating a control system that provides reasonable assurance that established objectives and goals will be achieved.

    C. Ensuring that external and internal auditors adequately monitor the control environment.

    D. Implementing and monitoring controls designed by the board of directors.

Answer (A) is correct.
    REQUIRED: The best description of senior management's responsibility.
    DISCUSSION: Senior management is primarily responsible for establishing a proper organizational culture and specifying a system of internal control.
    Answer (B) is incorrect. Senior management is not likely to be involved in the detailed design and day-to-day operation of a control system. **Answer (C) is incorrect.** Management administers risk and control processes. It cannot delegate this responsibility to the external auditors or to the internal audit activity. **Answer (D) is incorrect.** The board has oversight governance responsibilities but ordinarily does not become involved in the details of operations.

18. The COSO framework treats internal control as a process designed to provide reasonable assurance regarding the achievement of objectives related to

    A. Reliability of financial reporting.

    B. Effectiveness and efficiency of operations.

    C. Compliance with applicable laws and regulations.

    D. All of the answers are correct.

Answer (D) is correct.
    REQUIRED: The true statement regarding COSO's objectives in relation to internal control.
    DISCUSSION: The COSO framework treats internal control as a process designed to provide reasonable assurance regarding the achievement of objectives related to reliability of financial reporting, effectiveness and efficiency of operations, and compliance with applicable laws and regulations.

STUDY UNIT SEVEN

CONTROLS: APPLICATION

(35 pages of outline)

This study unit is the fourth of four covering **Domain V: Governance, Risk Management, and Control** from The IIA's CIA Exam Syllabus. This domain makes up 35% of Part 1 of the CIA exam and is tested at the **basic** and **proficient** cognitive levels. The four study units are

- Study Unit 4: Governance
- Study Unit 5: Risk Management
- Study Unit 6: Controls: Types and Frameworks
- **Study Unit 7: Controls: Application**

The **learning objectives** of Study Unit 7 are

- Interpret internal control concepts and types of controls
- Examine the effectiveness and efficiency of internal controls

7.1 FLOWCHARTS AND PROCESS MAPPING

Flowcharting is a useful auditing tool for both systems development and understanding internal control. A flowchart is a pictorial diagram of the definition, analysis, or solution of a problem in which symbols are used to represent operations, data flow, documents, records, etc. Questions on this topic will likely require you to interpret a flowchart.

Uses of Flowcharts

Process mapping represents a system or process as a diagram called a process map or flowchart. Flowcharts depict inputs by machines and/or humans and the outputs that result from those processes. Creating and updating process maps aids the auditor's understanding by facilitating discussion with the relevant auditee personnel.

Process mapping facilitates the identification of strengths and weaknesses in the process in the form of key controls that need to be tested. The auditor should conduct a walk-through to confirm that the process actually works in the manner depicted.

Flowchart Symbols

Due to the widespread use of flowcharts by auditors and other professionals such as business consultants and system engineers, the following standard flowchart symbols have been developed:

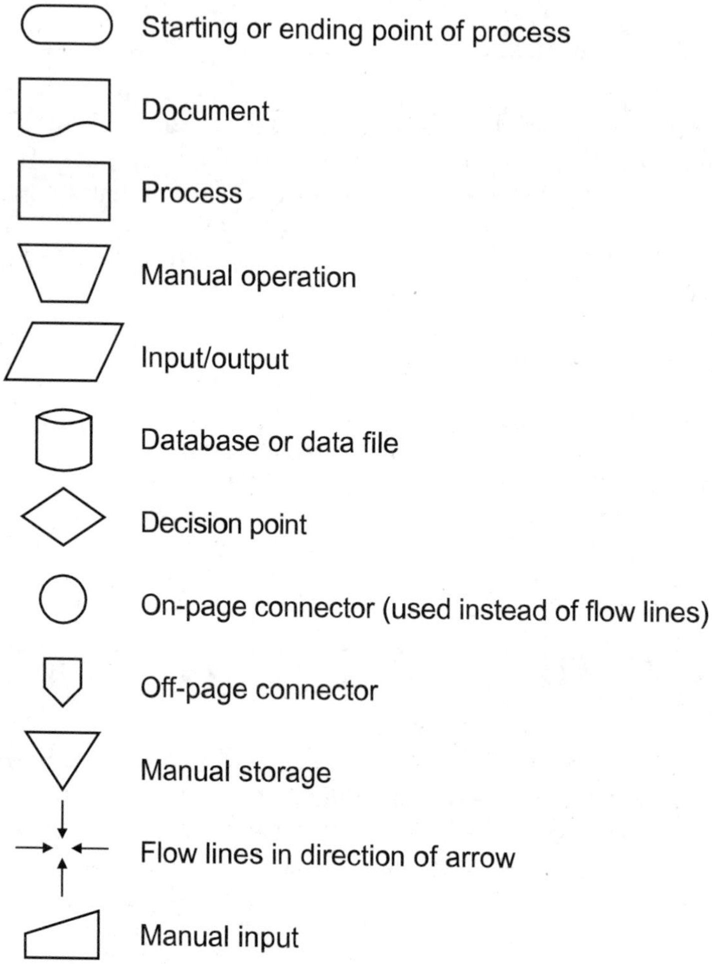

⬭	Starting or ending point of process
⬓	Document
▭	Process
▽	Manual operation
▱	Input/output
⬠	Database or data file
◇	Decision point
○	On-page connector (used instead of flow lines)
⬠	Off-page connector
▽	Manual storage
✛	Flow lines in direction of arrow
◹	Manual input

Figure 7-1

The layout or format of the flowchart, either vertical or horizontal, can be selected to best present the process.

Swim lanes can be used to delineate which function or department performs which process. In the flowchart below, for example, Purchasing, Computer Processing, Receiving, and Inventory Warehouse identify swim lanes.

- The example horizontal flowchart below shows the purchasing process starting with the identification of the need for additional inventory and ending with the receipt and recording of the new inventory and recognition of the amount due to the supplier.

Horizontal Flowchart

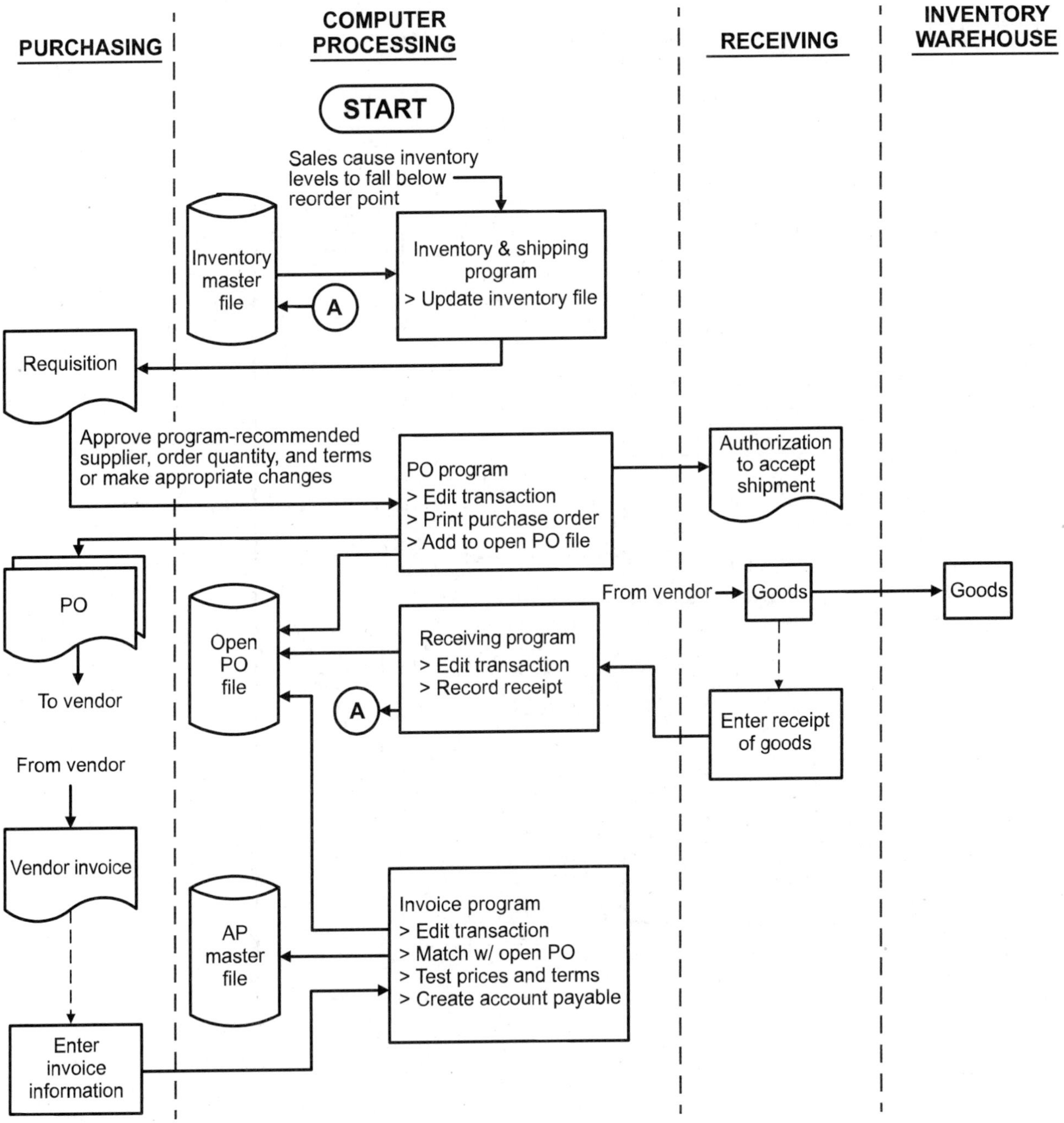

Figure 7-2

The flowchart below is an example of a vertical layout without flows across organizational units. In this instance, the process occurs entirely within the purchasing system.

Vertical Flowchart

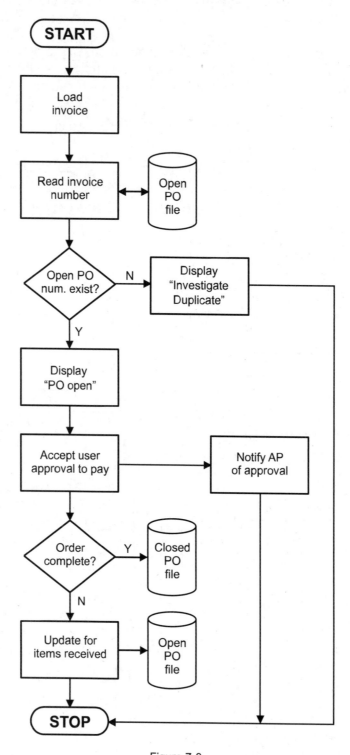

Figure 7-3

Other Charts

A **process narrative** is a tool that can be used alongside or instead of a flowchart. A narrative is a sequential description of the inputs, process steps, and outputs of a process. As with flowcharts, the objective of the auditor is to gain and document sufficient understanding of the process to identify areas of weakness and the key controls that will need to be evaluated. Narratives can provide more information than a flowchart at the expense of clarity.

A **block diagram** is similar to a process map in that it is used to depict a process in diagram form. It is easier to create and understand because it does not require knowledge of different symbols.

STOP & REVIEW

You have completed the outline for this subunit.
Study multiple-choice questions 1 through 7 beginning on page 241.

7.2 ACCOUNTING CYCLES AND ASSOCIATED CONTROLS

Internal Controls

A properly designed system of internal controls should reduce the risk of errors and prevent an individual from perpetrating and concealing fraud. The structure of an organization and the assignment of job duties should be designed to segregate certain functions within this environment.

- Cost-benefit criteria must be considered.

Segregation of Duties

For any given transaction, the following three functions preferably should be performed by separate individuals in different parts of the organization:

1. Authorization of the transaction
2. Recording of the transaction
3. Custody of the assets associated with the transaction

   ■ The following memory aid is for the functions that should be kept separate for proper segregation of duties:

A	**A**uthorization
R	**R**ecordkeeping
C	**C**ustody

The internal control system is designed to detect fraud by one person but not fraud by collusion or management override.

SUCCESS TIP

CIA candidates must understand segregation of duties, a basic principle of internal control. Expect multiple questions on this topic.

Organizational Hierarchy

In a medium-sized or larger organization, adequate segregation of duties can be achieved by separating the responsibilities of the following corporate-level executives:

VP of Operations	Chief Accounting Officer (Controller)	Treasurer	VP of Administration	VP of Human Resources
Sales Inventory warehouse Receiving Shipping Production Purchasing	Accounts receivable Billing Accounts payable General ledger Inventory control Cost accounting Payroll	Cash receipts Cash disbursements Credit	Mail room	Human resources

Please note that this is a generalization and, therefore, questions on the CIA exam may not follow this format.

Accounting Cycles

The accounting process can be described in terms of five cycles:

1. Sales to customers on credit and recognition of receivables
2. Collection of cash from customer receivables
3. Purchases on credit and recognition of payables
4. Payment (disbursement) of cash to satisfy trade payables
5. Payment of employees for work performed and allocation of costs

On the following pages are five flowcharts and accompanying tables depicting the steps in the cycles and the controls in each step for an organization large enough to have an optimal segregation of duties. In the diagrams that follow, documents that originate outside the organization are separated by a thick border.

- In small- and medium-sized organizations, some duties must be combined. The internal auditor must assess whether organizational segregation of duties is adequate.

- Except for manual checks and remittance advices, the flowcharts presented do not assume use of either a paper-based or an electronic system.

- Each document symbol represents a business activity or control, whether manual or computerized.

- The following detailed explanations of the accounting cycles do **not** need to be memorized. However, you should be able to understand them, and you may be able to relate these generic cycles to how the organization you work for handles them.

SUCCESS TIP

The precise details of accounting cycles and related internal controls will vary significantly across the organizations adopting them. As a result, this outline cannot cover all the possible approaches that may be tested on the exam. The best way to prepare for the exam is to answer as many practice questions as possible.

Sales-Receivables-Cash Receipts – Responsibilities of Personnel

The following are the responsibilities of personnel or departments in the sales-receivables-cash receipts cycle:

- **Sales** prepares sales orders based on customer orders.

- **Credit** reports to the treasurer, authorizes credit for all new customers, and initiates write-off of credit losses. Credit checks should be performed before credit approval.

- **Inventory Warehouse** maintains physical custody of products.

- **Inventory Control** maintains records of quantities of products in the Inventory Warehouse.

- **Shipping** prepares shipping documents and ships products based on authorized sales orders.

- **Billing** prepares customer invoices based on goods shipped.

- **Accounts Receivable** maintains the accounts receivable subsidiary ledger.

- **Mail Room** receives mail and prepares initial cash receipts records.

- **Cash Receipts** safeguards and promptly deposits cash receipts.

- **General Ledger** maintains the accounts receivable control account and records sales. Daily summaries of sales are recorded in a sales journal. Totals of details from the sales journal are usually posted monthly to the general ledger.

- **Receiving** prepares receiving reports and handles all receipts of goods or materials, including sales returns.

Sales-Receivables Flowchart

Study the flowchart below. Understand and visualize the sales-receivables process and controls. The flowchart begins at "Start." Read the business activity and internal control descriptions in the table on the next page as needed.

Sales-Receivables System Flowchart

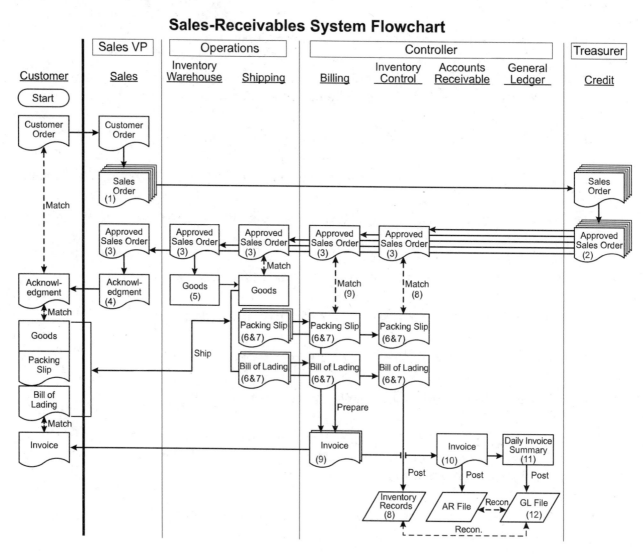

Figure 7-4

Sales-Receivables System Flowchart Table

Function	Authorization			Custody		Recording			
Department	Customer	Sales	Credit	Shipping	Inventory Warehouse	Billing	Inventory Control	Accounts Receivable	General Ledger

Step	Business Activity	Internal Control
1	Sales receives a **customer order** and prepares a multi-part **sales order** then forwards it to Credit.	Reconciling sequentially numbered sales orders helps ensure that orders are legitimate. (Recordkeeping)
2	Credit performs a credit check. If the customer is creditworthy, Credit approves the **sales order**.	Ensures that goods are shipped only to actual customers and that the account is unlikely to become delinquent. (Authorization & Recordkeeping)
3	Credit sends copies of the **approved sales order** to Sales, Inventory Warehouse, Shipping, Billing, and Inventory Control.	Notifies these departments that a legitimate sale has been made. (Authorization & Recordkeeping)
4	Upon receipt of the **approved sales order**, Sales sends an **acknowledgment** to the customer.	The customer's expectation of receiving goods reduces the chances of misrouting or misappropriation. (Recordkeeping & Custody)
5	Upon receipt of the **approved sales order**, the Inventory Warehouse pulls the goods and forwards them to Shipping.	Ensures that goods are removed from the Inventory Warehouse only as part of a legitimate sale. (Recordkeeping & Custody)
6	Shipping verifies that the goods received from Inventory Warehouse match the **approved sales order**, prepares a **packing slip** and a **bill of lading**, and ships the goods to the customer.	Ensures that the correct goods are shipped. (Recordkeeping & Custody)
7	Shipping forwards a copy of the **packing slip** and **bill of lading** to Inventory Control and Billing.	Notifies these departments that the goods have been shipped. (Recordkeeping & Custody)
8	Upon receipt of the **packing slip** and **bill of lading**, Inventory Control matches them with the **approved sales order** and updates the inventory records.	Ensures that inventory records are updated once the goods have been shipped. (Recordkeeping)
9	Upon receipt of the **packing slip** and **bill of lading**, Billing matches them with the **approved sales order**, prepares a multi-part **invoice**, and sends a copy to the customer. Typically, a **remittance advice** is included for use in the cash receipts cycle.	Ensures that customers are billed for all goods, and only those goods, that were actually shipped. Reconciling sequentially numbered invoices helps prevent misappropriation of goods. (Authorization, Recordkeeping, & Custody)
10	Accounts Receivable receives an **invoice** copy from Billing and posts a journal entry to the AR file.	Ensures that customer accounts are kept current. (Recordkeeping)
11	Accounts Receivable prepares a **daily invoice summary** for the day and forwards it to General Ledger for posting to the GL file.	Separation of the Accounts Receivable, Billing, and General Ledger helps assure integrity of recording. (Recordkeeping)
12	General Ledger receives a **daily invoice summary** from AR to post to the GL file.	Updating inventory, AR, and GL files separately provides an additional accounting control when they are periodically reconciled. (Recordkeeping)

Cash Receipts Flowchart

Study the flowchart below. Understand and visualize the cash receipts process and controls. The flowchart begins at "Start." Read the business activity and internal control descriptions in the table on the next page as needed.

Cash Receipts System Flowchart

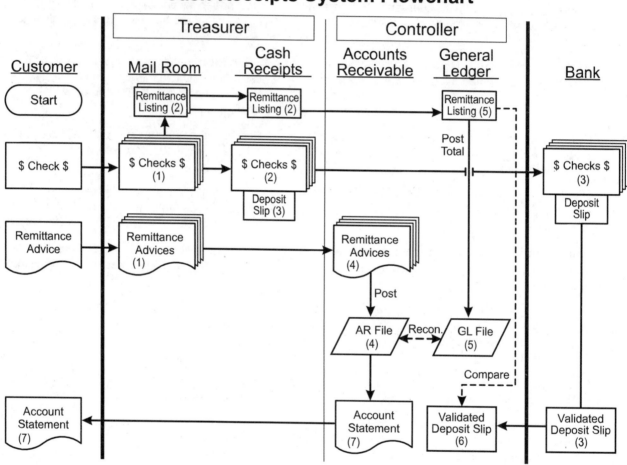

Figure 7-5

Cash Receipts System Flowchart Table

Function	Authorization		Custody		Recording	
Department	Customer	Bank	Mail Room	Cash Receipts	Accounts Receivable	General Ledger

Step	Business Activity	Internal Control
1	Mail Room opens customer mail with two clerks always present. Customer **checks** are immediately endorsed "For Deposit Only into Account XXX." **Remittance advices** are separated (one is prepared if not included in the payment).	Reduces risk of misappropriation by a single employee. Checks stamped "For Deposit Only into Account XXX" cannot be diverted. (Recordkeeping & Custody)
2	Mail Room prepares a **remittance listing** of all **checks** received during the day and forwards it with the checks to Cash Receipts.	Remittance listing provides a control total for later reconciliation. (Recordkeeping & Custody)
3	Cash Receipts prepares a **deposit slip** and deposits checks in Bank. Bank validates the **deposit slip**.	Bank provides independent evidence that the full amount was deposited. (Recordkeeping & Custody)
4	Mail Room sends **remittance advices** to Accounts Receivable for updating of customer accounts in the AR file.	Ensures that customer accounts are kept current. (Recordkeeping)
5	Mail Room also sends a copy of the **remittance listing** to General Ledger for posting of the total to the GL file.	Updating AR and GL files separately provides an additional accounting control when they are periodically reconciled. (Recordkeeping)
6	**Validated deposit slip** is returned to General Ledger to compare with **remittance listing**.	Ensures that all cash listed on the remittance listing from the Mail Room was deposited. (Recordkeeping & Custody)
7	Accounts Receivable periodically sends an **account statement** to customers showing all sales and payment activity.	Customers will complain about mistaken billings or missing payments. (Recordkeeping & Custody)

Purchases-Payables-Cash Disbursements – Responsibilities of Personnel

Responsibilities of personnel and departments in the purchases-payables-cash disbursements cycle include the following:

- **Inventory Control** provides authorization for the purchase of goods and performs an accountability function (e.g., Inventory Control is responsible for maintaining perpetual records for inventory quantities and costs).

- **Purchasing** issues purchase orders for required goods.

- **Receiving** accepts goods for approved purchases, counts and inspects the goods, and prepares the receiving report.

- **Inventory Warehouse** provides physical control over the goods.

- **Accounts Payable** (vouchers payable) assembles the proper documentation to support a payment voucher (and disbursement) and records the account payable.

- **Cash Disbursements** evaluates the documentation to support a payment voucher and signs and mails the check.

  - This department cancels the documentation to prevent duplicate payment.

- **General Ledger** maintains the accounts payable control account and other related general ledger accounts.

Study the flowchart below. Understand and visualize the purchases-payables process and controls. The flowchart begins at "Start." Read the business activity and internal control descriptions in the table on the next page as needed.

Purchases-Payables System Flowchart

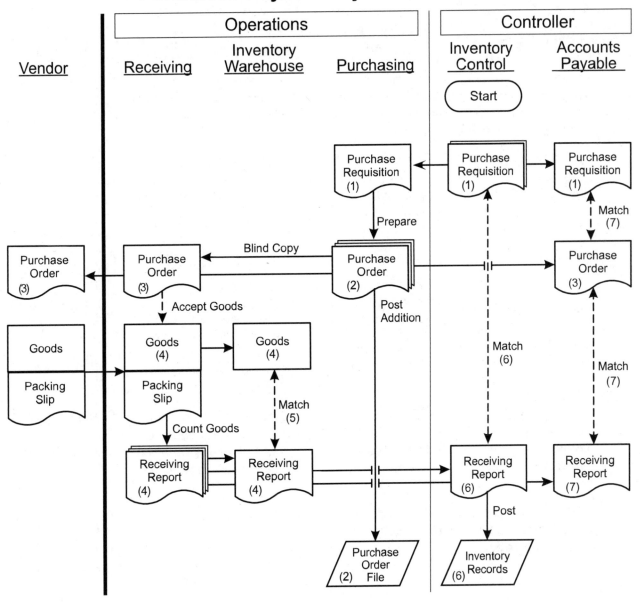

Figure 7-6

NOTE: Nothing is recorded in the general ledger for issuing a purchase order. A liability is not created until the goods and invoice are received (see the Cash Disbursements System Flowchart in Figure 7-7).

Purchases-Payables System Flowchart Table

Function	Authorization			Custody		Recording	
Department	Inventory Control	Purchasing	Vendor	Receiving	Inventory Warehouse	Accounts Payable	General Ledger

Step	Business Activity	Internal Control
1	Inventory Control prepares a **purchase requisition** when inventory reaches the reorder point due to sales and sends it to Purchasing and Accounts Payable.	Predetermined inventory levels trigger authorization to initiate a purchase transaction. (Authorization & Recordkeeping)
2	Purchasing locates the authorized vendor in the vendor file, prepares a **purchase order**, and updates the purchase order file.	• Purchasing ensures that goods are bought only from vendors who have been preapproved for reliability. (Authorization & Recordkeeping) • Reconciling sequentially numbered purchase orders helps ensure that orders are legitimate. (Authorization & Recordkeeping)
3	Purchasing sends the **purchase order** to Vendor, Receiving, and Accounts Payable. Receiving's copy has blank quantities.	• Receiving is put on notice to expect shipment. (Recordkeeping & Custody) • Accounts Payable is put on notice that liability to this vendor will increase when goods arrive. (Recordkeeping)
4	When goods arrive, Receiving accepts goods based on the file copy of the **purchase order**, prepares a **receiving report**, and forwards the **receiving report** with the goods to the Inventory Warehouse.	Because quantities are blank on Receiving's copy of the purchase order, employees must count items to prepare the receiving report. (Recordkeeping & Custody)
5	The Inventory Warehouse verifies that goods received match those listed on the **receiving report**.	Detects any loss or damage between Receiving and the Inventory Warehouse. Inventory Warehouse accepts responsibility for safeguarding receipted goods. (Recordkeeping & Custody)
6	Receiving sends the **receiving report** to Inventory Control for matching with the **purchase requisition** and updating of inventory records.	Ensures that inventory records are current. (Recordkeeping & Custody)
7	Receiving also sends a copy of the **receiving report** to Accounts Payable for matching with the **purchase order** and **purchase requisition**.	Accounts Payable ensures that all documents reconcile and will await the arrival of the vendor invoice to record the payable transaction (as shown in the Cash Disbursements System Flowchart on the next page). (Recordkeeping)

Study the flowchart below. Understand and visualize the cash disbursements process and controls. The flowchart begins at "Start." Read the business activity and internal control descriptions in the table on the next page as needed.

Cash Disbursements System Flowchart

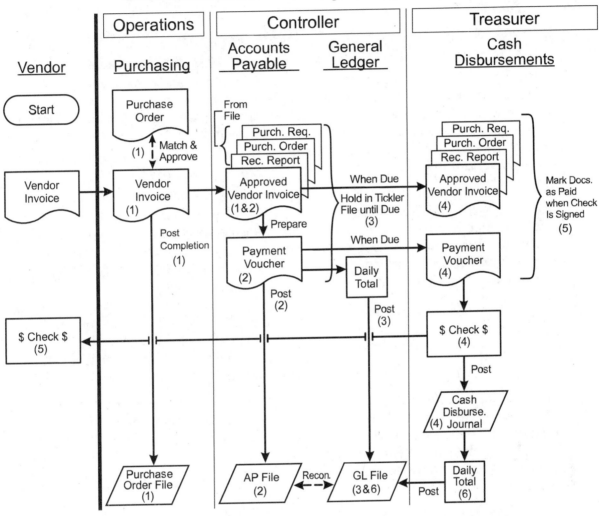

Figure 7-7

Cash Disbursements System Flowchart Table

Function	Authorization		Custody	Recording	
Department	Vendor	Purchasing	Cash Disbursements	Accounts Payable	General Ledger

Step	Business Activity	Internal Control
1	Purchasing receives a **vendor invoice**. The **vendor invoice** is matched with the **purchase order** and approved for payment. The **purchase order** is marked as closed in the purchase order file if completed, and the **approved vendor invoice** is forwarded to Accounts Payable.	• Purchasing ensures the vendor invoiced for the proper amount and the terms are as agreed. (Authorization, Recordkeeping, & Custody) • Purchasing can follow up on partially filled orders. (Recordkeeping)
2	Accounts Payable matches the **approved vendor invoice** with the file copies of the **purchase requisition, purchase order**, and **receiving report** and prepares a **payment voucher**. The **payment voucher** is recorded in the accounts payable file.	• Matching all documents provides assurance that only goods that were appropriately ordered, received, and invoiced are recorded as a liability. (Recordkeeping) • Periodic reconciliation with the payment vouchers in the tickler file (maintained by due date) with the accounts payable file (maintained by vendor) ensures proper recording. (Recordkeeping)
3	The **payment voucher**, with the attached documents, is filed in a tickler file by due date. The **daily total** of all payment vouchers is sent to the General Ledger to record the purchase (inventory) and liability (accounts payable).	Filing by due date ensures that payment will be made on a timely basis (e.g., to obtain discounts or avoid default). (Recordkeeping)
4	On the due date, the **payment voucher** and attached documents are removed from the tickler file sent to Cash Disbursements for **check** preparation, signing, and mailing. The **check** is recorded in the cash disbursements journal.	• Cash Disbursements cannot issue a check without an approved payment voucher. (Authorization, Recordkeeping, & Custody) • Large payments may require two signatures on the check to provide additional oversight. (Authorization & Custody)
5	The **payment voucher** and attached documents are stamped "Paid," and the **check** is mailed to the vendor.	Stamping the documents "Paid" prevents them from supporting a second, illicit payment voucher. (Recordkeeping & Custody)
6	The **daily total** of all checks written and mailed for the day is sent to General Ledger to record the reduction in accounts payable and cash.	Periodic reconciliation of the accounts payable and general ledger ensures proper recording. (Recordkeeping)

Other Payment Authorizations

This voucher disbursement system is applicable to virtually all required payments by the entity, not just purchases of inventory as described previously. The following are additional considerations:

- The authorizations may come from other departments based on a budget or policy (e.g., a utility bill might need authorization by the plant manager).

- Accounts Payable requires different document(s) (e.g., a utility bill with the signature of the plant manager) to support the preparation of the payment voucher and check.

- A debit other than inventory (e.g., utilities expense) is entered on the payment voucher and recorded in the general ledger. Accounts payable is still credited.

- The use of the tickler file and the functions of Cash Disbursements do not change when other types of payments are made.

Payroll – Responsibilities of Personnel

The following are the responsibilities of organizational subunits in the payroll cycle:

- **Human Resources** provides an authorized list of employees and associated pay rates, deductions, and exemptions.

- **Payroll** is an accounting function responsible for calculating the payroll (i.e., preparing the payroll register) based on authorizations from Human Resources and the authorized time records from Timekeeping.

- **Timekeeping** is an accounting function that oversees the employees' recording of hours on clock cards (using the time clock) and that receives and reconciles the job time tickets from Production.

- **Production** manufactures the products.

- **Cost Accounting** is an accounting function that accumulates direct materials, direct labor, and overhead costs on job order cost sheets to determine the costs of production.

- **Accounts Payable** prepares the payment voucher based on the payroll register prepared by Payroll.

- **Cash Disbursements** signs and deposits a check based on the payment voucher into a separate payroll account, prepares individual employee paychecks, and distributes paychecks.

- **General Ledger** records the payroll.

Study the flowchart below. Understand and visualize the payroll process and controls. The flowchart begins at "Start." Read the business activity and internal control descriptions in the table on the next page as needed.

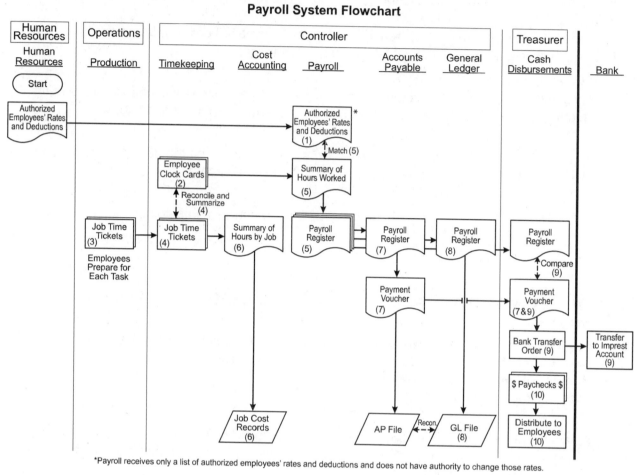

Payroll System Flowchart

*Payroll receives only a list of authorized employees' rates and deductions and does not have authority to change those rates.

Figure 7-8

Payroll System Flowchart Table

Function	Authorization		Custody		Recording				
Department	Human Resources	Production	Cash Disbursements	Bank	Timekeeping	Cost Accounting	Payroll	Accounts Payable	General Ledger

Step	Business Activity	Internal Control
1	Human Resources sends an **authorized employees' rates and deductions** list to Payroll.	Ensures that only actual employees are included on the payroll and that rates of pay and withholding amounts are accurate. (Authorization & Recordkeeping)
2	Employees record the start and end times of their workdays on **employee clock cards** held in Timekeeping.	The recording process mechanically or electronically captures employee work hours. (Recordkeeping)
3	Production employees record time worked on various tasks on **job time tickets**.	Allows accumulation of labor costs by job as well as tracking of direct and indirect labor. (Recordkeeping)
4	At the end of each day, a production supervisor approves the **job time tickets** and forwards them to Timekeeping, where they are reconciled with the **employee clock cards**.	Ensures that employees worked only authorized hours. Reconciles the time allocated to direct and indirect labor with total time worked. (Authorization & Recordkeeping)
5	Timekeeping prepares a **summary of hours worked** by employee and forwards it to Payroll. Payroll matches it with the **authorized employees' rates and deductions** list and prepares a **payroll register**.	Ensures that employees are paid the proper amount. (Recordkeeping & Custody)
6	Timekeeping prepares a **summary of hours worked by job** and forwards it to Cost Accounting for updating of the job cost records.	Ensures that direct labor costs are appropriately assigned to jobs. (Recordkeeping)
7	Accounts Payable receives the **payroll register** from Payroll, prepares a **payment voucher**, and forwards it along with the **payroll register** to Cash Disbursements.	Ensures that a payable is accrued. Authorizes the transfer of cash to the payroll imprest account. (Authorization, Recordkeeping, & Custody)
8	Payroll also forwards the **payroll register** to General Ledger for posting of the total to the GL file.	Updating AP and GL files separately provides an additional accounting control when they are periodically reconciled. (Recordkeeping)
9	Cash Disbursements compares the **payment voucher** with the **payroll register** total and initiates the bank transfer to the payroll imprest fund.	Ensures that the correct amount is transferred to the payroll imprest account (and governmental authorities). (Recordkeeping & Custody)
10	**Paychecks** are distributed to employees by the Treasurer function.	Treasurer has custody responsibility but no recording or authorization responsibility. This ensures that Payroll or supervisory personnel cannot perpetrate fraud by creating fictitious employees. (Custody)

You have completed the outline for this subunit.
Study multiple-choice questions 8 through 14 beginning on page 244.

STOP & REVIEW

7.3 MANAGEMENT CONTROLS

Roles and Responsibilities

Management

The chief executive officer (CEO) should establish the tone at the top. Organizations reflect the ethical values and control consciousness of the CEO.

The chief accounting officer also has a crucial role to play. Accounting staff have insight into activities across all levels of the organization.

Board of Directors

The entity's commitment to integrity and ethical values is reflected in the board's selections for senior management positions.

To be effective, board members should be capable of objective judgment, have knowledge of the organization's industry, and be willing to ask relevant questions about management's decisions.

Important subcommittees of the board in organizations of sufficient size and complexity include the audit committee, the compensation committee, the finance committee, and the risk committee.

Internal Auditors

Management is ultimately responsible for the design and function of the system of internal controls. However, an organization's internal audit function may play an important consulting and advisory role.

The internal audit function also evaluates the soundness of the system of internal control by performing systematic reviews according to professional standards.

To remain independent in the conduct of these reviews, the internal audit function cannot be responsible for selecting and executing controls.

Other Personnel

Everyone in the entity must be involved in internal control and is expected to perform his or her appropriate control activities.

In addition, all employees should understand that they are expected to inform those higher in the entity of instances of poor control when controls are not functioning as intended.

Organization

Organization, as a means of control, is an approved intentional structuring of roles assigned to people within the organization so that it can achieve its objectives efficiently and economically.

- Responsibilities should be divided so that no one person will control all phases of any transaction (this is discussed in further detail in Subunit 7.2).

- Managers should have the authority to take the action necessary to discharge their responsibilities.

- Individual responsibility always should be clearly defined so that it can be neither sidestepped nor exceeded.

- An official who assigns responsibility and delegates authority to subordinates should have an effective system of follow-up. Its purpose is to ensure that tasks assigned are properly carried out.

- The individuals to whom authority is delegated should be allowed to exercise that authority without close supervision. But they should check with their superiors in case of exceptions.

- People should be required to account to their superiors for the manner in which they have discharged their responsibilities.

- The organization should be flexible enough to permit changes in its structure when operating plans, policies, and objectives change.

- Organizational structures should be as simple as possible.

- Organization charts and manuals should be prepared. They help plan and control changes in, as well as provide better understanding of, the organization, chain of authority, and assignment of responsibilities.

Policies

A policy is any stated principle that requires, guides, or restricts action. Policies should follow certain principles.

- Policies should be clearly stated in writing in systematically organized handbooks, manuals, or other publications and should be properly approved. But when the organizational culture is strong, the need for formal, written policies is reduced. In a strong culture, substantial training results in a high degree of acceptance of the organization's key values. Thus, such values are intensely held and widely shared.

- Policies should be systematically communicated to all officials and appropriate employees of the organization.

- Policies must conform with applicable laws and regulations. They should be consistent with objectives and general policies prescribed at higher levels.

- Policies should be designed to promote the conduct of authorized activities in an effective, efficient, and economical manner. They should provide a satisfactory degree of assurance that resources are suitably safeguarded.

- Policies should be periodically reviewed. They should be revised when circumstances change.

Procedures

Procedures are methods employed to carry out activities in conformity with prescribed policies. The same principles applicable to policies also are applicable to procedures. In addition,

- To reduce the possibility of fraud and error, procedures should be coordinated so that one employee's work is automatically checked by another who is independently performing separate prescribed duties. The extent to which automatic internal checks should be built into the system of control depends on many factors. Examples are (1) degree of risk, (2) cost of preventive procedures, (3) availability of personnel, (4) operational impact, and (5) feasibility.

- For nonmechanical operations, prescribed procedures should not be so detailed as to stifle the use of judgment.

- To promote maximum efficiency and economy, prescribed procedures should be as simple and as inexpensive as possible.

- Procedures should not be overlapping, conflicting, or duplicative.

- Procedures should be periodically reviewed and improved as necessary.

Personnel

People hired or assigned should have the qualifications to do the jobs assigned to them. The best form of control over the performance of individuals is supervision. Hence, high standards of supervision should be established. The following practices help improve control:

- New employees should be investigated as to honesty and reliability.

- Employees should be given training that provides the opportunity for improvement and keeps them informed of new policies and procedures.

- Employees should be given information on the duties and responsibilities of other segments of the organization. They will better understand how and where their jobs fit into the organization as a whole.

- The performance of all employees should be periodically reviewed to see whether all essential requirements of their jobs are being met. Superior performance should be given appropriate recognition. Shortcomings should be discussed with employees so that they are given an opportunity to improve their performance or upgrade their skills.

Accounting

Accounting is the indispensable means of financial control over activities and resources. It is a framework that can be fitted to assignments of responsibility. Moreover, it is the financial scorekeeper of the organization. The problem lies in what scores to keep. Some basic principles for accounting systems follow:

- Accounting should fit the needs of managers for rational decision making rather than the dictates of a textbook or check list.

- Accounting should be based on lines of responsibility.

- Financial reports of operating results should parallel the organizational units responsible for carrying out operations.

- Accounting should permit controllable costs to be identified.

Budgeting

A budget is a statement of expected results expressed in numerical terms. As a control, it sets a standard for input of resources and what should be achieved as output and outcomes.

- Those who are responsible for meeting a budget should participate in its preparation.

- Those responsible for meeting a budget should be provided with adequate information that compares budgets with actual events and shows reasons for any significant variances.
    - Management should ensure it receives prompt feedback on performance variances.

- All subsidiary budgets should tie into the overall budget.

- Budgets should set measurable objectives. Budgets are meaningless unless managers know why they have a budget.

- Budgets should help sharpen the organizational structure. Objective budgeting standards are difficult to set in a confused combination of subsystems. Budgeting is therefore a form of discipline and coordination.

Reporting

In most organizations, management functions and makes decisions on the basis of reports it receives. Thus, reports should be timely, accurate, meaningful, and economical. The following are some principles for establishing a satisfactory internal reporting system:

- Reports should be made in accordance with assigned responsibilities.

- Individuals or units should be required to report only on those matters for which they are responsible.

- The cost of accumulating data and preparing reports should be weighed against the benefits to be obtained from them.

- Reports should be as simple as possible and consistent with the nature of the subject matter. They should include only information that serves the needs of the readers. Common classifications and terminology should be used as much as possible to avoid confusion.

- When appropriate, performance reports should show comparisons with predetermined standards of cost, quality, and quantity. Controllable costs should be segregated.

- When performance cannot be reported in quantitative terms, the reports should be designed to emphasize exceptions or other matters requiring management attention.

- For maximum value, reports should be timely. Timely reports based partly on estimates may be more useful than delayed reports that are more precise.

- Report recipients should be polled periodically to see whether they still need the reports they are receiving or whether the reports could be improved.

Examples of Management Controls

The following charts present examples of some management controls, their objectives, the related assertions, and the reasons for implementing the controls.

Production	
Objective	**Control(s)**
Only quality materials are used in production.	Require materials specifications for all purchases. (Recordkeeping)

WHY?

Materials specifications minimize defects in finished goods.

Identify the cause of defects in finished goods inventory.	Timely follow-up on all unfavorable usage variances. (Recordkeeping)

WHY?

Follow-up on unfavorable usage variances may lead to detection and correction of the use of substandard materials.

Detect production problems and excessive costs and inventories.	Compare actual production with management forecasts. (Recordkeeping)

WHY?

Comparing actual costs with budgeted costs detects unfavorable cost variances and production problems.

Debt and Equity Instruments

Objective	Control(s)
Safeguard debt and equity instruments from unauthorized use (e.g., pledge as security for personal financing).	Segregation of responsibility for custody of assets and recording of transactions. (Recordkeeping & Custody)

WHY?

One individual with no accounting responsibilities or power to authorize transactions should have custody of liquid assets.

Objective	Control(s)
The proper execution of debt and equity transactions in accordance with management's wishes.	Written policies requiring review of major funding or repayment proposals by the board. (Authorization & Custody)

WHY?

When a decision affects the capitalization of the entity, a policy should require review at the highest level.

Cash

Objective	Control(s)
Identify cash receipts recorded in the general ledger but not deposited.	Bank reconciliations performed by a third party. (Recordkeeping)

WHY?

A bank reconciliation compares the bank statement with the organization's records and resolves differences caused by deposits in transit, outstanding checks, NSF checks, bank charges, errors, etc. An independent third party should prepare bank reconciliations to detect unexplained discrepancies between recorded deposits and the bank statements.

Inventory	
Objective	**Control(s)**
Physically protect assets such as tools, equipment, and vehicles from unauthorized access.	Place tools, equipment, and vehicles in a secured area; install a keycard access system for all employees; and record each keycard access transaction on a report for the production superintendent. (Authorization, Recordkeeping, & Custody)

WHY?

Tools, equipment, and vehicles should be secured from theft using physical controls.

Safeguard tools, equipment, and vehicles from unauthorized use.	Tools, equipment, and vehicles inventory should be in the custody of inventory staging supervisors. Special requisitions should be required to issue tools, equipment, and vehicles to assist with recording the amount of tools removed from the inventory. (Authorization, Recordkeeping, & Custody)

WHY?

Assigning functional responsibility for custody of assets to one individual with no ability to authorize transactions or record them establishes accountability. Requiring that requisitions be submitted by appropriate persons is a control to ensure that their use is properly authorized. Moreover, items requisitioned should be consistent with the items typically used in the process performed.

Items ordered are received by authorized locations.	The receiving function verifies that the items received are those actually sent by the shipper. (Recordkeeping & Custody)

WHY?

Without verification of the receiving function, items could be lost, stolen, or sent to the wrong recipients.

Confirm that inventory items (including financial instruments) listed on inventory reports actually exist.	Physical inventories should be periodically reconciled with accounting records. (Recordkeeping & Custody)

WHY?

Auditors should make test counts of inventory.

-- Continued on next page --

Inventory (Continued)	
Objective	**Control(s)**
Reduce risks associated with disposal of obsolete and scrap materials.	Require managerial approval for materials to be declared scrap or obsolete. A commission is paid to the individual or organization assisting with selling obsolete or scrap materials. (Authorization, Recordkeeping, & Custody)

WHY?

Management approval of disposal reduces the risk of misappropriation of materials. Specifying that a commission be paid to the individual or organization assisting with selling the materials is an incentive to maximize the organization's return.

Ensure prompt delivery of out-of-stock items.	Match the back order file with goods received daily. (Recordkeeping)

WHY?

Matching back orders with daily receipts determines whether out-of-stock items are promptly replaced and identifies goods received that require immediate deliveries to customers.

Maintain adequate inventory quantities.	Increase inventory levels. Implement electronic data interchange (EDI) with suppliers. Reconcile the sum of filled and back orders with the total of all orders placed daily. (Recordkeeping & Custody)

WHY?

Determining appropriate inventory levels and economic order quantities, expediting deliveries by using EDI, and reconciling orders with filled and back orders minimize stockouts.

Safeguard raw materials.	Only storeroom personnel have custody of raw materials. (Custody)

WHY?

Access to raw materials should only be given to personnel responsible for the custody of assets, not to individuals responsible for execution functions, such as a production line supervisor.

-- Continued on next page --

Inventory (Continued)

Objective	Control(s)
Data entry is accurate and complete.	Inventory reconciliations of material requisitions and material receipts are performed daily. (Recordkeeping & Custody)

WHY?

The parts requested should be consistent with the parts used in the maintenance activities. Unexplained variances should be investigated.

Sales Invoices

Objective	Control(s)
Sales invoice amounts are properly reflected in accounting ledgers.	Generate a control total (total monetary amount of all sales invoices) and compare it with the total amount posted to the individual accounts. (Recordkeeping)

WHY?

Total monetary amounts listed on sales invoices should match the total amount posted to the general ledger and accounts receivable subsidiary ledger. Discrepancies should be investigated and resolved.

Compensation Programs

Objective	Control(s)
Long-term administration of a compensation program.	Job classifications based on predefined evaluation criteria. (Recordkeeping)

WHY?

Job classifications and grades are established during the job analysis phase, and the general level of compensation in the community and in the industry must be determined. Compensation is then fixed based on the job classifications, usually within a range for each grade. A range is necessary to allow for flexibility.

Insurance	
Objective	**Control(s)**
Prevent overcharging by service providers.	Develop a program that identifies services performed in excess of expectations for particular age categories, duplicate or equivalent services performed recently, and claims exceeding the average cost per claim. (Authorization & Recordkeeping)

WHY?

Unusual claims should be identified and followed up to determine whether they are legitimate. This control is a reasonableness test, a type of IT input control.

Effective administration of the insurance function.	Receipt of billings and the disbursement of payments should be segregated. Final settlements are negotiated after claims are submitted. (Recordkeeping & Custody)

WHY?

The maximum probable compensable loss that the insurer must pay should be assessed and reported. Adjustment for inflation alone is not sufficient to determine the degree of risk that should be insured.

Insurance coverage is adequate.	Policy coverage should be systematically evaluated each year (periodic appraisals). Safeguarding assets includes insuring them. The types and amounts of insurance should be supported by periodic appraisals. (Authorization & Recordkeeping)

WHY?

Policy coverage should be systematically evaluated each year. Coverage is a function of risk and the probability and amount of loss. They should be assessed to determine what insurance coverage is adequate. Adjustment for inflation alone is not sufficient.

Insurance carrier has the means to pay claims.	The financial resources of the carrier should be evaluated to determine whether the insurance carrier has the resources to pay claims. (Authorization & Recordkeeping)

WHY?

The ability of the insurance carrier to pay claims may necessitate a change in the insurance carrier.

You have completed the outline for this subunit.
Study multiple-choice questions 15 through 20 beginning on page 247.

STOP & REVIEW

QUESTIONS

7.1 Flowcharts and Process Mapping

1. An auditor's flowchart of a client's accounting system is a diagrammatic representation that depicts the auditor's

A. Assessment of the risks of material misstatement.

B. Identification of weaknesses in the system.

C. Assessment of the control environment's effectiveness.

D. Understanding of the system.

Answer (D) is correct.
REQUIRED: The purpose of an auditor's flowchart.
DISCUSSION: The auditor should document (1) the understanding of the entity and its environment and the components of internal control, (2) the sources of information regarding the understanding, and (3) the risk assessment procedures performed. The form and extent of this documentation are influenced by the nature and complexity of the entity's controls. For example, documentation of the understanding of internal control of a complex information system in which many transactions are electronically initiated, authorized, recorded, processed, or reported may include questionnaires, flowcharts, or decision tables.
Answer (A) is incorrect. The conclusions about the assessments of the risks of material misstatements should be documented. These are professional judgments of the auditor documented in the workpapers.
Answer (B) is incorrect. The flowchart is a tool to document the auditor's understanding of internal control, but it does not specifically identify weaknesses in the system. **Answer (C) is incorrect.** The auditor's judgment is the ultimate basis for concluding that controls are effective.

2. Of the following, which is the most efficient source for an auditor to use to evaluate a company's overall control system?

A. Control flowcharts.

B. Copies of standard operating procedures.

C. A narrative describing departmental history, activities, and forms usage.

D. Copies of industry operating standards.

Answer (A) is correct.
REQUIRED: The most efficient source for an auditor to use to evaluate a company's overall control system.
DISCUSSION: Control flowcharting is a graphical means of representing the sequencing of activities and information flows with related control points. It provides an efficient and comprehensive method of describing relatively complex activities, especially those involving several departments.
Answer (B) is incorrect. Copies of procedures and related forms do not provide an efficient overview of processing activities. **Answer (C) is incorrect.** A narrative review covering the history and forms usage of the department is not as efficient as flowcharting for the purpose of communicating relevant information about controls. **Answer (D) is incorrect.** Industry standards do not provide a picture of existing practice for subsequent audit activity.

Questions 3 and 4 are based on the following information.

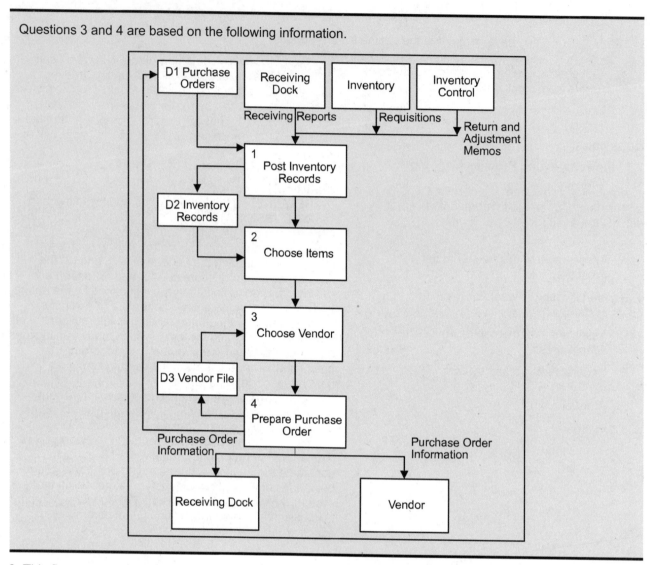

3. This figure shows how

    A. Physical media are used in the system.

    B. Input/output procedures are conducted.

    C. Data flow within and out of the system.

    D. Accountability is allocated in the system.

Answer (C) is correct.
    REQUIRED: The nature of the figure.
    DISCUSSION: A data flow diagram shows how data flow to, from, and within a system and the processes that manipulate the data.
    Answer (A) is incorrect. The figure does not show physical media or input/output procedures (manifestations of how the system works rather than what it accomplishes). Flowcharts depict these matters. **Answer (B) is incorrect.** The figure is a data flow diagram; it depicts the flow of data within and out of the system. Flowcharts show how input/output procedures are conducted. **Answer (D) is incorrect.** The figure does not show how accountability is allocated in the system. Accountability transfers are usually shown in flowcharts.

4. This data flow diagram could be expanded to show the

   A. Edit checks used in preparing purchase orders from stock records.

   B. Details of the preparation of purchase orders.

   C. Physical media used for stock records, the vendor file, and purchase orders.

   D. Workstations required in a distributed system for preparing purchase orders.

Answer (B) is correct.
   REQUIRED: The result that can be achieved by expanding the figure.
   DISCUSSION: A data flow diagram can be used to depict lower-level details as well as higher-level processes. A system can be divided into subsystems, and each subsystem can be further subdivided at levels of increasing detail. Thus, any process can be expanded as many times as necessary to show the required level of detail.
   Answer (A) is incorrect. A data flow diagram does not depict edit checks. **Answer (C) is incorrect.** Flowcharts, not data flow diagrams, show the physical media on which data such as stock records, the vendor file, and purchase orders are maintained. **Answer (D) is incorrect.** Flowcharts, not data flow diagrams, show the workstations through which data pass and the sequence of activities.

5. Which of the following tools would best give a graphical representation of a sequence of activities and decisions?

   A. Flowchart.

   B. Control chart.

   C. Histogram.

   D. Run chart.

Answer (A) is correct.
   REQUIRED: The best tool for a graphical representation of a sequence of activities and decisions.
   DISCUSSION: Flowcharting is an essential aid in the program development process that involves a sequence of activities and decisions. A flowchart is a pictorial diagram of the definition, analysis, or solution of a problem in which symbols are used to represent operations, data flow, equipment, etc.
   Answer (B) is incorrect. A control chart is used to monitor deviations from desired quality measurements during repetitive operations. **Answer (C) is incorrect.** A histogram is a bar chart showing conformance to a standard bell curve. **Answer (D) is incorrect.** A run chart tracks the frequency or amount of a given variable over time.

6. The diamond-shaped symbol is commonly used in flowcharting to show or represent a

   A. Process or a single step in a procedure or program.

   B. Terminal output display.

   C. Decision point, conditional testing, or branching.

   D. Predefined process.

Answer (C) is correct.
   REQUIRED: The meaning of the diamond-shaped symbol used in flowcharting.
   DISCUSSION: Flowcharts illustrate in pictorial fashion the flow of data, documents, and/or operations in a system. Flowcharts may summarize a system or present great detail, e.g., as found in program flowcharts. The diamond-shaped symbol represents a decision point or test of a condition in a program flowchart, that is, the point at which a determination must be made as to which logic path (branch) to follow.
   Answer (A) is incorrect. The rectangle is the appropriate symbol for a process or a single step in a procedure or program. **Answer (B) is incorrect.** A terminal display is signified by a symbol similar to the shape of a cathode ray tube. **Answer (D) is incorrect.** A predefined processing step is represented by a rectangle with double lines on either side.

7. When documenting internal control, the independent auditor sometimes uses a systems flowchart, which can best be described as a

- A. Pictorial presentation of the flow of instructions in a client's internal computer system.
- B. Diagram that clearly indicates an organization's internal reporting structure.
- C. Graphic illustration of the flow of operations that is used to replace the auditor's internal control questionnaire.
- D. Symbolic representation of a system or series of sequential processes.

Answer (D) is correct.
   REQUIRED: The best description of a systems flowchart.
   DISCUSSION: A systems flowchart is a symbolic representation of the flow of documents and procedures through a series of steps in the accounting process of the client's organization.
   Answer (A) is incorrect. A pictorial presentation of the flow of instructions in a client's internal computer system is a computer program flowchart. **Answer (B) is incorrect.** The organizational chart depicts the client's internal reporting structure. **Answer (C) is incorrect.** A flowchart does not necessarily replace the auditor's internal control questionnaire. Controls beyond those depicted on the systems flowchart must also be considered by the auditor, and information obtained from the questionnaire may be used to develop the flowchart.

7.2 Accounting Cycles and Associated Controls

8. An adequate system of internal controls is most likely to detect a fraud perpetrated by a

- A. Group of employees in collusion.
- B. Single employee.
- C. Group of managers in collusion.
- D. Single manager.

Answer (B) is correct.
   REQUIRED: The fraud most likely to be detected by an adequate system of internal controls.
   DISCUSSION: Segregation of duties and other control processes serve to prevent or detect a fraud committed by an employee acting alone. One employee may not have the ability to engage in wrongdoing or may be subject to detection by other employees in the course of performing their assigned duties. However, collusion may circumvent controls. For example, comparison of recorded accountability for assets with the assets known to be held may fail to detect fraud if persons having custody of assets collude with recordkeepers.
   Answer (A) is incorrect. A group has a better chance of successfully perpetrating a fraud than does an individual employee. **Answer (C) is incorrect.** Management can override controls. **Answer (D) is incorrect.** Even a single manager may be able to override controls.

9. Internal control should follow certain basic principles to achieve its objectives. One of these principles is the segregation of functions. Which one of the following examples does **not** violate the principle of segregation of functions?

A. The chief financial officer has the authority to sign checks but gives the signature block to the assistant chief financial officer to run the check-signing machine.

B. The warehouse clerk, who has the custodial responsibility over inventory in the warehouse, may authorize disposal of damaged goods.

C. The sales manager has the responsibility to approve credit and the authority to write off accounts.

D. The department time clerk is given the undistributed payroll checks to mail to absent employees.

Answer (A) is correct.
    REQUIRED: The situation that does not violate the principle of segregation of functions.
    DISCUSSION: The chief financial officer's department should have custody of assets but should not authorize or record transactions. Because the assistant chief financial officer reports to the chief financial officer, the chief financial officer is merely delegating an assigned duty related to asset custody.
    Answer (B) is incorrect. Authorization to dispose of damaged goods could be used to cover thefts of inventory for which the warehouse clerk has custodial responsibility. Transaction authorization is inconsistent with asset custody. **Answer (C) is incorrect.** The sales manager could approve credit to a controlled organization and then write off the account as a bad debt. The sales manager's authorization of credit is inconsistent with his or her indirect access to assets. **Answer (D) is incorrect.** The time clerk could conceal the termination of an employee and retain that employee's paycheck. Recordkeeping is inconsistent with asset custody.

10. Which of the following describes the most effective preventive control to ensure proper handling of cash receipt transactions?

A. Have bank reconciliations prepared by an employee not involved with cash collections and then have them reviewed by a supervisor.

B. One employee issues a prenumbered receipt for all cash collections; another employee reconciles the daily total of prenumbered receipts to the bank deposits.

C. Use predetermined totals (hash totals) of cash receipts to control posting routines.

D. The employee who receives customer mail receipts prepares the daily bank deposit, which is then deposited by another employee.

Answer (B) is correct.
    REQUIRED: The most effective preventive control to ensure proper handling of cash receipt transactions.
    DISCUSSION: Sequentially numbered receipts should be issued to maintain accountability for cash collected. Such accountability should be established as soon as possible because cash has a high inherent risk. Daily cash receipts should be deposited intact so that receipts and bank deposits can be reconciled. The reconciliation should be performed by someone independent of the cash custody function.
    Answer (A) is incorrect. The bank reconciliation is a detective, not a preventive, control. **Answer (C) is incorrect.** Use of hash totals is a control over the completeness of posting routines, not cash receipts. **Answer (D) is incorrect.** A cash remittance list should be prepared before a separate employee prepares the bank deposit. The list and deposit represent separate records based on independent counts made by different employees.

11. Which of the following activities performed by a payroll clerk is a control weakness rather than a control strength?

A. Has custody of the check signature stamp machine.

B. Prepares the payroll register.

C. Forwards the payroll register to the chief accountant for approval.

D. Draws the paychecks on a separate payroll checking account.

Answer (A) is correct.
   REQUIRED: The activity by a payroll clerk that is a control weakness.
   DISCUSSION: Payroll checks should be signed by someone who is not involved in timekeeping, recordkeeping, or payroll preparation. The payroll clerk performs a recordkeeping function.
   Answer (B) is incorrect. Preparing the payroll register is one of the recordkeeping tasks of the payroll clerk. **Answer (C) is incorrect.** The payroll register should be approved by an officer of the organization. This control is a strength. **Answer (D) is incorrect.** Paychecks should be drawn on a separate payroll checking account. This control is a strength.

12. One payroll engagement objective is to determine whether segregation of duties is proper. Which of the following activities is incompatible?

A. Hiring employees and authorizing changes in pay rates.

B. Preparing the payroll and filing payroll tax forms.

C. Signing and distributing payroll checks.

D. Preparing attendance data and preparing the payroll.

Answer (D) is correct.
   REQUIRED: The two activities that are incompatible.
   DISCUSSION: Attendance data are accumulated by the timekeeping function. Preparing the payroll is a payroll department function. For control purposes, these two functions should be separated to avoid the perpetration and concealment of irregularities.
   Answer (A) is incorrect. Hiring employees and authorizing changes in pay rates are both personnel functions. **Answer (B) is incorrect.** Preparing the payroll and filing payroll tax forms are both functions of the payroll department. **Answer (C) is incorrect.** Proper treasury functions include signing and distributing payroll checks.

13. Which of the following observations made during the preliminary survey of a local department store's disbursement cycle reflects a control strength?

A. Individual department managers use prenumbered forms to order merchandise from vendors.

B. The receiving department is given a copy of the purchase order complete with a description of goods, quantity ordered, and extended price for all merchandise ordered.

C. The chief financial officer's office prepares checks for suppliers based on vouchers prepared by the accounts payable department.

D. Individual department managers are responsible for the movement of merchandise from the receiving dock to storage or sales areas as appropriate.

Answer (C) is correct.
   REQUIRED: The observation about the disbursement cycle indicating a control strength.
   DISCUSSION: Accounting for payables is a recording function. The matching of the supplier's invoice, the purchase order, and the receiving report (and usually the purchase requisition) should be the responsibility of the accounting department. These are the primary supporting documents for the payment voucher prepared by the accounts payable section that will be relied upon by the chief financial officer in making payment.
   Answer (A) is incorrect. The managers should submit purchase requisitions to the purchasing department. The purchasing function should be separate from operations. **Answer (B) is incorrect.** To encourage a fair count, the receiving department should receive a copy of the purchase order from which the quantity has been omitted. **Answer (D) is incorrect.** The receiving department should transfer goods directly to the storeroom to maintain security. A copy of the receiving report should be sent to the storeroom so that the amount stored can be compared with the amount in the report.

14. Which one of the following situations represents an internal control weakness in the payroll department?

A. Payroll department personnel are rotated in their duties.

B. Paychecks are distributed by the employees' immediate supervisor.

C. Payroll records are reconciled with quarterly tax reports.

D. The timekeeping function is independent of the payroll department.

Answer (B) is correct.
    REQUIRED: The internal control weakness in the payroll department.
    DISCUSSION: Paychecks should not be distributed by supervisors because an unscrupulous person could terminate an employee and fail to report the termination. The supervisor could then clock in and out for the employee and keep the paycheck. A person unrelated to either payroll recordkeeping or the operating department should distribute checks.
    Answer (A) is incorrect. Periodic rotation of payroll personnel inhibits the perpetration and concealment of fraud. **Answer (C) is incorrect.** This analytical procedure may detect a discrepancy. **Answer (D) is incorrect.** Timekeeping should be independent of asset custody and employee records.

7.3 Management Controls

15. The most appropriate method to prevent fraud or theft during the frequent movement of trailers loaded with valuable metal scrap from the manufacturing plant to the organization's scrap yard about 10 miles away would be to

A. Perform complete physical inventory of the scrap trailers before leaving the plant and upon arrival at the scrap yard.

B. Require existing security guards to log the time of plant departure and scrap yard arrival. The elapsed time should be reviewed by a supervisor for fraud.

C. Use armed guards to escort the movement of the trailers from the plant to the scrap yard.

D. Contract with an independent hauler for the removal of scrap.

Answer (B) is correct.
    REQUIRED: The most appropriate method to prevent fraud or theft during the frequent movement of trailers loaded with valuable metal scrap.
    DISCUSSION: The cost of internal control must not be greater than its benefits. Logging the times of departure and arrival, and reviewing the elapsed time for material variances from the expected travel time, are cost-effective controls to prevent and detect fraud or theft during the movement of the scrap.
    Answer (A) is incorrect. The cost of internal control must not be greater than its benefits. The cost of performing a complete physical inventory of scrap at both locations would likely exceed its benefits. **Answer (C) is incorrect.** Hiring armed guards to escort the scrap trailers is unlikely to be cost-effective unless the scrap is extremely valuable. Logging departures and arrivals will be sufficient in most cases. **Answer (D) is incorrect.** Using an independent hauler would provide no additional assurance of prevention or detection of wrongdoing.

16. Which of the following would minimize defects in finished goods caused by poor quality raw materials?

A. Documented procedures for the proper handling of work-in-process inventory.

B. Required material specifications for all purchases.

C. Timely follow-up on all unfavorable usage variances.

D. Determination of the amount of spoilage at the end of the manufacturing process.

Answer (B) is correct.
    REQUIRED: The action to minimize defects in finished goods caused by poor quality materials.
    DISCUSSION: A preventive control is required in this situation, i.e., one that ensures an unwanted event does not take place. The most cost-effective way of achieving the goal is to keep poor quality raw materials from entering the warehouse to begin with. Of the controls listed, only required specifications will accomplish this.
    Answer (A) is incorrect. Documented procedures for handling work-in-process inventory do not ensure that materials are of sufficient quality. **Answer (C) is incorrect.** Follow-up on unfavorable usage variances may lead to detection and correction of use of substandard materials but does not prevent or minimize defects in products already processed. **Answer (D) is incorrect.** Determination of spoilage after raw materials have been used in production is not a preventive control.

17. An internal auditor notes year-to-year increases for small tool expense at a manufacturing facility that has produced the same amount of identical product for the last 3 years. Production inventory is kept in a controlled staging area adjacent to the receiving dock, but the supply of small tools is kept in an unsupervised area near the exit to the plant employees' parking lot. After determining that all of the following alternatives are equal in cost and are also feasible for local management, the internal auditor would best address the security issue by recommending that plant management

A. Move the small tools inventory to the custody of the production inventory staging superintendent and implement the use of a special requisition to issue small tools.

B. Initiate a full physical inventory of small tools on a monthly basis.

C. Place supply of small tools in a secured area, install a key-access card system for all employees, and record each key-access transaction on a report for the production superintendent.

D. Close the exit to the employee parking lot and require all plant employees to use a doorway by the receiving dock that also provides access to the plant employees' parking area.

Answer (A) is correct.
    REQUIRED: The best preventive control to reduce the risk of loss of small tools.
    DISCUSSION: Minimizing the loss of assets requires a preventive control. Giving responsibility for custody of small tools to one individual establishes accountability. Requiring that requisitions be submitted ensures that their use is properly authorized.
    Answer (B) is incorrect. A full physical inventory of small tools on a monthly basis is a periodic, detective control that is effective only in determining the amount of losses. **Answer (C) is incorrect.** Placing small tools in a secured area, installing a key-access system, and recording access transactions are preventive and detective controls but do not record the amount of tools removed from the inventory. **Answer (D) is incorrect.** Closing the exit to the employee parking lot does not limit access to the small tools inventory.

18. A utility with a large investment in repair vehicles would most likely implement which internal control to reduce the risk of vehicle theft or loss?

A. Review insurance coverage for adequacy.

B. Systematically account for all repair work orders.

C. Physically inventory vehicles and reconcile the results with the accounting records.

D. Maintain vehicles in a secured location with release and return subject to approval by a custodian.

Answer (D) is correct.
    REQUIRED: The internal control to reduce the risk of vehicle theft or loss.
    DISCUSSION: Physical safeguarding of assets is enacted through the use of preventive controls that reduce the likelihood of theft or other loss. Keeping the vehicles at a secure location and restricting access establishes accountability by the custodian and allows for proper authorization of their use.
    Answer (A) is incorrect. Insurance provides for indemnification if loss or theft occurs. It thus reduces financial exposure but does not prevent the actual loss or theft. **Answer (B) is incorrect.** An internal control designed to ensure control over repair work performed has no bearing on the risk of loss. **Answer (C) is incorrect.** Taking an inventory is a detective, not a preventive, control.

19. Obsolete or scrap materials are charged to a predefined project number. The materials are segregated into specified bin locations and eventually transported to a public auction for sale. To reduce the risks associated with this process, an organization should employ which of the following procedures?

1. Require managerial approval for materials to be declared scrap or obsolete.

2. Permit employees to purchase obsolete or scrap materials prior to auction.

3. Limit obsolete or scrap materials sales to a pre-approved buyer.

4. Specify that a fixed fee, rather than a commission, be paid to the auction firm.

   A. 2 and 3.

   B. 1 only.

   C. 2 and 4.

   D. 1, 3, and 4.

Answer (B) is correct.
   REQUIRED: The means of reducing risks associated with disposal of obsolete and scrap materials.
   DISCUSSION: A preventive control is needed. Management approval for materials to be declared scrap or obsolete reduces the risk of misappropriation. Otherwise, materials may be more easily misclassified.
   Answer (A) is incorrect. Permitting employees to purchase obsolete or scrap materials prior to auction provides even more incentive for misappropriation. Limiting obsolete or scrap materials sales to a pre-approved buyer does not mitigate the risk of misappropriation before the materials are sold. Moreover, these procedures may be less effective than an auction for obtaining the best price. **Answer (C) is incorrect.** Permitting employees to purchase obsolete or scrap materials prior to auction provides even more incentive for misappropriation. Specifying that a commission be paid to the auction firm creates an incentive to maximize the organization's return. **Answer (D) is incorrect.** Limiting obsolete or scrap materials sales to a pre-approved buyer does not mitigate the risk of misappropriation before the materials are sold. It also may be less effective than an auction for obtaining the best price. Specifying that a commission be paid to the auction firm creates an incentive to maximize the organization's return.

20. A system of internal control includes physical controls over access to and use of assets and records. A departure from the purpose of such procedures is that

   A. Access to the safe-deposit box requires two officers.

   B. Only storeroom personnel and line supervisors have access to the raw materials storeroom.

   C. The mailroom compiles a list of the checks received in the incoming mail.

   D. Only salespersons and sales supervisors use sales department vehicles.

Answer (B) is correct.
   REQUIRED: The departure from the purpose of control activities that limit access to assets.
   DISCUSSION: Storeroom personnel have custody of assets, and supervisors are in charge of execution functions. To give supervisors access to the raw materials storeroom is a violation of the essential internal control principle of segregation of functions.
   Answer (A) is incorrect. It is appropriate for two officers to be required to open the safe-deposit box. One supervises the other. **Answer (C) is incorrect.** The mailroom typically compiles a prelisting of cash. The list is sent to the accountant as a control for actual cash sent to the cashier. **Answer (D) is incorrect.** Use of sales department vehicles by only sales personnel is appropriate.

GLEIM

GO TO ONLINE COURSE

Access the **Gleim CIA Premium Review System** featuring our SmartAdapt technology from your Gleim Personal Classroom to continue your studies. You will experience a personalized study environment with exam-emulating multiple-choice questions.

STUDY UNIT EIGHT

FRAUD RISKS AND CONTROLS

(21 pages of outline)

This study unit covers **Domain VI: Fraud Risks** from The IIA's CIA Exam Syllabus. This domain makes up 10% of Part 1 of the CIA exam and is tested at the **basic** and **proficient** cognitive levels.

The **learning objectives** of Study Unit 8 are

- Interpret fraud risks and types of frauds and determine whether fraud risks require special consideration when conducting an engagement

- Evaluate the potential for occurrence of fraud (red flags, etc.) and how the organization detects and manages fraud risks

- Recommend controls to prevent and detect fraud and education to improve the organization's fraud awareness

- Recognize techniques and internal audit roles related to forensic auditing (interview, investigation, testing, etc.)

Study Unit 8 covers managing fraud risks through internal controls and the internal audit function. Management is responsible for establishing and maintaining internal control. Thus, management also is responsible for the fraud prevention program. Internal auditors must have sufficient knowledge to evaluate the risk of fraud and the manner in which it is managed by the organization. An internal auditor's responsibilities for the detection of fraud include

- Having sufficient knowledge to identify indicators that fraud may have been committed,

- Being alert to opportunities that could allow fraud (e.g., control weaknesses), and

- Being able to evaluate the indicators of fraud sufficiently to determine whether a fraud investigation should be conducted.

8.1 FRAUD -- RISKS AND TYPES

Fraud and Fraud Risk

Fraud is "any illegal act characterized by deceit, concealment, or violation of trust. These acts are not dependent upon the threat of violence or physical force. Frauds are perpetrated by parties and organizations to obtain money, property, or services; to avoid payment or loss of services; or to secure personal or business advantage."

Fraud risk is the possibility that fraud will occur and the potential effects to the organization when it occurs.

Characteristics of Fraud

Fraud is an intentional deception or misrepresentation. The three conditions ordinarily present when fraud exists include **pressure (incentive)** to commit fraud, an **opportunity**, and the capacity to **rationalize** misconduct.

1. **Pressure (incentive)** is the need a person tries to satisfy by committing the fraud.

    ■   Situational pressure can be personal (e.g., financial difficulties in an employee's personal life) or organizational (e.g., the desire to release positive news to the financial media).

2. **Opportunity** is the ability to commit the fraud.

    ■   Opportunity is a factor in low-level employee fraud. Lack of controls over cash, goods, and other organizational property, as well as insufficient segregation of duties, are enabling factors.

    ■   Opportunity is the characteristic that the organization can most influence, e.g., by means of controls.

3. **Rationalization** is the ability to justify the fraud. It occurs when a person attributes his or her actions to rational and creditable motives without analysis of the true and, especially, unconscious motives.

    ■   Feeling underpaid is a common rationalization for low-level fraud.
    ■   Fraud awareness training minimizes rationalization by

        ‣   Supporting the ethical tone at the top,
        ‣   Promoting an environment averse to fraud, and
        ‣   Emphasizing that the organization does not tolerate misconduct of any kind.

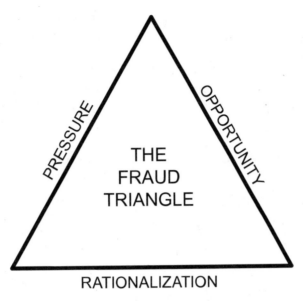

Figure 8-1

Effects of Fraud

Monetary losses from fraud are significant, but its full cost is immeasurable in terms of time, productivity, and reputation, including customer relationships.

Thus, an organization should have a fraud program that includes awareness, prevention, and detection programs. It also should have a fraud risk assessment process to identify fraud risks.

Types of Fraud

Asset misappropriation is stealing cash or other assets (supplies, inventory, equipment, and information). The theft may be concealed, e.g., by adjusting records.

- For example, entering fraudulent journal entries can help conceal asset theft (e.g., when an asset is purchased, the perpetrator debits an expense account instead of an asset account).

- However, selecting a vendor based on a blanket purchase order with an approved vendor(s) is a common business practice.

Skimming is theft of cash before it is recorded, for example, accepting payment from a customer but not recording the sale.

Payment fraud involves payment for fictitious goods or services, overstatement of invoices, or use of invoices for personal reasons.

Expense reimbursement fraud is payment for fictitious or inflated expenses, for example, an expense report for personal travel, nonexistent meals, or extra mileage.

Payroll fraud is a false claim for compensation, for example, overtime for hours not worked or payments to fictitious employees. One control used to detect the addition of fictitious persons to the payroll is for the auditor to make periodic comparisons of the names on the payroll with persons observed working for the company.

Financial statement misrepresentation often overstates assets or revenue or understates liabilities and expenses. Management may benefit by selling stock, receiving bonuses, or concealing another fraud.

Information misrepresentation provides false information, usually to outsiders in the form of fraudulent financial statements.

Corruption is an improper use of power, e.g., bribery. It often leaves little accounting evidence. These crimes usually are uncovered through tips or complaints from third parties. Corruption often involves the purchasing function.

Bribery is offering, giving, receiving, or soliciting anything of value to influence an outcome (e.g., kickbacks). Bribes may be offered to key employees such as purchasing agents. Those paying bribes tend to be intermediaries for outside vendors.

A **conflict of interest** is an undisclosed personal economic interest in a transaction that adversely affects the organization or its shareholders.

A **diversion** redirects to an employee or outsider a transaction that normally benefits the organization.

Wrongful use of confidential or proprietary information is fraudulent.

A **related-party fraud** is receipt of a benefit not obtainable in an arm's-length transaction.

Tax evasion is intentionally falsifying a tax return.

Low-Level Fraud vs. Executive Fraud

Fraud committed by staff or line employees most often consists of theft of property or embezzlement of cash. The incentive might be relief of economic hardship, the desire for material gain, or a drug or gambling habit. This type of fraud is intended to benefit individuals and is generally committed by an individual or individuals living outside their apparent means of support.

- Stealing petty cash or merchandise, lapping accounts receivable, and creating nonexistent vendors are common forms of low-level fraud.

Fraud at the executive level is different in that it often benefits both the self and the organization. The incentive is usually either maintaining or increasing the stock price, receiving a large bonus, or both.

- Executive level fraud ordinarily consists of materially misstating financial statements because promotion and compensation are tied to profits.

Symptoms of Fraud

A **document symptom** is any tampering with the accounting records to conceal a fraud. Keeping two sets of books or forcing the books to reconcile are examples.

A **lifestyle symptom** is an unexplained rise in an employee's social status or level of material consumption.

A **behavioral symptom** (i.e., a drastic change in an employee's behavior) may indicate the presence of fraud. Guilt and other forms of stress associated with perpetrating and concealing the fraud may cause noticeable changes in behavior.

Some Indicators (Red Flags) of Possible Fraud

Even the most effective internal control can sometimes be circumvented, for example, by collusion of two or more employees. Thus, an auditor must be sensitive to conditions that might indicate the existence of fraud. The following are examples:

- Lack of employee rotation in sensitive positions, such as cash handling

- Inappropriate combination of job duties (e.g., cash collections and disbursements responsibilities)

- Unclear lines of responsibility and accountability

- Unrealistic sales or production goals

- An employee who refuses to take vacations or refuses promotion

- Established controls not applied consistently

- High reported profits when competitors are suffering from an economic downturn

- High turnover among supervisory positions in finance and accounting areas

- Excessive or unjustifiable use of sole-source procurement

- An increase in sales far out of proportion to the increase in cost of goods sold (e.g., sales increase by 30% and cost of goods sold increase by 3%)

- Material contract requirements in the actual contract differ from those in the request for bids

- Petty cash transactions are not handled through an imprest fund

- Business arrangements are difficult to understand and do not seem to have any practical applicability to the entity

- End-of-period transactions are complex, unusual, or significant

Types of Fraudulent Processes

Lapping Receivables

In this fraud, a person (or persons) with access to customer payments and accounts receivable records steals a customer's payment. The shortage in that customer's account then is covered by a subsequent payment from another customer.

The process continues until

- A customer complains about his or her payment not being posted,
- An absence by the perpetrator allows another employee to discover the fraud, or
- The perpetrator covers the amount stolen.

Check Kiting

Kiting exploits the delay between (a) depositing a check in one bank account and (b) clearing the check through the bank on which it was drawn. This practice is only possible when manual checks are used. The widespread use of electronic funds transfer and other networked computer safeguards make electronic kiting difficult.

A check is kited when (a) a person (the kiter) writes an insufficient funds check on an account in one bank and (b) deposits the check in another bank.

The second bank immediately credits the account for some or all of the amount of the check, enabling the kiter to write other checks on that (nonexistent) balance. The kiter then covers the insufficiency in the first bank with another source of funds. The process can proceed in a circle of accounts at any number of banks.

Roles of Internal Auditors

Internal auditors are not responsible for the detection of all fraud, but they always must be alert to the possibility of fraud.

Implementation Standard 1210.A2

Internal auditors must have sufficient knowledge to evaluate the risk of fraud and the manner in which it is managed by the organization, but are not expected to have the expertise of a person whose primary responsibility is detecting and investigating fraud.

- According to Implementation Standard 1220.A1, internal auditors must exercise due professional care by, among other things, considering the "probability of significant errors, fraud, or noncompliance."

- Internal auditors therefore must consider the probability of fraud when developing engagement objectives (Implementation Standard 2210.A2).

Implementation Standard 2120.A2

The internal audit activity must evaluate the potential for the occurrence of fraud and how the organization manages fraud risk.

The internal auditor should consider the potential for fraud risks in the assessment of control design and the choice of audit procedures.

- Internal auditors should obtain reasonable assurance that objectives for the process under review are achieved and material control deficiencies are detected.

- The consideration of fraud risks and their relation to specific audit work are documented.

Internal auditors should have sufficient knowledge of fraud to identify indicators of fraud (red flags). However, internal auditors do not normally perform procedures specifically to gather red flag information.

- This knowledge includes
    - The characteristics of fraud,
    - The methods used to commit fraud, and
    - The various fraud schemes associated with the activities reviewed.

Internal auditors should be alert to opportunities that could allow fraud, such as control deficiencies.

- If significant control deficiencies are detected, additional procedures may be performed to determine whether fraud has occurred.

Internal auditors should evaluate the indicators of fraud and decide whether any further action is necessary or whether an investigation should be recommended.

Internal auditors should evaluate whether

- Management is actively overseeing the fraud risk management programs,

- Timely and sufficient corrective measures have been taken with respect to any noted control deficiencies, and

- The plan for monitoring the program is adequate.

If appropriate, internal auditors should recommend an investigation.

STOP & REVIEW

You have completed the outline for this subunit.
Study multiple-choice questions 1 through 11 beginning on page 272.

8.2 FRAUD -- CONTROLS

Fraud Management Program

The components of an effective fraud management program include the following:

- Company ethics policy
- Fraud awareness
- Fraud risk assessment
- Ongoing reviews
- Prevention and detection
- Investigation

Controls

Control is the principal means of managing fraud and ensuring the components of the fraud management program are present and functioning. (Control and types of control are covered in detail in Study Unit 6.)

The **COSO Internal Control Framework** (covered in detail in Study Unit 6, Subunit 3) can be applied in the fraud context to promote an environment in which fraud is effectively managed.

- The **control environment** includes such elements as a code of conduct, ethics policy, or fraud policy to set the appropriate tone at the top; hiring and promotion guidelines and practices; and board oversight.

- A **fraud risk assessment** generally includes the following:

    - Identifying and prioritizing fraud risk factors and fraud schemes
    - Determining whether existing controls apply to potential fraud schemes and identifying gaps
    - Testing operating effectiveness of fraud prevention and detection controls
    - Documenting and reporting the fraud risk assessment

- **Control activities** are policies and procedures for business processes that include authority limits and segregation of duties.

- **Fraud-related information and communication practices** promote the fraud risk management program and the organization's position on risk. The means used include fraud awareness training and confirming that employees comply with the organization's policies.

- **Monitoring** evaluates antifraud controls through independent evaluations of the fraud risk management program and use of it.

Preventing fraud. Essential elements in preventing fraud are setting the correct tone at the top and instilling a strong ethical culture. The following are preventative controls:

- **Safeguarding of assets** protects entities against the unauthorized use and disposal of assets. Examples include theft of assets and intellectual property.

- Computer access controls such as passwords and device authorization tables are used to prevent improper use or manipulation of data files and programs.

- A lockbox system can ensure that cash receipts are not stolen by mail clerks or other employees.

Detecting fraud. An essential element in detecting fraud is employee feedback, as fraud tips from employees is the most common way to detect fraud. Sources of employee feedback include a whistleblower hotline, exit interviews, and employee surveys.

Responsibility for Controls

Management is primarily responsible for establishing and maintaining control.

Internal auditors must assist the organization by evaluating the effectiveness and efficiency of controls and promoting continuous improvement (Performance Standard 2130).

- In an assurance engagement, internal auditors must assist the organization by evaluating the adequacy and effectiveness of controls in responding to risks (Implementation Standard 2130.A1).

- Internal auditors are not responsible for designing and implementing fraud prevention controls.

- However, internal auditors acting in a consulting role can help management identify and assess risk and determine the adequacy of the control environment.

  - Internal auditors also are in a unique position within the organization to recommend changes to improve the control environment.

Fraud Awareness

Fraud awareness is having an understanding of the nature, causes, and characteristics of fraud.

- Fraud awareness is developed through periodic fraud risk assessments, training of employees, and communications between management and employees.

Employee training about fraud should be tailored to each organization's fraud risks.

- Training typically covers the organization's values and code of conduct, types of fraud, and employee roles and responsibilities to report violations of ethical behavior.

Fraud essentially is the falsification of transactions. Thus, an auditor's examination of transactions for fraud tests the existence assertion.

Management override takes place when management circumvents an entity's controls for an illegitimate purpose, such as personal gain or enhanced presentation of the entity's position.

EXAMPLE 8-1 Examples of Management Override

- Management could approve the sale of goods to a customer who does not meet the company's credit policies in order to increase revenue. In doing so, management overrides the credit approval control that was in place.
- Management requests the controller leave the period open and overrides the control in place related to closing in order to manipulate cutoff.
- Management alters adjusting entries that have been reviewed and approved at department levels prior to posting to decrease current-period expenses, overriding controls related to adjustments to the financial statements.

- The following controls address management override risks (detailed examples of controls are included on the following pages):
  - Controls over significant, unusual transactions, particularly those that result in late or unusual journal entries
  - Controls over journal entries and adjustments made in the period-end financial reporting process
  - Controls over related party transactions
  - Controls related to significant management estimates
  - Controls that mitigate incentives for, and pressures on, management to falsify or inappropriately manage financial results

- Assessing the risk of management override is part of the assessment of fraud risk. The board of directors or audit committee oversees this assessment.

The following charts describe examples of some controls (including their objectives) and provide a reason for their existence.

Purchases	
Objective	**Control**
Confirm purchases are properly authorized.	Prepare an Accounts Payable signature authorization list showing the signatures for authorized individuals who may initiate and approve purchase orders.
	Persons authorized to initiate or approve purchase orders have full responsibility for ensuring that each purchase, including the price, specifications, quality, and quantity, is appropriate.
	Purchases can only be transacted by approved vendors or evidenced by approved contracts.
	A policy prohibits receipt of kickbacks, gifts, and other items of value from vendors.
	Expenditures transacted via credit or debit cards and electronic payments (Venmo, PayPal, Zelle, Square, etc.) are subject to expense-type code restrictions.
	Separation of duties between the ordering and receiving of merchandise.
	Receiving department does not accept goods unless it has a blind copy of a properly approved purchase order for the items.
	Credit card charges are subject to the expenditure controls used on purchases transacted through the accounts payable process cycle.
	Receiving reports and vendor invoices are required to be sent to accounts payable.

WHY?

Prevent a purchasing agent from purchasing items for personal use with the organization's funds.

Computer Fraud

Objective	Control
Only those persons with a bona fide purpose and authorization have access to data files and programs.	Programmers do not have access to programs used in processing. Lists of authorized persons are maintained online and should constantly be updated after personnel changes (e.g., promotion or resignation).

WHY?

The risk of inappropriate use is reduced when only authorized personnel access programs used in processing. Use should be necessary to fulfill job obligations.

Objective	Control
Only those persons with a bona fide purpose and authorization have access to data files and programs.	Use a device authorization table to grant access only to those physical devices that should logically need access. Restrict the ability of employees to gain access to and change sensitive information.

WHY?

For example, it is illogical for anyone to access the accounts receivable file from a manufacturing terminal. Accordingly, the device authorization table should deny access to the accounts receivable file even when a valid password is used from a manufacturing terminal.

Objective	Control
Convert data into unreadable code so that unauthorized individuals cannot use the data inappropriately.	Encrypt data so that only authorized users can decode (decipher) the information.

WHY?

Encoding data before transmission over communication lines makes understanding or modifying the content more difficult for someone with access.

Objective	Control
Adequate control over program changes.	Redesign programs using a working copy, not the version in use. Systems analyst is made responsible for communicating the purpose of the design to the programmer. Actual users test new programs. Programmers do not have access to operational processes, and librarians are not able to program.

WHY?

Prevent opportunities for an individual with malicious or fraudulent intent to create and insert code within the program under development.

Segregation of Duties

Objective	Control
Minimize the opportunities for a person to be able to perpetrate and conceal fraud or errors in the normal course of his or her duties.	Separate contract negotiation from approval of invoices for payment.
	Person(s) responsible for signing checks or approving electronic payments verify that a service or product was received.
	Separate contract negotiation, approval of invoices for payment, and budget preparation.
	Separate vendor setup responsibility from the purchasing function.
	Separate employee and contractor setup from the position responsible for processing payroll and contractor payments.

WHY?

When feasible, segregation of duties divides responsibility for recording of the transaction, authorization, and custody of the assets associated with the transaction. The effect is to minimize the opportunities for a person to be able to perpetrate and conceal fraud or error.

STOP & REVIEW

You have completed the outline for this subunit.

Study multiple-choice questions 12 through 17 beginning on page 275.

8.3 FRAUD -- INVESTIGATION

Forensic auditing uses accounting and auditing knowledge and skills in matters having civil or criminal legal implications. Engagements involving fraud, litigation support, and expert witness testimony are examples. Forensic auditing procedures include interviewing, investigating, and testing.

Fraud Investigation

A fraud investigation should discover the full nature and extent of the fraud. An investigation gathers sufficient information to determine

1. Whether fraud has occurred,
2. The loss exposures,
3. Who was involved, and
4. How fraud occurred.

Internal auditors, lawyers, and other specialists usually conduct fraud investigations.

The investigation and resolution activities must comply with local law, and the auditors should work effectively with legal counsel and become familiar with relevant laws.

Management implements controls over the investigation. They include (1) developing policies and procedures, (2) preserving evidence, (3) responding to the results, (4) reporting, and (5) communications.

*   These matters may be documented in a **fraud policy** that the internal auditors may assist in evaluating.

*   Policies and procedures address

    *   The rights of individuals;
    *   The qualifications of investigators;
    *   The relevant laws; and
    *   The disciplining of employees, suppliers, or customers, including legal measures.

*   The authority and responsibilities of those involved in the investigation, especially the investigator and legal counsel, should be clear.

*   Internal communications about an ongoing investigation should be minimized.

*   A policy should specify the investigator's responsibility for determining whether a fraud has been committed. Either the investigator or management decides whether fraud has occurred, and management decides whether to notify outside authorities.

The responsibility of the **internal audit activity** for investigations should be defined in its charter and in fraud policies and procedures.

- For example, internal auditing may
    - Be primarily responsible,
    - Act as a resource, or
    - Avoid involvement because it is responsible for assessing investigations or lacks resources.

- Any role is acceptable if its effect on independence is recognized and managed appropriately.

- Internal auditors typically not only assess investigations but also advise management about the process, including control improvements.

- To be proficient, fraud investigation teams must obtain sufficient knowledge of
    - Fraud schemes,
    - Investigation methods, and
    - The applicable law.

- The internal audit activity may use in-house staff, outsourcing, or both.

An **investigation plan** is developed for each investigation.

- The lead investigator determines the knowledge, skills, and other competencies needed.

- The process includes obtaining assurance that no potential conflict of interest exists with those investigated or any employees of the organization.

- Planning should consider the following:
    - Gathering evidence using surveillance, interviews, or written statements
    - Documenting and preserving evidence, the legal rules of evidence, and the business uses of the evidence
    - Determining the extent of the fraud
    - Determining the methods used to perpetrate the fraud
    - Evaluating the cause of the fraud
    - Identifying the perpetrators

- All evidence obtained should be recorded chronologically in a log or inventory. Examples of evidence include the following:

    - Letters, memos, and correspondence (in hard copy or electronic form)
    - Financial records
    - IT or systems access records
    - Phone records
    - Customer or vendor information (e.g., contracts, invoices, and payment information)
    - Public records (e.g., property records or business registrations filed with government agencies)
    - News articles
    - Websites (e.g., social networking sites)

- The investigation should be coordinated with management, legal counsel, and other specialists.

- Investigators need to be prudent, consistent, and knowledgeable of the rights of persons within the scope of the investigation and the reputation of the organization itself.

- The level and extent of complicity in the fraud throughout the organization needs to be assessed. This assessment can be critical to avoid

    - Destroying or tainting crucial evidence and
    - Obtaining misleading information from persons who may be involved.

- The investigation needs to secure evidence collected and follow chain-of-custody procedures.

Interrogation of Employees

A fraud-related interrogation differs significantly from a normal interview.

- The purpose of a typical interview is to gather facts.

    - In an interrogation, the internal auditor has already gathered pertinent facts and is seeking confirmation.

- At no time should the internal auditor accuse the employee of committing a crime.

    - If the accusation is unprovable, the organization could have legal liability.

- The accused generally is interrogated after most relevant evidence has been obtained.

    - The objective often is to use the evidence to obtain a confession.

- All information received during the interview must be correctly documented.

    - All evidence should be subject to effective chain-of-custody procedures.

- Two persons should conduct the interview, one of whom takes notes and may serve as a witness.

The internal auditor should guide the conversation from the general to the specific.

- Open questions generally are used early in the interrogation, and closed questions are used later as the auditor comes closer to obtaining a confession.

    - Open questions are of the type, "Describe your role in the vendor approval process."

    - Closed questions are of the type, "Do you personally verify the existence of every vendor who seeks approval?"

- Normal interviewing methods regarding nonthreatening tone and close observation of body language apply.

The employee should not be allowed to return to his or her normal work area upon completion of the interrogation.

- Because the employee is now alert to the fraud investigation, (s)he might be tempted to destroy valuable evidence.

Fraud Reporting

The chief audit executive is responsible for fraud reporting. It consists of the various oral or written, interim or final communications to management or the board regarding the status and results of fraud investigations.

- A formal communication may be issued at the conclusion of the investigation that includes
    - Time frames,
    - Observations,
    - Conclusions,
    - Resolution, and
    - Corrective action to improve controls.

- It may need to be written to protect the identities of some of the people involved.

- The needs of the board and management, legal requirements, and policies and procedures should be considered.

A draft of the proposed final communication should be submitted to legal counsel for review. To be covered by the attorney-client privilege, the report must be addressed to counsel.

Any incident of significant fraud, or incident that leads the internal auditors to question the level of trust placed in one or more individuals, must be timely reported to senior management and the board.

If previously issued financial statements for 1 or more years may have been adversely affected, senior management and the board also should be informed.

Resolution of Fraud Incidents

Resolution consists of determining actions to be taken after the investigation is complete.

- Management and the board are responsible for resolving fraud incidents.

Resolution may include the following:

- Providing closure to persons who were found innocent or reported a problem

- Disciplining an employee

- Requesting voluntary financial restitution

- Terminating contracts with suppliers

- Reporting the incident to law enforcement or regulatory bodies, encouraging them to prosecute, and cooperating with them

- Filing a civil suit to recover the amount taken

- Filing an insurance claim

- Complaining to the perpetrator's professional association

- Recommending control improvements

Communication of Fraud Incidents

Management or the board determines whether to inform parties outside the organization after consultation with such individuals as legal counsel, human resources personnel, and the CAE.

- The organization may need to notify government agencies of certain types of fraudulent acts. It also may need to notify its insurers, bankers, and external auditors of instances of fraud.

Internal communications are a strategic tool used by management to reinforce its position relating to integrity and to show why internal controls are important.

Opinion on Fraud-Related Controls

The internal auditor may be asked by management or the board to express an opinion on internal controls related to fraud. The following provide relevant guidance:

- Standards and Implementation Guides applying to communication of results (Performance Standard 2400, etc.)

- Practice Guide, *Formulating and Expressing Internal Audit Opinions*

An opinion on fraud-related controls is acceptable, but it is inappropriate for an internal auditor to express an opinion on the culpability of a fraud suspect.

STOP & REVIEW

You have completed the outline for this subunit.
Study multiple-choice questions 18 through 20 on page 278.

QUESTIONS

8.1 Fraud -- Risks and Types

1. In the course of their work, internal auditors must be alert for fraud and other forms of white-collar crime. The important characteristic that distinguishes fraud from other varieties of white-collar crime is that

- A. Fraud is characterized by deceit, concealment, or violation of trust.
- B. Unlike other white-collar crimes, fraud is always perpetrated against an outside party.
- C. White-collar crime is usually perpetrated for the benefit of an organization, but fraud benefits an individual.
- D. White-collar crime is usually perpetrated by outsiders to the detriment of an organization, but fraud is perpetrated by insiders to benefit the organization.

Answer (A) is correct.
   REQUIRED: The trait distinguishing fraud from other white-collar crimes.
   DISCUSSION: Fraud is defined in The IIA Glossary as "any illegal act characterized by deceit, concealment, or violation of trust. These acts are not dependent upon the threat of violence or physical force."
   Answer (B) is incorrect. Fraud may be perpetrated internally. **Answer (C) is incorrect.** Fraud may be perpetrated for the organization's benefit or for otherwise unselfish reasons. **Answer (D) is incorrect.** Fraud may be perpetrated by insiders and outsiders, and it may be either beneficial or detrimental to an organization.

2. A key feature that distinguishes fraud from other types of crime or impropriety is that fraud always involves the

- A. Violent or forceful taking of property.
- B. Deceitful wrongdoing of management-level personnel.
- C. Unlawful conversion of property that is lawfully in the custody of the perpetrator.
- D. False representation or concealment of a material fact.

Answer (D) is correct.
   REQUIRED: The key distinguishing feature of fraud.
   DISCUSSION: Fraud is defined in The IIA Glossary as "any illegal act characterized by deceit, concealment, or violation of trust. These acts are not dependent upon the threat of violence or physical force."
   Answer (A) is incorrect. Fraud usually does not involve force or violence. **Answer (B) is incorrect.** Employees at any level in an organization can commit fraud. **Answer (C) is incorrect.** Embezzlement is the unlawful conversion of property that is lawfully in the custody of the perpetrator.

3. What is the responsibility of the internal auditor with respect to fraud?

- A. The internal auditor should have sufficient knowledge to identify the indicators of fraud but is not expected to be an expert.
- B. The internal auditor should have the same ability to detect fraud as a person whose primary responsibility is detecting and investigating fraud.
- C. An internal auditor should have sufficient knowledge and training so that (s)he is able to detect fraud.
- D. An internal auditor's primary role is to detect and investigate fraud.

Answer (A) is correct.
   REQUIRED: The internal auditor's responsibility with respect to fraud.
   DISCUSSION: Internal auditors must have sufficient knowledge to evaluate the risk of fraud and the manner in which it is managed by the organization. They are not expected to have the expertise of a person whose primary responsibility is detecting and investigating fraud (Impl. Std. 1210.A2).
   Answer (B) is incorrect. The internal auditor is not expected to have the expertise of a person whose primary responsibility is detecting and investigating fraud. **Answer (C) is incorrect.** An internal auditor must have sufficient knowledge to identify the indicators of fraud but is not required to have sufficient knowledge and training to be able to detect fraud. **Answer (D) is incorrect.** Detecting and investigating fraud is not a primary role of an internal auditor.

4. Internal auditors should have knowledge about factors (red flags) that have proven to be associated with management fraud. Which of the following factors have generally **not** been associated with management fraud?

   A. Generous performance-based reward systems.

   B. A domineering management.

   C. Regular comparison of actual results with budgets.

   D. A management preoccupation with increased financial performance.

Answer (C) is correct.
   REQUIRED: The factor not associated with management fraud.
   DISCUSSION: Regular comparison of actual results to budgets provides feedback and is a normal and necessary part of the control loop. Ineffective control is an indicator of possible fraud.
   Answer (A) is incorrect. Generous reward systems provide incentives for management to distort performance. **Answer (B) is incorrect.** Pressure from superiors provides an incentive for management to distort performance. **Answer (D) is incorrect.** A management preoccupation with increased financial performance provides an incentive for managers to distort performance.

5. When auditing the award of a major contract, which of the following should an internal auditor suspect as a red flag for a bidding fraud scheme?

   A. Subsequent change orders increase requirements for low-bid items.

   B. Material contract requirements are different on the actual contract than on the request for bids.

   C. A high percentage of employees are charged to indirect accounts.

   D. Losing bidders are not given feedback.

Answer (B) is correct.
   REQUIRED: The red flag for a bidding fraud scheme.
   DISCUSSION: The internal audit activity must evaluate the potential for the occurrence of fraud and how the organization manages fraud risk (Impl. Std. 2120.A2). According to The IIA Glossary, fraud is any illegal act characterized by deceit, concealment, or violation of trust. It is fraudulent for the material contract requirements on the request for bids to differ from the actual contract. This type of fraud inflates bid amounts by having more bidder-friendly requirements on the request for bids than on the actual contract.
   Answer (A) is incorrect. Subsequent change orders that increase requirements for low-bid items are routine occurrences. **Answer (C) is incorrect.** A high percentage of employees may perform work resulting in costs properly classified as overhead. **Answer (D) is incorrect.** Not providing losing bidders with feedback is a common business practice.

6. A medium-sized regional firm distributes packaged snack foods to convenience stores. A routine inventory has revealed significant amounts of inventory missing from the delivery trucks. Which of the following suggests a control weakness that may provide an opportunity for fraud?

   A. The policy and procedure manual clearly defines allowed and prohibited actions.

   B. Careful counts are made as inventory is loaded on the trucks.

   C. Access to the warehouse is restricted to a few trusted employees.

   D. Truck drivers are allowed to use the trucks for personal reasons, including taking them home at night, as a benefit of employment.

Answer (D) is correct.
   REQUIRED: The control weakness that may provide an opportunity for fraud.
   DISCUSSION: Unrestricted access to the trucks creates opportunities for theft of merchandise by the drivers.
   Answer (A) is incorrect. A detailed policy and procedure manual is a control strength. **Answer (B) is incorrect.** Inventory counts made at the time the trucks are loaded will help to bring the shortages to management's attention but will not prevent them. **Answer (C) is incorrect.** Restricting access to the warehouse is a control strength.

7. In an organization with a separate division that is primarily responsible for the prevention of fraud, the internal audit activity is responsible for

A. Examining and evaluating the adequacy and effectiveness of that division's actions taken to prevent fraud.

B. Establishing and maintaining that division's system of internal control.

C. Planning that division's fraud prevention activities.

D. Controlling that division's fraud prevention activities.

Answer (A) is correct.
   REQUIRED: The responsibility of the internal audit activity in an organization with a separate fraud prevention division.
   DISCUSSION: Control is the principal means of preventing fraud. Management is primarily responsible for the establishment and maintenance of control. Internal auditors must assist the organization by evaluating the effectiveness and efficiency of controls and promoting continuous improvement. Internal auditors should be alert to opportunities that could allow fraud and evaluate the indicators of fraud. For example, internal auditors can evaluate whether management is actively overseeing the fraud risk management programs.
   Answer (B) is incorrect. Establishing and maintaining control is a responsibility of management. **Answer (C) is incorrect.** Planning fraud prevention activities is a responsibility of management. **Answer (D) is incorrect.** Controlling fraud prevention activities is a responsibility of management.

8. Which of the following wrongful acts committed by an employee constitutes fraud?

A. Libel.

B. Embezzlement.

C. Assault.

D. Harassment.

Answer (B) is correct.
   REQUIRED: The employee act constituting fraud.
   DISCUSSION: Fraud is defined in The IIA Glossary as "any illegal act characterized by deceit, concealment, or violation of trust. These acts are not dependent upon the threat of violence or physical force. Frauds are perpetrated by parties and organizations to obtain money, property, or services; to avoid payment or loss of services; or to secure personal or business advantage." Embezzlement is the intentional appropriation of property entrusted to one's care. The embezzler converts property to his or her own use and conceals the theft.
   Answer (A) is incorrect. Libel is defamation published in a relatively permanent form (newspaper, letter, film, etc.). **Answer (C) is incorrect.** The tort of assault entails placing another in reasonable fear of a harmful or offensive bodily contact. **Answer (D) is incorrect.** Harassment is the act of persistently annoying another.

9. Which of the following fraudulent entries is most likely to be made to conceal the theft of an asset?

A. Debit expenses and credit the asset.

B. Debit the asset and credit another asset account.

C. Debit revenue and credit the asset.

D. Debit another asset account and credit the asset.

Answer (A) is correct.
   REQUIRED: The fraudulent entry most likely to be made to conceal theft of an asset.
   DISCUSSION: Most fraud perpetrators attempt to conceal their theft by charging it against an expense account. The result is that the recorded asset balance equals the actual amount on hand, and applying procedures to it will not detect the theft.
   Answer (B) is incorrect. Debiting the stolen asset account simply increases the discrepancy between the recorded amount and the amount on hand. **Answer (C) is incorrect.** An entry decreasing revenue is unusual and would attract attention. **Answer (D) is incorrect.** This entry would not permanently conceal the fraud. It would simply shift the irreconcilable balance to another asset account.

10. An upcoming internal audit engagement involves the possibility of fraud. The *Standards* require the internal auditors to possess which of the following skills?

A. To hold a current Certified Fraud Examiner certification.

B. To hold a current Certified Internal Auditor certification.

C. To be able to identify indicators that fraud may have been committed.

D. To possess technical expertise in a particular area of fraud examination, such as computer hacking.

Answer (C) is correct.
REQUIRED: The skills requirements for an internal auditor on a possible fraud engagement.
DISCUSSION: An internal auditor's responsibilities for the detection of fraud include (1) having sufficient knowledge to identify indicators that fraud may have been committed, (2) being alert to opportunities that could allow fraud (e.g., control weaknesses), and (3) being able to evaluate the indicators of fraud sufficiently to determine whether a fraud investigation should be conducted.
Answer (A) is incorrect. The *Standards* do not require an internal auditor to hold a Certified Fraud Examiner certification to serve on an engagement in which possibility of fraud exists. **Answer (B) is incorrect.** The *Standards* do not require an internal auditor to hold a Certified Internal Auditor certification to serve on an engagement in which possibility of fraud exists. **Answer (D) is incorrect.** The *Standards* do not require an internal auditor to have technical expertise in a particular area of fraud examination to serve on an engagement in which a possibility of fraud exists.

11. One factor that distinguishes fraud from other employee crimes is that fraud involves

A. Intentional deception.

B. Personal gain for the perpetrator.

C. Collusion with a party outside the organization.

D. Malicious motives.

Answer (A) is correct.
REQUIRED: The factor that distinguishes fraud from other employee crimes.
DISCUSSION: Fraud is defined in The IIA Glossary as "any illegal act characterized by deceit, concealment, or violation of trust. These acts are not dependent upon the threat of violence or physical force."

8.2 Fraud -- Controls

12. A programmer's accumulation of roundoff errors into one account, which is later accessed by the programmer, is a type of computer fraud. The best way to prevent this type of fraud is to

A. Build in judgment with reasonableness tests.

B. Independently test programs during development and limit access to the programs.

C. Segregate duties of systems development and programming.

D. Use control totals and check the results of the computer.

Answer (B) is correct.
REQUIRED: The best way to prevent computer fraud.
DISCUSSION: Programmers should not have access to programs used in processing. The accumulation of roundoff errors into one person's account is a procedure written into the program. Independent testing of a program will lead to discovery of this programmed fraud.
Answer (A) is incorrect. Reasonableness tests will not detect this irregularity. In this particular type of fraud, all of the amounts will balance. **Answer (C) is incorrect.** Segregation of duties between systems development and programming would not prevent this type of error. The skills required to construct the program are possessed by programmers. **Answer (D) is incorrect.** This particular fraud will result in balanced entries. Thus, control totals would not detect the fraud.

13. Internal auditors have a responsibility for helping to deter fraud. Which of the following best describes how this responsibility is usually met?

A. By coordinating with security personnel and law enforcement agencies in the investigation of possible frauds.

B. By testing for fraud in every engagement and following up as appropriate.

C. By assisting in the design of control systems to prevent fraud.

D. By evaluating the adequacy and effectiveness of controls in light of the potential exposure or risk.

Answer (D) is correct.
    REQUIRED: The responsibility of internal auditing to deter fraud.
    DISCUSSION: Control is the principal means of preventing fraud. Management is primarily responsible for the establishment and maintenance of control. In an assurance engagement, internal auditors must assist the organization by evaluating the adequacy and effectiveness of controls in responding to risks (Impl. Std. 2130.A1).
    Answer (A) is incorrect. Investigating possible frauds involves detection, not deterrence. **Answer (B) is incorrect.** Testing for fraud in every engagement is not required. **Answer (C) is incorrect.** Designing control systems impairs an internal auditor's objectivity.

14. Which of the following controls is the **least** effective in preventing a fraud conducted by sending purchase orders to bogus vendors?

A. Require that all purchases be made from an authorized vendor list maintained independently of the individual placing the purchase order.

B. Require that only approved vendors be paid for purchases.

C. Require contracts with all major vendors from whom production components are purchased.

D. Require that total purchases for a month not exceed the total budgeted purchases for that month.

Answer (D) is correct.
    REQUIRED: The control least effective in preventing a fraud involving bogus vendors.
    DISCUSSION: Requiring that total purchases for a month not exceed the total budgeted purchases for that month controls the total amount of expenditures, not whether a purchase has been requested and authorized, with whom the purchase orders are placed, or whether goods purchased are received.

15. A potential problem for a manufacturer is that purchasing agents may take kickbacks or receive gifts from vendors in exchange for favorable contracts. Which of the following is the **least** effective in preventing this problem?

A. A specific organizational policy prohibiting the acceptance of anything of value from a vendor.

B. An organizational code of ethics that prohibits such activity.

C. A requirement for the purchasing agent to develop a profile of all vendors before the vendors are added to the authorized vendor list.

D. The establishment of long-term contracts with major vendors, with the contract terms approved by senior management.

Answer (C) is correct.
    REQUIRED: The least effective control to prevent purchasing agents from taking kickbacks or gifts from vendors.
    DISCUSSION: A requirement for the purchasing agent to develop a profile of all vendors is the least effective approach. It applies only to the authorization of vendors, a function that should be performed independently of the purchasing agent. It does not address the purchasing agent's relationships with approved vendors.
    Answer (A) is incorrect. A policy prohibiting kickbacks and gifts from vendors provides guidance and influences behavior. **Answer (B) is incorrect.** A code of ethics gives direction to the purchasing agents and is helpful in influencing behavior. **Answer (D) is incorrect.** Approval of long-term vendor contracts by senior management is an effective procedure that is increasingly being used by many organizations.

16. A significant employee fraud took place shortly after an internal auditing engagement. The internal auditor may not have properly fulfilled the responsibility for the prevention of fraud by failing to note and report that

A. Policies, practices, and procedures to monitor activities and safeguard assets were less extensive in low-risk areas than in high-risk areas.

B. A system of control that depended upon separation of duties could be circumvented by collusion among three employees.

C. There were no written policies describing prohibited activities and the action required whenever violations are discovered.

D. Divisional employees had not been properly trained to distinguish between bona fide signatures and cleverly forged ones on authorization forms.

Answer (C) is correct.
   REQUIRED: The way in which the internal auditor may not have properly fulfilled the responsibility for the prevention of fraud.
   DISCUSSION: Management is responsible for establishing and maintaining internal control. Thus, management also is responsible for the fraud prevention program. The control environment element of this program includes a code of conduct, ethics policy, or fraud policy to set the appropriate tone at the top. Moreover, organizations should establish effective fraud-related information and communication practices, for example, documentation and dissemination of policies, guidelines, and results.
   Answer (A) is incorrect. For cost-benefit reasons, controls should be more extensive in high-risk areas. **Answer (B) is incorrect.** Even the best system of control can often be circumvented by collusion. **Answer (D) is incorrect.** Forgery, like collusion, can circumvent even an effective control.

17. A purchasing agent received expensive gifts from a vendor in return for directing a significant amount of business to that vendor. Which of the following organizational policies most effectively prevents such an occurrence?

A. All purchases exceeding specified monetary amounts should be approved by an official who determines compliance with budgetary requirements.

B. Important high-volume materials should regularly be purchased from at least two different sources in order to afford supply protection.

C. The purchasing function should be decentralized so each department manager or supervisor does his or her own purchasing.

D. Competitive bids should be solicited on purchases to the maximum extent that is practicable.

Answer (D) is correct.
   REQUIRED: The policy that most effectively prevents or detects bribery by a vendor.
   DISCUSSION: In the absence of special circumstances, competitive bidding is a legitimate and effective means of obtaining the lowest price consistent with quality. It is a practice that exploits competition in the market place. Competitive bidding also serves as a control over fraud by restricting the ability of a purchasing agent to reward a favored vendor.
   Answer (A) is incorrect. The problem is vendor selection, not authorization of purchases. **Answer (B) is incorrect.** A purchasing agent could still display favoritism to one of the vendors. **Answer (C) is incorrect.** Decentralization creates more opportunities for buyer fraud.

8.3 Fraud -- Investigation

18. Which of the following gives the internal auditor the authority to investigate fraud?

A. The *Standards*.

B. Common law.

C. Management.

D. The IIA's Code of Ethics.

Answer (C) is correct.
REQUIRED: The source of an internal auditor's authority to investigate fraud.
DISCUSSION: Any fraud investigation undertaken by internal auditors must be authorized by management.
Answer (A) is incorrect. The internal auditor has authority only to recommend an investigation. Answer (B) is incorrect. An internal auditor has no authority under common law. Answer (D) is incorrect. The IIA's Code of Ethics does not mention fraud investigation.

19. When conducting fraud investigations, internal auditors should

A. Clearly indicate the extent of the internal auditors' knowledge of the fraud when questioning suspects.

B. Assign personnel to the investigation in accordance with the engagement schedule established at the beginning of the fiscal year.

C. Perform its investigation independently of lawyers, security personnel, and specialists from outside the organization who are involved in the investigation.

D. Assess the probable level of, and the extent of complicity in, the fraud within the organization.

Answer (D) is correct.
REQUIRED: The role of the internal auditors in fraud investigations.
DISCUSSION: When conducting fraud investigations, internal auditors or others should assess the level of, and the extent of complicity in, the fraud within the organization. This assessment can be critical to ensuring that (1) crucial evidence is not tainted or destroyed and (2) misleading information is not obtained from persons who may be involved.
Answer (A) is incorrect. By always giving the impression that additional evidence is in reserve, the internal auditors are more apt to obtain complete and truthful answers. Answer (B) is incorrect. Fraud investigations usually occur unexpectedly and cannot be scheduled in advance. Also, the fraud investigation must be conducted by individuals having the appropriate expertise, even if another engagement must be delayed. Answer (C) is incorrect. The internal auditors should coordinate their activities with management, legal counsel, and other specialists.

20. Questions used to interrogate individuals suspected of fraud should

A. Adhere to a predetermined order.

B. Cover more than one subject or topic.

C. Move from the general to the specific.

D. Direct the individual to a desired answer.

Answer (C) is correct.
REQUIRED: The method of asking questions used to interrogate individuals suspected of fraud.
DISCUSSION: Internal auditors should be skilled in dealing with people and in communicating effectively. One important communications skill is the ability to conduct an effective interview. For example, initial questions in a fraud interview should be broad. In contrast with a directive approach emphasizing narrowly focused questions, this nondirective approach is more likely to elicit clarifications and unexpected observations from employees who are under suspicion.
Answer (A) is incorrect. The interviewee's answer may suggest a follow-up question that should be asked before asking the next planned question. Answer (B) is incorrect. This interviewing technique may be confusing for the respondent. Answer (D) is incorrect. The interrogator should avoid leading questions, that is, questions that suggest an answer.

APPENDIX A
THE IIA GLOSSARY

This appendix contains the Glossary appended to the *Standards*.

Activity-level controls – Controls that operate for the entire activity (area, process, or program). Examples are review of cost center reports, inventory counts, and the soft controls that influence the mini-control environment within the activity, which may or may not be consistent with that of the organization as a whole.

Add value – Value is provided by improving opportunities to achieve organizational objectives, identifying operational improvement, and/or reducing risk exposure thorough both assurance and consulting services.

Adequate control – Present if management has planned and organized (designed) in a manner that provides reasonable assurance that the organization's risks have been managed effectively and that the organization's goals and objectives will be achieved efficiently and economically.

Advisory services – Service activities provided by the internal audit function, the nature and scope of which are agreed with the recipients of the services, are intended to add value and improve an organization's governance, risk management, and control processes without the internal auditor assuming management responsibility. Examples include counsel, advice, facilitation, and training.

Analytical procedures – The activities of comparing client information with expectations for that information obtained from an independent source, identifying variances, and investigating the cause of significant variances.

Application controls – Fully automated (i.e., performed automatically by the systems) IT controls designed to ensure effective business process enablement and the complete and accurate processing of data, from input through output.

Application systems – Sets of programs that are designed for end users such as payroll, accounts payable, and, in some cases, large applications such as enterprise resource planning (ERP) systems that provide many business functions.

Appropriate evidence – Any piece or collection of evidence gained during an engagement that provides relevant and reliable support for the judgments and conclusions reached during the engagement.

Asset misappropriation – Acts involving the theft or misuse of an organization's assets (for example, skimming revenues, stealing inventory, or payroll fraud).

Assurance layering – A technique of coordinating multiple assurance activities designed to mitigate a known risk to a needed or desired level within an established risk tolerance.

Assurance map – A visual depiction of the different assurance activities and assurance functions within an organization. Such a depiction can help identify gaps or overlaps in assurance activities and help assess that risk is managed consistent with the board's and management's expectations.

Assurance services – An objective examination of evidence for the purpose of providing an independent assessment on governance, risk management, and control processes for the organization. Examples may include financial, performance, compliance, system security, and due diligence engagements.

Attribute sampling – A statistical sampling approach, based on binomial distribution theory, that enables the user to reach a conclusion about a population in terms of a rate of occurrence.

Audit committee – A committee of the board charged with recommending to the board the approval of auditors and financial reports.

Audit engagement/engagement – A specific internal audit assignment, task, or review activity, such as an internal audit, control self-assessment review, fraud examination, or consultancy. An engagement may include multiple tasks or activities designed to accomplish a specific set of related objectives.

Audit observation – Any identified and validated gap between the current and desired state arising from an assurance engagement.

Audit risk – The risk of reaching invalid audit conclusions and/or providing faulty advice based on the audit work conducted.

Audit sampling – The application of an audit procedure to less than 100 percent of the items in a population for the purpose of drawing an inference about the entire population.

Audit universe – A compilation of the subsidiaries, business units, departments, groups, processes, or other established subdivisions of an organization that exist to manage one or more business risks.

Auditee/audit client/audit customer – The subsidiary, business unit, department, group, or other established subdivision of an organization that is the subject of an assurance engagement.

Big data – A term used to refer to the large amount of constantly streaming digital information, massive increase in the capacity to store large amounts of data, and the amount of data processing power required to manage, interpret, and analyze the large volumes of digital information.

Blank confirmations – Confirmation that asks the third party to fill in a blank with the information requested. This provides stronger evidence than other confirmations.

Board – The highest level governing body (e.g., a board of directors, a supervisory board, or a board of governors or trustees) charged with the responsibility to direct and/or oversee the organization's activities and hold senior management accountable. Although governance arrangements vary among jurisdictions and sectors, typically the board includes members who are not part of management. If a board does not exist, the word "board" in the *Standards* refers to a group or person charged with governance of the organization. Furthermore, "board" in the *Standards* may refer to a committee or another body to which the governing body has delegated certain functions (e.g., an audit committee).

Bottom-up approach – To begin by looking at all processes directly at the activity level, and then aggregating the identified processes across the organization.

Bring your own device (BYOD) – A policy whereby organizations allow associates to access business email, calendars, and other data on their personal laptops, smartphones, tablets, or other devices.

Business acumen – Savviness and experience with regard to business management in general, and more specifically, with the way the organization and, in particular, specific business units operate.

Business process – The set of connected activities linked with each other for the purpose of achieving one or more business objectives.

Business process outsourcing (BPO) – The act of transferring some of an organization's business processes to an outside provider to achieve cost reductions, operating effectiveness, or operating efficiency while improving service quality.

Capability maturity model – A tool used to measure today's capability and define the characteristics of higher levels of capability. Largely used in business to assess and develop operations and services.

Cause – The reason for the difference between the expected and actual conditions (why the difference exists).

Chief audit executive (CAE) – Chief audit executive describes the role of a person in a senior position responsible for effectively managing the internal audit activity in accordance with the internal audit charter and the mandatory elements of the International Professional Practices Framework. The chief audit executive or others reporting to the chief audit executive will have appropriate professional certifications and qualifications. The specific job title and/or responsibilities of the chief audit executive may vary across organizations.

Classical variables sampling – A statistical sampling approach based on normal distribution theory that is used to reach conclusions regarding monetary amounts.

Cloud computing – The use of various computer resources–both hardware and software–that are delivered through a network like the Internet. The cloud can be configured with various options of services along with configurations for the network. It allows for a great deal of flexibility in network, software, and hardware utilization. Cloud computing also provides options for remote storage of data and use of remote applications.

COBIT – An IT governance framework and supporting toolset that allows managers to bridge the gap between control requirements, technical issues, and business risks.

Code of Ethics – The Code of Ethics of The Institute of Internal Auditors (IIA) are principles relevant to the profession and practice of internal auditing and Rules of Conduct that describe behavior expected of internal auditors. The Code of Ethics applies to both parties and entities that provide internal audit services. The purpose of the Code of Ethics is to promote an ethical culture in the global profession of internal auditing.

Combined assurance – Aligning various assurance activities within an organization to ensure assurance gaps do not exist and assurance activities minimize duplication and overlap but still manage risk consistent with the board's and management's expectations.

Compensating control – An activity that, if key controls do not fully operate effectively, may help to reduce the related risk. Such controls also can back up or duplicate multiple controls and may operate across multiple processes and risks. A compensating control will not, by itself, reduce risk to an acceptable level.

Compliance – Adherence to policies, plans, procedures, laws, regulations, contracts, or other requirements.

Computer-assisted audit techniques (CAATs) – Automated audit techniques, such as generalized audit software, utility software, test data, application software tracing and mapping, and audit expert systems, that help the internal auditor directly test controls built into computerized information systems and data contained in computer files.

Condition – The factual evidence that the internal auditor found in the course of the examination (what does exist).

Confirmations – Document sent to independent third parties asking them to verify the accuracy of client information in the course of audit testing.

Conflict of interest – Any relationship that is, or appears to be, not in the best interest of the organization. A conflict of interest would prejudice an individual's ability to perform his or her duties and responsibilities objectively.

Consulting services – Advisory and related client service activities, the nature and scope of which are agreed with the client, are intended to add value and improve an organization's governance, risk management, and control processes without the internal auditor assuming management responsibility. Examples include counsel, advice, facilitation, and training.

Continuous auditing – Using computerized techniques to perpetually audit the processing of business transactions.

Continuous monitoring – The automated review of business processes and controls by associates in the business unit. It helps an organization detect errors, fraud, abuse, and system inefficiencies.

Control – Any action taken by management, the board, and other parties to manage risk and increase the likelihood that established objectives and goals will be achieved. Management plans, organizes, and directs the performance of sufficient actions to provide reasonable assurance that objectives and goals will be achieved.

Control activities – Policies and procedures put in place to ensure that risk management actions are effectively carried out.

Control environment – The attitude and actions of the board and management regarding the importance of control within the organization. The control environment provides the discipline and structure for the achievement of the primary objectives of the system of internal control. The control environment includes the following elements:

- Integrity and ethical values
- Organizational structure
- Management's philosophy and operating style
- Assignment of authority and responsibility
- Human resource policies and practices
- Competence of personnel

Control processes – The policies, procedures (both manual and automated), and activities that are part of a control framework, designed and operated to ensure that risks are contained within the level that an organization is willing to accept.

Control risk – The potential that controls will fail to reduce controllable risk to an acceptable level.

Controllable risk – The portion of inherent risk that management can reduce through day-to-day operations and management activities.

Controls are adequately designed – Present if management has planned and organized (designed) the controls or the system of internal controls in a manner that provides reasonable assurance that the organization's entity-level and process-level risks can be managed to an acceptable level.

Controls are operating effectively – Present if management has executed (operated) the controls or the system of internal controls in a manner that provides reasonable assurance that the organization's entity-level and process-level risks have been managed effectively and that the organization's goals and objectives will be achieved efficiently and economically.

Core Principles for the Professional Practice of Internal Auditing – The Core Principles for the Professional Practice of Internal Auditing are the foundation for the International Professional Practices Framework (IPPF) and support internal audit effectiveness.

Corporate governance – The exercise of ethical and effective leadership by the board toward the achievement of ethical culture, good performance, effective control, and legitimacy.

Corporate social responsibility – The term commonly associated with the movement to define and articulate the responsibility of private enterprise for nonfinancial performance.

Corruption – Acts in which individuals wrongfully use their influence in a business transaction to procure some benefit for themselves or another person, contrary to their duty to their employer or the rights of another (for example, kickbacks, self-dealing, or conflicts of interest).

COSO – The Committee of Sponsoring Organizations of the Treadway Commission is a joint initiative of five private sector organizations dedicated to providing thought leadership through the development of frameworks and guidance on enterprise risk management, internal control, and fraud deterrence.

Cosourcing – Activity of contracting with a third party to collaborate in the provision of assurance and consulting services.

Criteria – The standards, measures, or expectations used in making an evaluation and/or verification of an observation (what should exist).

Customer – The subsidiary, business unit, department, group, individual, or other established subdivision of an organization that is the subject of a consulting engagement.

Data analytics – A process of inspecting, cleaning, transforming, and modeling data with the goal of highlighting useful information, suggesting conclusions, and supporting decision-making.

Data visualization – Making complex data more understandable through visual depiction in terms of statistical graphics, plots, information graphics, tables, and charts.

Database – A large repository of data typically contained in many linked files and stored in a manner that allows it to be easily accessed, retrieved, and manipulated.

Descriptive analytics – The reporting of past events to characterize what has happened. It condenses large chunks of data into smaller, more meaningful bits of information.

Design evaluation – A detailed risk assessment of the activities within the audit scope, including identification of the controls and other risk management techniques over the major risks, and evaluation of the design of these controls and techniques.

Detective control – An activity that is designed to discover undesirable events that have already occurred. A detective control must occur on a timely basis (before the undesirable event has had a negative impact on the organization) to be considered effective.

Developmental objectives – Objectives that require enhancement or transformation to something new with a start and end date.

Diagnostic analytics – A process that provides insight into why certain trends or specific incidents occurred and helps analysts gain a better understanding of business performance, market dynamics, and how different inputs affect the outcome.

Directive control – A control that causes or encourages a desirable event to occur. Examples are guidelines, training programs, and incentive compensation plans. Also included in this category are soft controls like tone at the top.

Effect – The risk or exposure the organization and/or others encounter because the condition is not consistent with the criteria (the consequence of the difference).

Engagement – A specific internal audit assignment or project that includes multiple task or activities designed to accomplish a specific set of objectives. Also see Assurance Services and Consulting Services.

Engagement objectives – Broad statements developed by internal auditors that define intended engagement accomplishments.

Engagement opinion – The rating, conclusion, and/or other description of results of an individual internal audit engagement, relating to those aspects within the objectives and scope of the engagement.

Engagement work program – A document that lists the procedures to be followed during an engagement, designed to achieve the engagement plan.

Enterprise risk management (ERM) – Enterprise risk management is a process, effected by an entity's board of directors, management and other personnel, applied in strategy setting and across the enterprise, designed to identify potential events that may affect the entity, and manage risk to be within its risk appetite, to provide reasonable assurance regarding the achievement of entity objectives.

Entity-level control – A control that operates across an entire entity and, as such, is not bound by, or associated with, individual processes.

External auditor – See Independent Outside Auditor.

External service provider – A person or firm outside of the organization that has special knowledge, skill, and experience in a particular discipline.

Framework – A body of guiding principles that form a template against which organizations can evaluate a multitude of business practices. These principles are comprised of various concepts, values, assumptions, and practices intended to provide a yardstick against which an organization can assess or evaluate a particular structure, process, or environment or a group of practices or procedures.

Fraud – Any illegal act characterized by deceit, concealment, or violation of trust. These acts are not dependent upon the threat of violence or physical force. Frauds are perpetrated by parties and organizations to obtain money, property, or services; to avoid payment or loss of services; or to secure personal or business advantage.

Fraudulent financial reporting – Acts that involve falsification of an organization's financial statements (for example, overstating revenues, or understating liabilities and expenses).

General information technology controls – Controls that operate across all IT systems and are in place to ensure the integrity, reliability, and accuracy of the application systems. Also represents a specific example of an "entity-level control."

Governance – The combination of processes and structures implemented by the board to inform, direct, manage, and monitor the activities of the organization toward the achievement of its objectives.

Haphazard sampling – A non-statistical sample selection technique used to select a sample without intentional bias to include or exclude a sample item that is expected to be representative of the population.

Hard controls – The tangible elements of governance controls, such as policies and procedures, accounting reconciliations, and management signoffs.

Illegal acts – Activities that violate laws and regulations of particular jurisdictions where a company is operating.

Impairment – Impairment to organizational independence and individual objectivity may include personal conflict of interest, scope limitations, restrictions on access to records, personnel, and properties, and resource limitations (funding).

Impairment to independence or objectivity – The introduction of threats that may result in a substantial limitation, or the appearance of a substantial limitation, to the internal auditor's ability to perform an engagement without bias or interference.

Incremental objective – Improving the quality or efficiency of the existing operational outcome by enhancing one or more of the components (people, process, technology, or deliverable).

Independence – The freedom from conditions that threaten the ability of the internal audit activity to carry out internal audit responsibilities in an unbiased manner.

Independent outside auditor – A registered public accounting firm, hired by the organization's board or executive management, to perform a financial statement audit providing assurance for which the firm issues a written attestation report that expresses an opinion about whether the financial statements are fairly presented in accordance with applicable Generally Accepted Accounting Principles.

Information technology general controls – Controls that apply to all systems components, processes, and data present in an organization or systems environment. The objectives of these controls are to ensure the appropriate development and implementation of applications, as well as the integrity of program and data files and of computer operations.

Information technology governance – The leadership, structure, and oversight processes that ensure the organization's IT supports the objectives and strategies of the organization.

Information technology operations – The department or area in an organization (people, processes, and equipment) that performs the function of running the computer systems and various devices that support the business objectives and activities.

Inherent limitations of internal control – The confines that relate to the limits of human judgment, resource constraints and the need to consider the cost of controls in relation to expected benefits, the reality that breakdowns can occur, and the possibility of collusion or management override.

Inherent risk – The combination of internal and external risk factors in their pure, uncontrolled state, or, the gross risk that exists, assuming there are no internal controls in place.

Insight – An end product or result from the internal audit function's assurance and consulting work designed to provide valued input or information to an auditee or customer. Examples include identifying entity-level root causes of control deficiencies, emerging risks, and suggestions to improve the organization's governance process.

Internal audit activity – A department, division, team of consultants, or other practitioner(s) that provides independent, objective assurance and consulting services designed to add value and improve an organization's operations. The internal audit activity helps an organization accomplish its objectives by bringing a systematic, disciplined approach to evaluate and improve the effectiveness of governance, risk management and control processes.

Internal audit charter – The internal audit charter is a formal document that defines the internal audit activity's purpose, authority, and responsibility. The internal audit charter establishes the internal audit activity's position within the organization; authorizes access to records, personnel, and physical properties relevant to the performance of engagements; and defines the scope of internal audit activities.

Internal control – A process, effected by an entity's board of directors, management, and other personnel, designed to provide reasonable assurance regarding the achievement of objectives in the following categories:

- Effectiveness and efficiency of operations.
- Compliance with applicable laws and regulations.

International Organization for Standardization (ISO) – A network of national standards institutes of 162 countries that issues globally accepted standards for industries, processes, and other activities.

International Professional Practices Framework (IPPF) – The conceptual framework that organizes the authoritative guidance promulgated by The IIA. Authoritative Guidance is composed of two categories - (1) mandatory and (2) strongly recommended.

Intrusion detection systems (IDS) – Network security appliances that monitor network or system activities and report the activities to management.

Intrusion prevention systems (IPS) – Network security appliances that monitor network or system activities and prevent malicious activities from happening on the network.

ISACA – Professional organization that provides practical guidance, benchmarks, and other effective tools for all enterprises that use information systems.

Judgmental sample – A nonrandom sample selected using the auditor's judgment in some way.

Key controls – Controls that must operate effectively to reduce a significant risk to an acceptable level.

Key performance indicator – A metric or other form of measuring whether a process or individual tasks are operating within prescribed tolerances.

Logical access – Tools used in computer systems for identification, authentication, authorization, and accountability.

Management action plan – What the audit customer, alone or in collaboration with others, intends to do to address the cause, correct the condition, and–if appropriate–recover from the condition.

Management control – Actions carried out by management to assure the accomplishment of their objectives, including the setting up of oversight for an objective and the alignment of people, processes, and technology to accomplish that objective.

Management trail – Processing history controls, often referred to as an audit trail, that enable management to identify the transactions and events they record by tracking transactions from their source to their output and by tracing backward.

Material observation – An individual observation, or a group of observations, is considered "material" if the control in question has a reasonable possibility of failing and the impact of its failure is not only significant, but also exceeds management's materiality threshold.

Monitoring – A process that assesses the presence and functioning of governance, risk management, and control over time.

Narrative – Free-form compositions used to describe processes. They have no inherent discipline like risk/control matrices and flowcharts, but they are useful for things that require an explanation too lengthy to fit within the confines of the disciplined tools.

Negative confirmations – Confirmations that ask for a response only if the information is not accurate.

Network – A configuration that enables computers and devices to communicate and be linked together to efficiently process data and share information.

Network firewall – A device or set of devices designed to permit or deny network transmissions based upon a set of rules. It is frequently used to protect networks from unauthorized access while permitting legitimate communications to pass.

Nonsampling risk – The risk that occurs when an internal auditor fails to perform his or her work correctly (for example, performing inappropriate auditing procedures, misapplying an appropriate procedure, or misinterpreting sampling results).

Objectives – What an entity desires to achieve. When referring to what an organization wants to achieve, these are called business objectives, and may be classified as strategic, operations, reporting, and compliance. When referring to what an audit wants to achieve, these are called audit objectives or engagement objectives.

Objectivity – An unbiased mental attitude that allows internal auditors to perform engagements in such a manner that they believe in their work product and that no quality compromises are made. Objectivity requires that internal auditors do not subordinate their judgment on audit matters to others.

Observation – A finding, determination, or judgment derived from the internal auditor's test results from an assurance or consulting engagement.

Observation (as an audit test) – An audit test that involves simply watching something being done.

Operating system – Software programs that run the computer and perform basic tasks, such as recognizing input from the keyboard, sending output to the printer, keeping track of files and directories on the hard drive, and controlling various computer peripheral devices.

Opinion – The auditor's evaluations of the effects of the observations and recommendations on the activities reviewed; also called a micro opinion or conclusion. The opinion usually puts the observations and recommendations in perspective based on their overall implications.

Opportunity – The possibility that an event will occur and positively affect the achievement of objectives.

Organizational independence – The chief audit executive's line of reporting within the organization that allows the internal audit function to fulfill its responsibilities free from interference. Also see Independence.

Other assurance providers – Other entities within the organization whose principal mission is to test compliance or assess business activities to confirm that risks are effectively evaluated and managed.

Outsourcing – Activity of contracting with an independent third party to provide assurance services.

Overall opinion – The rating, conclusion, and/or other description of results provided by the chief audit executive addressing, at a broad level, governance, risk management, and/or control processes of the organization. An overall opinion is the professional judgment of the chief audit executive based on the results of a number of individual engagements and other activities for a specific time interval.

Positive confirmations – Confirmations that ask for a response regarding whether the information is accurate or not.

Predictive analytics – Type of analytics that allows users to extract information from large volumes of existing data, apply certain assumptions, and draw correlations to predict future outcomes and trends.

Preventive control – An activity that is designed to deter unintended events from occurring.

Primary control – An activity designed to reduce risk associated with a critical business objective.

Principle – A fundamental proposition that serves as the foundation for a system of belief or a chain of reasoning.

Probability-proportional-to-size (PPS) sampling – A modified form of attribute sampling that is used to reach a conclusion regarding monetary amounts rather than rates of occurrence.

Process map (flowchart) – A tool that shows the process flow visually, which highlights the control points and therefore helps internal auditors to identify missing controls and assess whether existing controls are adequate.

Processing controls – Controls that provide an automated means to ensure processing is complete, accurate, and authorized.

Process-level control – An activity that operates within a specific process for the purpose of achieving process-level objectives.

Professional skepticism – The state of mind in which internal auditors take nothing for granted; they continuously question what they hear and see and critically assess audit evidence.

Random sample – A sample in which every item in the population has an equal chance of being selected.

Random sampling – A sampling technique in which each item in the defined population has an equal opportunity of being selected.

Rating – A component of an audit opinion or conclusion. Such a rating typically reflects the auditor's conclusion about residual risk.

Ratio analysis – Calculating financial or nonfinancial ratios. For example, the auditor could calculate the percent of products produced that were returned as defective, or the percent of sick days taken to the number of sick days allowed.

Reasonable assurance – A level of assurance that is supported by generally accepted auditing procedures and judgments. Reasonable assurance can apply to judgments surrounding the effectiveness of internal controls, the mitigation of risks, the achievement of objectives, or other engagement-related conclusions.

Reasonableness tests – The act of comparing information to the internal auditor's general knowledge of the organization or industry, rather than another specific piece of information.

Recommendation – The auditor's call for action to correct or improve operations. A recommendation may suggest approaches to correcting or enhancing performance as a guide for management in achieving desired results. The recommendation answers the question, "What is to be done?"

Regression analysis – Statistical technique used to establish the relationship of a dependent variable to one or more independent variables. For example, an internal auditor might estimate payroll expense based on the number of employees, average rate of pay, and the number of hours worked, and then compare the result to the recorded payroll expense.

Residual risk – The portion of inherent risk that remains after management executes its risk responses (sometimes referred to as net risk).

Risk – The possibility of an event occurring that will have an impact on the achievement of objectives. Risk is measured in terms of impact and likelihood.

Risk appetite – The level of risk that an organization is willing to accept.

Risk assessment – The identification and analysis (typically in terms of impact and likelihood) of relevant risks to the achievement of an organization's objectives, forming a basis for determining how the risks should be managed.

Risk capacity – The maximum risk a firm may bear and remain solvent.

Risk management – A process to identify, assess, manage, and control potential events or situations to provide reasonable assurance regarding the achievement of the organization's objectives.

Risk mitigation – An action, or set of actions, taken by management to reduce the impact and/or likelihood of a risk to a lower, more acceptable level.

Risk tolerance – The acceptable variation relative to performance to the achievement of objectives.

Risk treatment/risk response – An action, or set of actions, taken by management to achieve a desired risk management strategy. Risk responses can be categorized as risk avoidance, reduction, sharing, or acceptance. Exploiting opportunities that, in turn, enable the achievement of objectives, is also a risk response. ISO 31000 refers to this step in risk management as risk treatment.

Risk/control matrix – An audit tool that facilitates risk-based auditing. It usually consists of a series of columns, including columns for business objectives, risks to the objectives, controls or risk management techniques, and other columns that aid in the analysis.

Sampling risk – The risk that the internal auditor's conclusion based on sample testing may be different than the conclusion reached if the audit procedure was applied to all items in the population.

Secondary control – An activity designed to either reduce risk associated with business objectives that are not critical to the organization's survival or success or serve as a backup to a key control.

Significance – The relative importance of a matter within the context in which it is being considered, including quantitative and qualitative factors, such as magnitude, nature, effect, relevance, and impact. Professional judgment assists internal auditors when evaluating the significance of matters within the context of the relevant objectives.

Significant observation – An individual observation, or a group of observations, is considered "significant" if the control activity in question has a reasonable possibility of failing and the impact of its failure is significant.

Smart mobile devices – Intelligent mobile devices like smart phones and tablets.

Social media – Web-based and mobile technologies used to turn communication into interactive dialogue.

Social networks – The social network sites that are commonly used. Examples include Facebook, Google+, and Twitter.

Soft controls – The intangible, inherently subjective elements of governance control like tone at the top, integrity and ethical values, and management philosophy and operating style.

Standard – A professional pronouncement promulgated by the Internal Audit Standards Board that delineates the requirements for performing a broad range of internal audit activities and for evaluating internal audit performance.

Statistical sampling – A sampling technique that allows the auditor to define with precision how representative the sample will be. After applying the technique and testing the sample, the auditor can state the conclusion in terms of being "%" confident that the error rate in the population is less than or equal to "%."

Strategic objectives – What an entity desires to achieve through the value creation choices management makes on behalf of the organization's stakeholders.

Strategy – Refers to how management plans to achieve the organization's objectives.

Sufficient evidence – A collection of evidence gained during an engagement that, in its totality, is enough to support the judgments and conclusions made in the engagement.

System of internal controls – Comprises the five components of internal control–the control environment, risk assessment, control activities, information and communication, and monitoring–that are in place to manage risks related to the financial reporting, compliance, and operational objectives of an organization. Also see Internal Control.

Third-party service provider – A person or firm, outside the organization, who provides assurance and/or consulting services to an organization.

Three Lines Model – A model of assurance that helps organizations identify structures and processes that best assist the achievement of objectives and facilitate strong governance and risk management. The model applies to all organizations and is optimized by:

- Adopting a principles-based approach and adapting the model to suit organizational objectives and circumstances.
- Focusing on the contribution risk management makes to achieving objectives and creating value, as well as to matters of "defense" and protecting value.
- Clearly understanding the roles and responsibilities represented in the model and the relationships among them.
- Implementing measures to ensure activities and objectives are aligned with the prioritized interests of stakeholders.

Tolerance – The boundaries of acceptable outcomes related to achieving business objectives.

Tone at the top – The entity-wide attitude of integrity and control consciousness, as exhibited by the most senior executives of an organization. Also see Control Environment.

Top-down approach – To begin at the entity level, with the organization's objectives, and then identify the key processes critical to the success of each of the organization's objectives.

Tracing – Taking information from one document, record, or asset forward to a document or record that was prepared later. For example, if auditors count inventory, they would trace their count forward to the client's inventory records to verify the completeness of the records.

Transaction-level control – Controls that operate within a transaction-processing system. Examples are authorizations, segregation of duties, and exception reports.

Transformational objective – An objective that requires significantly altering operational components of people, processes, and/or technology to accomplish a new, higher objective or value-adding opportunity.

Transparency – Communicating in a manner that a prudent individual would consider to be fair and sufficiently clear and comprehensive to meet the needs of the recipient(s) of such communication.

Trend analysis – Comparing information from one period with the same information from the prior period.

Val IT – A governance framework and supporting publications addressing the governance of IT-enabled business investments.

Virtualization – When a physical IT component is partitioned into multiple "virtual" components; for example, when a physical server is logically partitioned into two virtual servers.

Vouching – The act of taking information from one document or record backward to an asset, document, or record that was prepared earlier. For example, auditors might vouch information on a computer report to the source documents from which the information was input to the system to verify the validity of the information.

Web content filtering – The technique whereby content is blocked or allowed based on analysis of its content, rather than its source or other criteria. It is most widely used on the Internet to filter email and web access.

APPENDIX B
THE IIA CIA EXAM SYLLABUS
AND CROSS-REFERENCES

For your convenience, we have reproduced verbatim The IIA's CIA Exam Syllabus for Part 1 of the CIA exam. Note that the "basic" cognitive level means the candidate must retrieve relevant knowledge from memory and/or demonstrate basic comprehension of concepts or processes. Those levels labeled "proficient" mean the candidate must apply concepts, processes, or procedures; analyze, evaluate, and make judgments based on criteria; and/or put elements or material together to formulate conclusions and recommendations.

We also have provided cross-references to the study units and subunits in this book that correspond to The IIA's more detailed coverage. Please visit The IIA's website for updates and more information about the exam. Rely on the Gleim materials to help you pass each part the exam. We have researched and studied The IIA's CIA Exam Syllabus as well as questions from prior exams to provide you with an excellent review program.

PART 1 – ESSENTIALS OF INTERNAL AUDITING

		Domain	Cognitive Level	Gleim Study Unit(s) or Subunit(s)
I		**Foundations of Internal Auditing (15%)**		
	A	Interpret The IIA's Mission of Internal Audit, Definition of Internal Auditing, and Core Principles for the Professional Practice of Internal Auditing, and the purpose, authority, and responsibility of the internal audit activity	Proficient	1.1
	B	Explain the requirements of an internal audit charter (required components, board approval, communication of the charter, etc.)	Basic	1.7
	C	Interpret the difference between assurance and consulting services provided by the internal audit activity	Proficient	1.1
	D	Demonstrate conformance with the IIA Code of Ethics	Proficient	1.2-1.6
II		**Independence and Objectivity (15%)**		
	A	Interpret organizational independence of the internal audit activity (importance of independence, functional reporting, etc.)	Basic	2.1
	B	Identify whether the internal audit activity has any impairments to its independence	Basic	2.3
	C	Assess and maintain an individual internal auditor's objectivity, including determining whether an individual internal auditor has any impairments to his/her objectivity	Proficient	2.2-2.3
	D	Analyze policies that promote objectivity	Proficient	2.2-2.3
III		**Proficiency and Due Professional Care (18%)**		
	A	Recognize the knowledge, skills, and competencies required (whether developed or procured) to fulfill the responsibilities of the internal audit activity	Basic	2.4-2.5
	B	Demonstrate the knowledge and competencies that an internal auditor needs to possess to perform his/her individual responsibilities, including technical skills and soft skills (communication skills, critical thinking, persuasion/negotiation and collaboration skills, etc.)	Proficient	2.4
	C	Demonstrate due professional care	Proficient	3.1
	D	Demonstrate an individual internal auditor's competency through continuing professional development	Proficient	3.1

Domain		Cognitive Level	Gleim Study Unit(s) or Subunit(s)
Quality Assurance and Improvement Program (7%)			
IV	A	Describe the required elements of the quality assurance and improvement program (internal assessments, external assessments, etc.)	Basic	3.2-3.3
	B	Describe the requirement of reporting the results of the quality assurance and improvement program to the board or other governing body	Basic	3.4
	C	Identify appropriate disclosure of conformance vs. nonconformance with The IIA's *International Standards for the Professional Practice of Internal Auditing*	Basic	3.4
Governance, Risk Management, and Control (35%)			
V	A	Describe the concept of organizational governance	Basic	4.1-4.2
	B	Recognize the impact of organizational culture on the overall control environment and individual engagement risks and controls	Basic	4.1
	C	Recognize and interpret the organization's ethics and compliance-related issues, alleged violations, and dispositions	Basic	4.1
	D	Describe corporate social responsibility	Basic	4.3
	E	Interpret fundamental concepts of risk and the risk management process	Proficient	5.1
	F	Describe globally accepted risk management frameworks appropriate to the organization (COSO - ERM, ISO 31000, etc.)	Basic	5.2-5.4
	G	Examine the effectiveness of risk management within processes and functions	Proficient	SU 5
	H	Recognize the appropriateness of the internal audit activity's role in the organization's risk management process	Basic	5.1
	I	Interpret internal control concepts and types of controls	Proficient	SUs 6-7
	J	Apply globally accepted internal control frameworks appropriate to the organization (COSO, etc.)	Proficient	6.3
	K	Examine the effectiveness and efficiency of internal controls	Proficient	SUs 6-7
Fraud Risks (10%)			
VI	A	Interpret fraud risks and types of frauds and determine whether fraud risks require special consideration when conducting an engagement	Proficient	8.1
	B	Evaluate the potential for occurrence of fraud (red flags, etc.) and how the organization detects and manages fraud risks	Proficient	8.1-8.2
	C	Recommend controls to prevent and detect fraud and education to improve the organization's fraud awareness	Proficient	SUs 6-7, 8.2
	D	Recognize techniques and internal audit roles related to forensic auditing (interview, investigation, testing, etc.)	Basic	8.3

APPENDIX C
INTERNATIONAL ENGLISH
ACCOUNTING TERMINOLOGY

Terminology Clarification

In accounting and finance, different terms are sometimes used for the same or similar concepts. Some of these differences result from national differences, especially between the U.S. and Commonwealth countries. Others are the personal preference of the professionals involved. These differences are becoming less pronounced with the adoption of International Financial Reporting Standards (IFRS) in most countries around the world and the collaboration between the International Accounting Standards Board (IASB) and the U.S. Financial Accounting Standards Board (FASB). The following is a guide to commonly used synonyms as well as terms that are understood differently by some preparers and users of financial information.

Accounts always means a unit of classification to accumulate accounting transactions of the same kind to enable subsequent reporting. Although the classifications adopted by different organizations will often differ widely depending on their business context and information needs, they will all relate to one of the fundamental elements of financial reporting, such as assets and liabilities. Examples of accounts include travel expenses and interest income. In the United Kingdom, the Companies Act uses the term **annual accounts** to describe what is more commonly called, in the United Kingdom as well as elsewhere, financial statements. **Financial statements** is the term used under both IFRS and U.S. GAAP. Other terms may be used, such as annual financial report or annual accounting statement.

The terms **accounts payable, amounts owing to suppliers, bills payable,** and **trade creditors** may be used interchangeably.

- Similarly, **accounts receivable, amounts due from customers, bills receivable,** and **trade debtors** may also be used interchangeably.

Business combinations are also referred to as **mergers and acquisitions** and **takeovers**.

Cost of goods sold and **cost of sales** are synonymous.

Equity is the difference between assets and liabilities. In theory, it represents the stake of the owners in the business. However, given that the price that could be obtained for selling the business or the proceeds that could be realized from liquidating the assets and settling the liabilities will likely differ from the book value, it is of limited relevance. It is relevant in confirming the maximum that could be paid out as dividends to shareholders. The term **ownership** can be used interchangeably with equity. In addition to common stock and capital in excess of par value (or ordinary shares plus share premium), equity also includes **accumulated profits, retained earnings**, or **distributable reserves**. These all represent the cumulative profits less any dividends that have been paid. In addition, equity will typically include accumulated other comprehensive income such as a revaluation reserve arising on the unrealized gain from writing up the value of an asset to its fair value. This is a **non-distributable reserve** which cannot be paid out as dividends. Equity can also be referred to as **shareholders' funds**.

Expenses are decreases in assets or increases in liabilities resulting from the activities of the business. They are not the same as expenditures. **Expenditures** may be expenses, but they can also relate to the acquisition of assets.

Financial statements under both IFRS and U.S. GAAP are comprised of

- The **statement of financial position**, which is often and traditionally called a **balance sheet**. Other names used to describe this statement include statement of financial condition and statement of assets and liabilities. This presents the assets, liabilities, and equity of the organization at a point in time.

- The **statement of financial performance**, which is an IFRS term for what is more commonly called the **statement of profit or loss and other comprehensive income** or the **statement of comprehensive income**, which may be presented as one statement or as two separate statements. The statement of profit or loss is often referred to as an **income statement**. Other terms include statement of earnings and statement of operations. Irrespective of what they are called, these statements present the income and expenses from routine business activities. In contrast, other comprehensive income comprises items that impact the interest of owners in the business but are considered not to be indicative of the ongoing performance of the business and therefore inappropriate to include in determining the profit or loss. Examples of items that appear in other comprehensive income are gains or losses from translation of foreign subsidiaries, gains and losses on certain financial assets, and remeasurements of defined pension plans.

- **Profit or loss** is income less expenses. This may be called **net profit or loss, profit after tax, earnings,** or **net income**. Confusingly, it may also be called income, which conflicts with the core element called income. The context of the income statement should help to clarify whether income excludes the deduction of any expenses or is effectively profit or earnings. The income statement may have subtotals before arriving at net income, net profit, or earnings, proverbially known as the bottom line. These subtotals may include gross profit (sales less cost of sales) or operating profit (profit before taxes).

NOTE: These financial statements may be presented using different layouts and conventions. Negative numbers may be explicitly used or may be implied which can cause confusion to inexperienced readers. The way to overcome this confusion is to become familiar with a range of approaches and be able to understand how the information is presented. Other statements that may be included in the financial statements are the statement of changes in equity and the statement of cash flows.

Income is the increase in assets from the activities of the business. This income may be described by a variety of names. **Sales** or **revenue** are the two most common. Sales may imply the selling of a product whereas revenue may be more generic and include fee and service income. **Turnover** is a term used in some Commonwealth countries and generally can be considered synonymous with sales or revenue. This can cause confusion as turnover is also a term used in financial analysis for a ratio used to assess asset utilization.

Liabilities are amounts owed to other parties. **Debt** is typically a type of **liability** that results from **borrowing**. The terms **loans** and **financing obligations** may also be used. Debt may be in the form of **bonds** or **debentures**, which are securities entitling the holder to interest and principal payments. **Notes payable** and **promissory notes** are also debt. Other liabilities such as amounts owed to suppliers or taxation payable are typically not regarded as debt. This is because they arise from the normal course of business rather than a deliberate decision to borrow.

Listed and **quoted** are interchangeable terms describing shares or stocks traded on an exchange.

The terms **long-lived assets, fixed assets,** and **tangible noncurrent assets** are all used interchangeably with the term **property, plant and equipment**. These terms describe assets used in the production of goods or services, for rental to others, or for administrative purposes.

The term **provision for bad debts** may be used to denote an entry for an **expected credit loss allowance** for amounts receivable that are considered to have been impaired.

- **Provision** under IFRS also means the recognition of a probable liability, which is referred to as a **contingent liability** under U.S. GAAP. Contingent liability is used under IFRS to denote a possible but not probable liability which is disclosed but not presented in the notes to the financial statements.

Stock and **shares** can be used interchangeably. These are units of ownership in a **company** equivalent to a **corporation**. However, stock or stocks can also be used to refer to **inventory**, being items held to sell, be used to manufacture goods for sale, or consumed in the production or delivery of goods or services. Stock is a traditional Commonwealth term though the term inventory is increasingly used. Stock count and inventory count are synonymous terms.

- The term **ordinary stock** is used in the U.S. to denote the ownership stake that has the rights to vote at **stockholder meetings**, receive dividends when declared, and receive proceeds on any dissolution of the corporation. The term **common shares** denotes the same ownership stake by owners known as **shareholders**. The shares may have a **par value** or **nominal value**. Shares will typically be issued at a price greater than the par or nominal value. This surplus is known as **capital in excess of par value** or **share premium**. **Preferred stock** or **preference shares** describe a security that combines aspects of debt and equity. It is included in debt if there is a provision for it to be redeemed. If there is no provision for redemption, it is included in equity. A fixed-percentage dividend must be paid to preferred stockholders before ordinary stockholders or common shareholders are able to receive a dividend.

Taxation payable, **tax due**, and **income tax payable** are synonymous in denoting amounts due to taxation authorities. Similarly, **taxation expense** and **income tax expense** are synonymous in denoting the change in amounts due to taxation authorities as a result of current year activities.

INDEX

Notes

Notes

Notes

Notes

311